The Pre-Christian Paul

MARTIN HENGEL

The Pre-Christian Paul

in collaboration with
Roland Deines

SCM PRESS
London

TRINITY PRESS INTERNATIONAL
Philadelphia

Translated by John Bowden from the German
'Der vorchristliche Paulus',
first published in M.Hengel and U. Heckel (eds.), *Paulus, Missionar und Theologe und das antike Judentum*, WUNT, by J.C.B.Mohr (Paul Siebeck), Tübingen 1991.

This edition first published 1991

SCM Press Ltd
26-30 Tottenham Road
London N1 4BZ

Trinity Press International
3725 Chestnut Street
Philadelphia PA 19104

British Library Cataloguing in Publication Data

Hengel, Martin
The pre-Christian Paul.
1. Saint Paul, the Apostle
I. Title   II. Deines, Roland
225.92

ISBN 0-334-02497-8

Library of Congress Cataloging-in-Publication Data

Hengel, Martin
[Vorchristliche Paulus. English]
The pre-Christian Paul / Martin Hengel in collaboration with
Roland Deines.
p. cm.
Translation of: Der vorchristliche Paulus.
Includes bibliographical references and index.
ISBN 1-56338-009-9
1. Paul, the Apostle, Saint. 2. Bible. N.T.—Criticism,
interpretation, etc. 3. Church history—Primitive and early church,
ca. 30–600. 4. Christian saints—Turkey—Tarsus—Biography.
I. Deines, Roland. II. Title.
BS2506.H4713 1991
225.9′2—dc20
[B]
91–12154
CIP

Phototypeset by Input Typesetting Ltd, London
and printed in Great Britain by
Clays Ltd, St Ives plc, Bungay, Suffolk

For
Marc Philonenko
Pierre Prigent
my Strasbourg Friends

Contents

Preface

An abbreviated form of this study was first given at a symposium to commemorate the fiftieth anniversary of the death of Adolf Schlatter (16 August 1852-19 May 1938) in September 1988, in Tübingen. The theme of this joint meeting of Durham and Tübingen New Testament scholars was 'Paul, Missionary and Theologian, and Ancient Judaism'. The German version of the text here translated by John Bowden is being published as part of the symposium in the series Wissenschaftliche Untersuchungen zum Neuen Testament, by Mohr-Siebeck in Tübingen. An abbreviated version was given as a lecture in late autumn 1988 in University College, London, and at the Oxford Centre for Postgraduate Hebrew Studies, Yarnton.

Roland Deines has been extraordinarily helpful to me in providing the original contribution to the symposium with extensive notes. The often substantial bibliographical details and in part also the text of the major notes are his work. I recall with gratitude the fruitful discussions with him which have similarly found expression in this study. After he left for a study year in Israel, Jörg Frey helped me with the final editorial work.

The study follows on almost without a break from earlier investigations, like my studies 'Between Jesus and Paul' and 'The "Hellenists"', "The Seven" and Stephen (Acts 6.1-15; 7.54-8.3)', in *Between Jesus and Paul. Studies in the Earliest History of Christianity*, London and Philadelphia 1983, 1-30, 128-56, and *The 'Hellenization' of Judaea in the First Century after Christ*, London and Philadelphia 1989. They are all bricks in the construction of a history of early Christianity, which is growing slowly and which will attempt to correct at decisive points that earlier picture of primitive Christianity developed by the history of religions school and continued by its successors down to the present day. As a result of the numerous archaeological discoveries in Jerusalem and in Jewish Palestine, the historical profile of the original home of Christianity at the time of Jesus and the apostles is emerging more clearly today than it could in the time of our parents and grandparents. So we can also have a better grasp than before of the cultural and spiritual milieu in which the earliest community was formed and therefore understand our sources – Paul, the much misunderstood Luke, and also Josephus and the early rabbinic accounts – in a more approriate way than had been possible earlier from the perspective of an often incomprehensible radical criticism.

Nevertheless, I am aware that in many details the attempt made here to describe the pre-Christian development of the apostle to the Gentiles and first Christian theologian rests on hypotheses, though these are always based directly or indirectly on statements in the sources. Here Luke in particular, if he is understood against the Jewish background of his time, proves to be a more reliable witness than many people nowadays assume under the influence of an all too cheap criticism of his writings. We are just not aware of how much basic knowledge we owe to the first Christian 'historian' and 'apologist'.

Although I have tried to argue strictly in historical terms, the aim of this investigation is nevertheless ultimately a theological one. My concern is for a better understanding of the apostle's doctrine of justification, which nowadays is often misinterpreted and disputed, against the background of his own career and his encounter with the risen Christ which changed this radically. Because of our familiarity with Paul, we often easily overlook what an extraordinary, indeed in a way unique, religious figure he was – the kind of person given to humanity perhaps only once in many centuries. He was of absolutely fundamental significance for the rise of Christianity. Something of his personality is already visible – albeit still in a very veiled form – in the accounts which we have of his pre-Christian period: the tension between Hellenistic and Jewish-scribal education, between the Roman citizen and the Pharisaic Jew, between the zealot for the law and the ambitious young teacher and preacher.

That Paul was able to teach to the Gentile Christian community that he founded the meaning of God's radical grace – 'But if it is by grace, then it does not rest on deeds done, or grace would cease to be grace' (Rom.11.6) – is connected with his special past.

The question of the unconditional character of grace, raised by Paul for the first time with this clarity and sharpness, is one of the foundations of the Christian faith – and yet at that time it could be raised only by a Jew on the basis of his Old Testament-Jewish heritage. So its significance lies on quite a different fundamental level from the historical question over which there is so much argument today, whether the apostle rightly interpreted the view of the Law in the Palestinian Judaism of his time.

Perhaps there was no such thing as this *one* Palestinian Judaism with the *one* binding view of the law. Be that as it may, my view is that the apostle gave expression to his own – personally thought-out – view, which at the same time was quite appropriate for those circles in which he moved. In reality, however, what we have here is a problem within Christianity: Paul was already discussing – controversially – with *Christian* brothers the view that salvation rests only on God's free grace and not on human actions. The actions are 'the fruit of the Spirit' (Gal.5.22), and as such are God's own work: '...for it is God who works in you, inspiring both the will and the deed, for his own chosen purpose' (Phil.2.13). One could also say that they are signs of overwhelming gratitude to the one to whom we owe everything.

In this dispute within Christianity, which runs through the whole of church history down to the present day and in which all too often the law triumphed over the gospel and works over grace, if we are still concerned with the Christian truth we have to make a decision: in the end one cannot really mediate between Augustine and Pelagius, Luther and Erasmus, Jansen and Molina. Conversely, the message of the grace of God, which does not require any human presupposition, but gives what it demands, already meets us in the Old Testament and in individual Jewish texts, for example in Deutero-Isaiah and the Yahwistic patriarchal history. Here I would simply refer to the fine study by my Tübingen colleague Otfried Hofius, 'Rechtfertigung des Gottlosen als Thema biblischer Theologie' (in *Paulusstudien*, WUNT 51, 1989, 121-47): the 'new' feature in Paul lies in the fact that he 'sees the "justification of the godless", promised and attested in "scripture", fulfilled in the atoning and reconciling event of the death and

resurrection of Jesus Christ and therefore understands it as the
"righteousness of faith" which is effectively promised and appropriated in the gospel as the saving word of God' (146). This grace
which becomes manifest here is at work in the old covenant as well
as the new. It is especially with Jewish conversation partners that
nowadays one often finds more understanding of the unfathomable
grace of God, *rab ḥesed we'met* (Ex.34.6), than in a Christianity
which because of its sheer pluralism has lost its binding character
and now only moralizes. Thus I read in Michael Wyschogrod:

> 'Every Jew knows, or should know, that if God were to pay him
> what he deserves, neither more nor less, he would be lost. His
> only chance depends on the mercy of God. If God decides to
> overlook his sorry record and to bestow mercy rather than justice
> on him, then he has a chance. But certainly not otherwise' ('The
> Impact of Dialogue with Christianity on My Self-Understand-
> ing as a Jew', in *Die Hebräische Bibel und ihre zweifache Nachge-
> schichte, Festschrift für Rolf Rendtorff zum 65. Geburtstag*, Neukir-
> chen-Vluyn 1990, 371).

That also applies to the Christian, who can learn in Paul that God
in Christ has put grace before justice.

At a time when it has become almost fashionable to interpret Paul
'untheologically' and only 'historically' and thus to misinterpret
his real intention, the present apparently 'untheological' study,
arguing completely in historical terms, is meant to help towards a
better understanding of Paul's career up to that change which
altered the whole history of the world and thus make clear why his
doctrine of justification was necessarily so fundamental to his later
preaching as a missionary to the Gentiles. At the same time I hope
it will become evident how deeply his gospel is moulded by the
language and spirit of the old people of God.

Tübingen, January 1991

Introduction[1]

As the first *Christian* author, theologian and missionary to the Gentiles, who not only brought the Gentile Christian church into being but founded Christian theology in the real sense, Paul has always attracted the attention of theologians concerned with the New Testament – perhaps more than any other figure of early Christianity. However, these theologians have almost forgotten the *Jew* Saulus/*šā'ūl*. Whereas the literature of the past century about the Christian apostle is too vast to cover, relatively little attention has been paid to the Pharisee and persecutor of the churches. Granted, his verdict on his own *pre*-Christian past (as on the past of any Christian) is that 'the old has passed away' (II Cor.5.17), but at the same time he gives the readers of his letters information about that past, sometimes very personal information – more so than any other Christian author before the middle of the second century. Nevertheless, the usual monographs on Paul seldom devote more than a couple of pages to the apostle's pre-Christian period.[2] Only Justin, and before him perhaps at best Hermas, give an account of themselves at such length.[3]

In addition to Paul's well-known autobiographical testimonies,[4] indirect conclusions can be drawn from his theological argumentation, which – and I deliberately put this in a pointed way – cannot be understood as *Christian* theology without attention to its *Jewish* roots, indeed I would venture to say its latent '*Jewish*' character. Knowledge of Saul the *Jew* is a precondition of understanding Paul the *Christian*. The better we know the former, the more clearly we shall understand the latter.[5]

Paul's own testimony is supplemented by the numerous accounts of Luke in his Acts of the Apostles, which scholars nowadays are fond of denigrating as being largely or completely unreliable, though it is a valuable addition to Paul's own accounts.[6] Granted, even such an otherwise sympathetic Jewish scholar as Leo Baeck thought that 'the Third Gospel and the Acts of the Apostles offer us more historical *belles lettres* than history',[7] but he forgets that, measured by modern standards, this could be said of the majority of ancient historians, not least including Josephus, as they were always biassed writers who also wrote with rhetorical drama and, since they were intent on the impact they made on their hearers and readers, never reported in a strict, positivistic sense along the lines of Ranke's 'as it really happened'.[8] A Hellenistic historian always at the same time wanted to provide good entertainment for his readers (or to edify them), and here Luke was no exception.[9] But we should never forget how difficult, indeed virtually impossible, it would be to give Paul a historical setting if we did *not* have Acts.

I Origin and Citizenship

Let us plunge straight in and begin with Paul's origins. It must be stressed quite emphatically, against a current trend in scholarship which seeks to see Paul exclusively as a 'Hellenistic Diaspora Jew', that in his own testimonies, in the letters, the Pharisee connected with Jewish Palestine stands in the foreground, to whom Jerusalem seems to be more important than anywhere else. Only from Luke do we learn that he came from Tarsus, the capital of Cilicia, and that he was a citizen of both Tarsus and Rome.[10] Paul the author of the letters no longer thinks this part of his past worth mentioning; it seems to him to be much more remote than his time as a Pharisee in Palestine.

1 Tarsus as a cultural metropolis[11]

In other words, only Luke describes Paul as a Diaspora Jew who was already privileged by virtue of his origins. Paul comes from a major Hellenistic city famed for its high culture, which in his youth achieved a special degree of pre-eminence as a result of the favour of Augustus and was elevated to become the 'metropolis' of Cilicia. This development makes more comprehensible Paul's later mission focussed on the provincial capitals.[12] Whereas much is said in the Gospels about the open country and villages, and (with the exception of Jerusalem) hardly anything is said of cities,[13] precisely the opposite is the case in the letters of Paul. It is remarkable that despite the present widespread tendency to question almost everything that Luke says, this information that Paul came from Tarsus is, as far as I can see, barely doubted.[14] And that despite the fact that the apostle never speaks of his home city, and on the basis of his letters we should have, rather, to assume that he came from the Jewish mother country or somewhere

nearby.[15] If we did not have Luke's account, why should Paul not
have come from Caesarea, Tiberias, Damascus, the Decapolis, or
from Jerusalem itself?[16] In Paul's autobiographical account in
Galatians 1 and 2, which might be called a brief 'Acts of the
Apostles of a special kind', he first mentions Damascus, and then
the region of Nabataea – which is probably what he means by
Arabia.[17] He then speaks of Jerusalem, though only in connection
with a brief stay; only after that does he talk of the 'regions of Syria
and Cilicia'. Then he comes back to Jerusalem in connection with
the Apostolic Council; only now and at this point is Antioch
mentioned, as the scene of the clash with Peter. Tarsus plays no
part in any of this, in complete contrast to Jerusalem, which Paul
mentions relatively often. One simply cannot assume on the basis
of the letters that Paul came from the capital of Cilicia. At any
rate, Jerusalem is mentioned nine times in the authentic letters[18]
and Judaea four times;[19] by contrast, Corinth is mentioned only
three times,[20] Ephesus and Damascus twice,[21] and Antioch only
once.[22] Here, however, for once people have been ready to believe
Luke, because if Paul came from Tarsus it was possible to connect
him broadly with Hellenistic education and culture and with the
syncretistic practices of Syria and Asia Minor from his earliest
youth. For it was the verdict of Strabo that in the capital of Cilicia
'there was so much zeal for philosophy and all the other aspects of
education generally among the inhabitants that in this respect
they surpassed even Alexandria, Athens, and any other place'.[23]

However, it is an open question whether and how far the young
Paul in Tarsus acquired any of this 'general education' that
flourished there, in contrast to his older contemporary Philo of
Alexandria, whose nature was so different.[24] Certainly in Paul's
letters we meet a few maxims and commonplaces from the popular
philosophers, but these go with the style of missionary and apologetic preaching in the synagogues;[25] by contrast, we find virtually
none of the knowledge of the classical Greek literature which
formed part of the general canon of education in his letters.[26] It is
completely uncertain whether he had every seen a *Greek* tragedy
or a mime. The most popular drama of the Hellenistic period was
Euripides' *Bacchae* – an abomination to strict Jews, certainly, and
the same went for the lascivious mime. The pious Pharisaic Jew
rejected the pagan theatre hardly any less bitterly than the orator

and Christian Tertullian in his *de spectaculis*.[27] At best one might perhaps assume that Paul had occasionally heard one of the recitations of poetry which were popular at the time. However, there are no references to this in his letters. His language shows no trace of any knowledge of Greek poetry, i.e. of epics, drama and poetry. The only lyric which he quotes, in I Corinthians 15.33, comes from Menander's *Thais* and – like many other verses of the comic poet – had long since become a detached saying.[28] The language of Homer and the Greek tragedians is as alien to Paul as the imitation of the Attic orators or the purity of classical language. Nor does the pseudo-classical verse of the Jews play any part in his argumentation. It only became significant again a century later, for the Christian apologists, through whom early Christianity deliberately made its way into the world of Greek education.[29]

Strabo concludes his hymn of praise to Tarsus by saying that the city also had 'all kinds of schools of the rhetorical arts',[30] and intrinsically it would be conceivable that the young Saul also mastered literary Greek at a very early stage, so thoroughly, that for him, 'the true master of the speech, to whom ideas came in an overwhelming flood', it became 'an appropriate instrument'.[31] The only question is how long he lived in Tarsus.

I doubt whether Paul was trained in one of the usual schools of rhetoric, since a clear distinction must be made between the Greek elementary school and instruction in rhetoric. Even the question where he received his Greek elementary education must remain open. Both Jerusalem and Tarsus are possibilities, since in Paul it is impossible to separate Greek education from Jewish. Even in Greek garb he remains a Jew through and through. So Paul does not adopt the course of the Syrian Lucian of Samosata (in the second century CE), who was a 'barbarian' in origins and language.[32] He ran away from his uncle, who was teaching him to be a sculptor, and went to Greece to get 'education' and become an orator – succeeding admirably.[33] Possibly the negative verdict of the Corinthians in II Cor.10.10 (cf.11.6) on Paul's way of speaking developed from a similar attitude to that adopted by Lucian to an oriental man of letters active in Athens, whose knowledge of Greek had evidently not reached the heights of elegance achieved by Lucian himself. Lucian describes this man's way of talking as an

incessant monotone, Greek, but in intonation and pronunciation
betraying his (barbarian) origins.[34]

Although to outward appearance Paul is a 'wanderer between
two worlds',[35] his theological thinking displays a quite astonishing
unity. That will already have been the case with the Jew Saul, and
the two periods of his life, the Jewish and the Christian, are closely
interlocked. This makes it clear that faith in the Messiah Jesus
was not something alien to the Jew, something which came from
outside.

Today hardly anyone argues that the later Paul, as H.J.Schoeps
and L.Goppelt conjecture, was at least indirectly influenced in his
christology by impressions from his youth, going back to the
public cult of the vegetation god Sandon-Heracles[36] worshipped in
Tarsus, or to titles used in the Hellenistic-Roman ruler cult;[37] this
is extremely improbable. Traces of a Cilician 'syncretism', or even
a syncretism from Asia Minor and Syria, are simply not to be
found in the Pauline letters that have come down to us.

2 The political situation of Tarsus and citizenship of the city

According to Luke, as I have already pointed out, Paul was not
only born in Tarsus but was a citizen of the city as well as being a
Roman citizen. Both these assertions have been constantly disputed in recent times. The question of the origin and social status
of Paul's family is closely connected with this.

There are problems in deciding whether Paul was a citizen of
the city in which he was born. It is striking that scholars have
either completely failed to discuss this question or – with few
exceptions – have treated it quite superficially when they have
done so. In the context of the tense narrative about Paul's arrest
in Jerusalem, Luke constructs a dialogue. When the tribune Lysias
asks in amazement in the Antonia citadel, 'Do you understand
Greek? Are you not that Egyptian who recently sparked off a
rebellion', Paul describes himself as a Jew and 'from Tarsus in
Cilicia, the citizen of no mean city'.[38] The question is how we are
to understand the words Ταρσεύς and πολίτης. Already in the
third century BCE, under Antiochus II or III, Tarsus was called
'Antioch on the Cydnus' and was given the constitution of a Greek
polis, though we do not know much of the details.[39] Caesar came

to Tarsus in 47 BCE and evidently showed such great favours to the city that in return it adopted the name Juliopolis.[40] After the murder of Caesar, his supporters gained the upper hand in the city, and for that Cassius, one of his murderers, imposed a heavy tribute on them in summer 43. All the resources of the city and temple were used to make the payment, and in addition a large number of the population had to be sold into slavery. The city's fortunes changed only with the victory of Caesar's party. Because of its loyalty to Caesar's cause, after the battle of Philippi in 42 BCE against Caesar's murderers Brutus and Cassius the city was given the status of a *civitas libera*[41] and exemption from taxes, and its territory was substantially enlarged at the expense of other cities so that it also included part of the Cilician coast. Although Tarsus was about eight miles inland, Tarsus became a port (cf. Acts 9.30). In the north its territory may have reached as far as the gates of Cilicia.

Those who had been sold into slavery at the time were freed again, and in some cases could have been given Roman citizenship at the same time.[42] Tarsus also had many ties with Augustus. Because of its positive attitude to Rome in the period between Pompey and Augustus, Roman citizenship was bestowed on a large number of citizens of the city. One of its citizens was Athenodorus, son of Sandon, who taught Augustus philosophy. In his old age he became head of the city, in order to implement necessary reforms. During the empire a census of 500 drachmae was a requisite for citizenship of Tarsus,[43] or, as seems to me more likely, citizenship could be bought for this sum.

Since citizenship was not readily bestowed on aliens in Greek *poleis* conscious of their traditions, Ramsay conjectured that right from the time of the refounding of the city by the early Seleucids, the Jews had had their own *phyle*,[44] and that Paul's family had settled there at that time. In his view an alternative was that citizenship could have been granted to Paul's father or grandfather for special services.[45] However, the close connection between Paul's family and the mother country tells against the first hypothesis, since it makes descent from an old Diaspora family improbable;[46] it is much more likely that Paul's father or grandfather had been given citizenship of Tarsus as a Roman citizen or freedman. The problem is that we do not know the constitution of the city,

which had been reformed by Athenodorus. We might further
suppose that from his birth Paul had been a member of the Jewish
community in Tarsus. We have quite a number of hints that there
were special political, economic and personal links between Cilicia,
particularly Tarsus, and Jewish Palestine. Josephus identifies the
famous biblical Tarshish in Spain with Tarsus in Cilicia.[47] As in
other places in the East, the Jews probably had certain privileges,
but not full citizenship, there, and *polites*[48] in Luke, as in the
Septuagint and in some passages in Josephus, does not denote full
legal citizenship but origin.[49] The very question of the *isopoliteia* of
the Jewish minority over against the 'Greek' citizens was vigorously
disputed[50] in some Eastern cities like Alexandria,[51] Caesarea,[52]
and Antioch.[53]

We can infer again from Dio Chrysostom that in some circumstances there were gradations in citizenship in Tarsus; he speaks
of a large proletarian group who were called 'textile workers'
(λινουργοί) and had 'an obscure constitutional status'.[54] On
the one hand they did not have full citizenship (ὥσπερ ἔξωθεν
πολιτείας), but on the other they could take part in assemblies of
the *demos*. Dio advises that they should all be given full citizenship
(τοὺς ἅπαντας ἀναγράψαι).

If we are to take Luke at his word, in view of the sources it seems
to me most plausible that Paul's citizenship of Tarsus came
through purchase, especially as we also have other reports about
the purchase of citizenship in Greek *poleis*.[55] Augustus is said to
have banned the Athenians from engaging in such trade, which
served above all to fill the state coffers and increase the number of
those liable to taxation and liturgy.[56] So what is said about Luke's
Paul in Acts 21.39 cannot be held to be either incorrect or certainly
correct.[57]

3 Roman citizenship and the names Paul and Saul

Still less is there adequate reason for doubting Luke's reports that
Paul was a Roman citizen.[58] The reasons recently once more
brought forward against this are not at all convincing.[59] Thus Paul
may have been flogged three times (II Cor.11.25) because he kept
quiet about his Roman citizenship deliberately in order to follow
Christ in his suffering. For him the 'marks of Jesus on his body'

(Gal.6.17) were tokens won in an honourable battle. Moreover, for his proclamation of the *Kyrios Iesous* crucified by the Roman authorities, mention of his possession of Roman citizenship would have been more of a hindrance. We must also consider the possibility that in acute states of emergency individual city magistrates and Roman magistrates were not very bothered about the fact of Paul's citizenship,[60] not to mention the difficulties there would have been in demonstrating this citizenship during the kind of tumult which usually preceded his arrests. At that time people did not go around with a personal passport in their pockets.[61] Moreover we have a whole series of accounts from the first century of Roman citizens having been crucified – a much more serious matter than a mere flogging.[62] Before the outbreak of the Jewish War in 66 CE, the procurator Gessius Florus had two Jews who were Roman *equites* publicly flogged and executed by crucifixion.[63] Some Romans suffered the same fate on Rhodes in 44 CE, having been condemned to death by the city authorities of the old *civitas libera et foederata*.[64] By contrast, flogging was merely an act of local police *coercitio*, which was performed much more frequently and more swiftly. Moreover the fact that Paul never speaks of the privilege of his citizenship does not mean anything, since he keeps quiet about almost all of his family matters. Had Paul been a mere *peregrinus*, he would very probably have been condemned in Judaea without much fuss and would not have been sent for the verdict of the emperor in Rome. Indeed perhaps his citizenship of Tarsus also played some part in this.[65] Moreover a trial lasting around five years is almost inconceivable in the case of a Jewish provincial without means. The claim of Wolfgang Stegemann that this was because of the 'political significance of the case' and because the apostle was 'accused of causing a riot by the supreme self-governing body in Jerusalem' replaces clear statements with incredible hypotheses. We should not confuse Paul with a long-standing, successful and therefore politically dangerous bandit leader like Eleazar ben Dinai or a popular agitator in a big way like the weaver Jonathes in Cyrene, who as *Moses redivivus* led a large number of people into the wilderness in order to show them 'signs and wonders'. Eleazar was sent to Rome by Felix as an example of his military successes; Jonathes, because matters had got out of hand

for the governor as a result of the numerous denunciations of the
prisoner, which had reached as far as Rome.[66]

If Paul's Roman citizenship and thus the basis of his trial is a
Lukan invention, then one should finally come clean and regard
the *whole* of Acts as romantic fiction. But even its severest critics
do not want to draw this conclusion. Only W.Schmithals, who is
unsurpassed in imaginative, speculative, 'radical' criticism, is also
consistent here. He conjectures that Paul was first arrested in
Rome.[67] But even he is not yet radical and consistent enough. For
if Luke is deceptive to this degree, did Paul have to come to Rome
at all? Perhaps he had already been liquidated in Jerusalem or
disappeared without trace somewhere else in the East. It is
remarkable that where there is radical mistrust of the ancient
sources because of their 'bias', the possibilities of a scholar's own
biassed imagination extend all the further because all the boundary
posts have been taken down.

Nor does the objection that Paul nowhere mentions his complete
three-part Roman name mean anything. First, this usage was
seldom customary in Greek-speaking circles and went against the
usage of Judaism and early Christianity even more. We do not
have the Roman names for many other early Christians, for
example already in the list of people whom Paul greets in Romans
16,[68] in Clement of Rome, in the list of bishops of Rome until well
into the third century, and even in the case of such prominent
teachers as Hippolytus. Such information first emerges with
African notables like Tertullian and Cyprian.[69] The important
thing for Christians was not the privilege of an earthly citizenship
but the fact that they were brothers and sisters.[70] So we can
certainly say that Paul did not attach any special value to his
citizenship. However, that does not exclude the possibility that he
was a Roman citizen who made use of the fact in particular
circumstances, especially when they were threatening. As he
urgently wanted to get to Rome, he will have thrown his Roman
citizenship on to the scales at the decisive moment to achieve his
purpose.

It has to be said that the name 'Paul' itself is not very common
among Romans;[71] it was extremely rare among non-Romans,
above all in the Greek East, and does not occur at all among Jews.
In the substantially later Jewish inscriptions of Beth She'arim in

Galilee (second to fourth century), all we find is a spice-seller with the name Paulinus, which is more frequent only from the third to fourth centuries.[72] It continues to be unclear why the young Jew with the proud biblical-Palestinian name Sha'ul, which at the same time emphasized the descent of his family from the tribe of Benjamin, was given this Latin *cognomen*. The most plausible conjecture is still that it may be connected with the personal associations of Paul's father, perhaps with his patron.[73] However, further speculations, for example that Paul's family had as patrons the family of Sergius Paulus in Pisidian Antioch, should not be pursued.[74] It seems to me to be questionable whether the unusual name was chosen because of the assonance between Saulus and Paulus, as Sherwin-White conjectured.[75] One might rather suppose that the usual Greek way of writing Sha'ul Σαούλ (LXX) or Σαουλος in Josephus and in a later Jewish foundation inscription from Apamea[76] was assimilated to the pronunciation of the Roman name Παυλος in the form of the simplified Σαυλος. Luke was fully aware of this difference in writing the name. In the threefold description of the vision at the apostle's call Paul is always addressed by the Lord with the biblical form of the name.[77] It is also worth mentioning that with two very late exceptions, the inscription from Syrian Apamea mentioned above and a second from Phthiotic Thebes on the borders of Thessaly, *Saul(os)* never appears among Diaspora Jews but does so quite often in Josephus, in rabbinic texts, and on ostraca and in inscriptions in Palestine.[78]

Luke is also our sole source of information about the Hebrew name. Why should he not also have invented this in order to make Paul a Palestinian Jew through and through – something of which he is often accused – so that he could then shape the shift in Paul's life with dramatic effect? Sometimes the radical critics seem to be afraid of their own courage. Here, however, there is a striking connection between the name Sha'ul, the most famous of the Benjaminites, and the quite extraordinary information, given twice by Paul himself, that he was a member of the tribe.[79] At the only point at which Luke mentions the two names together he does so connecting them in the way in which *nomen* and *cognomen* are often connected in papyri and inscriptions.[80] So the transition to the new name does not take place at the call but at the point where for the first time Paul moves from a Jewish-Christian to a pagan environment as missionary to the Gentiles; and at the same time an eminent 'namesake', Sergius Paulus the governor of Cyprus, appears as the first 'Gentile Christian' convert of Paul's to be mentioned by name.[81] From the time of the early church on, certain speculations have been associated with this link between the change of name and the emergence of Sergius Paulus.[82] Here it is probably enough to suppose that this coincidence derives from the narrator Luke, who while knowing how to arrange facts effectively, need not necessarily have made them up himself.

But there is possibly a connection between Sergius Paulus the governor of Cyprus and the Sergii Pauli attested by inscriptions in the Roman colony of Antiochia Caesarea in Pisidia; and it could be that the visit to Pisidian Antioch on the so-called first missionary journey is connected with Paul's missionary success with the governor of Cyprus. However, as I have already said, we need not infer any wider client relationship between this high official and his family and the family of the Jew Paul from Tarsus.[83]

That the missionary to the Gentiles uses only his non-Jewish name in the letters may well be an indication that in this more external point he wanted to put himself on the same footing with the non-Jews to whom he proclaimed the gospel (I Cor.9.21). His own Hebrew name Saul, linked to the first king of Israel, had now become unimportant to him, as had his descent from the tribe of Benjamin (Phil.3.5,7).

Finally, the reality of Paul's Roman citizenship is also supported by the fact that geographically this bearer of a rare Roman name thinks entirely in Roman categories,[84] and in his world-wide plans for mission has only the empire and its provinces in view: the Parthian east, the barbarian north and the Arab-Libyan south are unimportant to him (for Luke things are different). The Hellenistic-Jewish metropolis of Alexandria (the great rival, indeed the ideological enemy of Rome[85]) plays no role in his concerns. At a very early stage his gaze focusses on the Roman capital (Rom.1.10ff.), and then extends further to the Western provinces of the Iberian peninsula (Rom.15.24), the end of the world, where people spoke predominantly Latin. It is quite conceivable that as a Roman citizen Paul himself spoke some Latin. His travel strategy is orientated on the names of the Roman provinces – starting from Judaea with its capital Jerusalem (Rom.15.25), through the double province of Syria and Cilicia, Galatia (I firmly support the hypothesis of a southern Galatian province), Asia, Macedonia and Achaea (Rom.15.26), going on to Illyricum (15.19). Here he concentrates on the provincial capitals, and it is probably no coincidence that Roman colonies like Antioch in Pisidia, Iconium, Lystra, Troas and Philippi also play an important role.[86] Philippians 3.20f. becomes particularly significant in a letter from a Roman citizen to the Christian community of that famous Roman foundation in the East: it is about 'our citizenship' (πολίτευμα) which is common to both.[87] That Romans 13.1-7, which many people find so offensive (and which must be judged in the wider context of 12.1-13.14 with its focal point in 13.8a) fits admirably into this picture of Paul the Roman citizen need hardly be mentioned.

We can only venture hypotheses with relative degrees of probability about how Paul's father (or his ancestors) acquired Roman citizenship.[88] It is relatively improbable that it was bestowed on them for political or military services, though this cannot be ruled out completely. Caesar on his Egyptian adventure already received powerful support from Jewish troops of the high priest Hyrcanus II under the leadership of Antipater and showed himself particularly well disposed towards the Jews. After his death the Jews especially are said to have mourned him and to have 'come to visit his funeral pyre night after night'.[89] As early as 50 BCE a large number of Jews were already Roman citizens and had been exempted from military service by the consul Lucius Lentulus.[90] In Sardes, as Roman citizens they were granted freedom of assembly and their own judicature.[91]

A more important reason for extending this privilege, particularly among Jews who came from Palestine, was, however, the emancipation of Jewish slaves by Roman citizens, even if there were still certain restrictions on the citizenship of the *libertus* in the first (and possibly second) generation.[92] Here purchasing freedom by relatives and friends may have played a part. In ancient Judaism it was regarded as a religious duty.[93] Stegemann overlooks this decisive point, either because he misunderstands its significance or because he deliberately wants to play it down. According to Philo's well-known report, which has to be taken very seriously by historians, the majority of Jews living in Rome were Roman

citizens. Having been carried off to Italy as prisoners of war, in
due course they were freed by their owners who 'did not compel
them to corrupt their ancestral laws'. Augustus, on being given
precise information about their religious practices, 'did not expel
them from Rome nor deprive them of Roman citizen rights because
they were concerned to keep their Jewish faith'.[94] Despite some
sporadic compulsory measures on the part of individual emperors
against the Jews, especially in Rome, this toleration towards new
citizens (which was typically Roman) was not abandoned in the
case of a strange and exclusive religion. As a rule they were exempt
from military service, though it must be stressed here that in the
late Republic and the period of the early Empire the Roman
army was made up of volunteers. Notice was taken of religious
peculiarities in a variety of other ways. Unless he held office, a
Jew, whether a Roman citizen or not, did not have to perform any
religious actions in connection with the emperor cult, either in
Rome or in the Greek-speaking East, where the emperor cult
flourished more strongly after the period of the Hellenistic mon-
archies than in the capital itself. Some exemptions merely confirm
this rule, and in times of crisis they did not so much affect Roman
citizens as *peregrini*. Only the short period of the reign of Caligula
is an exception here. However, even such an educated Jew as
Philo, who came from the richest Jewish family in Egypt, as a
Roman citizen never moved an inch in the direction of the demands
of the ruler cult, but produced vigorous polemic against it in his
Legatio ad Gaium. His nephew Tiberius Julius Alexander became
an apostate not because of external compulsion, but for the sake
of his brilliant career. With the tendency which existed in the early
principate to encourage citizens who came from the East and
citizens of Rome without means to emigrate to the East, Jewish
freedmen will have been quite ready to follow this course.

In attributing to Jews with Roman citizenship 'a high degree of
adaptation to paganism' and nurturing 'the greatest doubt as to
whether Paul's father and Paul himself can have been orthodox
Jews and Roman citizens at the same time',[95] Stegemann is
completely overlooking what the sources say; clearly he does not
know them well enough. In fact Roman Jewry with its high
proportion of Roman citizens was much closer to the 'orthodox'
mother country than the Alexandrians, who were more indepen-

dent of it – and they too, or at least the great majority of them, were not negligent in questions of their faith. Moreover the Jewish community in Rome carried on a successful mission among pagan citizens, about which Roman writers like Horace, Seneca and Juvenal complained bitterly.[96] Finally, the freeing of a Jewish slave and the acquisition of citizenship which went with it was not up to the slave, but his master, who often derived financial benefit from it.

In addition we have much information about the return of Jewish freedmen to Judaea; they then lived there as Roman citizens. Probably the Roman authorities even encouraged such a return, because it gave them the possibility of reducing the number of supporters of the many oriental cults in the imperial capital, who were suspect to them.[97] Certainly[98] the nucleus of the συν-αγωγή...Λιβερτίνων mentioned in Acts 6 consisted of such Roman *libertini* and their families – how else could such a designation have arisen?[99] The Theodotus son of Vettenus who founded a synagogue in Jerusalem was also presumably a descendant of such a person; his patronym indicates Roman origin and the title priest that he was one of the Jewish nobility by birth.[100] When Pompey captured the Temple in 63 BCE many priests were taken as prisoners to Rome; when they were later emancipated, they eagerly looked for possible ways of returning to the Holy City.

According to Luke, Silas-Silvanus of Jerusalem, who accompanied Paul on the so-called second missionary journey, was also a Roman citizen.[101] How respectable a Roman freedman could be in Judaea is evident from the tomb of the 'Goliath' family in Jericho, where the ossuary of a son of the ancestor of the family bears the inscription: Θεοδότου ἀπελευθέρου βασιλίσσης Ἀγριππείνης σόρος. This Theodotus belonged to the 'house of Caesar' (οἶκος Καίσαρος); the 'empress Agrippina' was the wife of Claudius and mother of Nero. His Hebrew name was Nath(an)'el (*ntn'l*), and people seem to have been proud of the high rank of this member of the family even in Jewish Palestine – otherwise it would not have been mentioned at such length on the ossuary.[102]

Although the majority of inscriptions are Greek, despite the preponderance of Semitic names, the ossuary of Theodotus' daughter has an Aramaic inscription: 'Mary, daughter of Nath(an)el daughter of Shlomsion (*šlmsywn*)'. The official Roman name of this freedman – who as a *libertus* of the empress belonged to the *gens Iulia* – is missing. It was unusual in Judaea and indeed throughout the Roman East.[103] However, beyond question it can be seen that Roman citizenship – which as a rule was acquired unasked for – and nationalist fidelity to ancestral religion could very easily be interconnected.

So it seems most likely that Paul's forebears, too, were given the privileged status of citizenship – unasked for – when they were freed by a Roman citizen. Jerome reports in his commentary on Philemon that Paul's parents came from the neighbourhood of Gischala and that they had been carried off to Tarsus in the upheavals of war which laid waste to Judaea. The young Paul had accompanied his parents into their new situation. In *De viris illustribus* 5 Jerome says even more briefly and clearly that Paul himself came from Gischala in Judaea and had emigrated from there to Tarsus with his parents as a Roman prisoner of war.[104] However, this contradicts Acts 22.28 (cf.22.3), where Luke explicitly makes Paul tell Claudius Lysias that he was born a Roman citizen. If Jerome, whose presumably written source remains unknown,[105] were right, we might presuppose that Paul was only a *libertus* and not a full Roman citizen. The widely read patriarch Photius, who perhaps drew on the same source as Jerome, attempted to resolve the contradiction by claiming that Paul was conceived in Gischala and born in Tarsus.[106] This enigmatic piece of information cannot now be verified historically, but it does show that at a relatively early stage it was assumed in the early church that the legal position of Paul or that of his family had come about through emancipation. It seems quite plausible that Paul's forebears became prisoners and slaves as the result of hostilities which kept flaring up after the sacking of the Temple by Pompey in 63 BCE. How and why Paul's parents or ancestors came to Tarsus remains open. The reason might be connected with their Roman master or patron, and they could have come by a roundabout route, even via Rome. Tarsus was a significant metropolis, only slightly inferior to Antioch, in which numerous Roman citizens lived: some had migrated there, and some were resident Greeks who had earned their citizenship by merit. Paul's father (or grandfather) could have been the freedman of such a Roman or Greek, but it is also conceivable that he was the administrator in Tarsus of the property of a rich Roman who himself lived elsewhere, possibly even in the imperial court. Here there are many possibilities, but no probabilities.

4 Social origin and profession

There is also great uncertainty about the apostle's social origins. Ramsay's assumption was that Paul 'belonged to a family of wealth and position';[107] Lietzmann conjectured 'that the boy grew up in a well-to-do house';[108] Eduard Meyer even assumed that 'his father had a factory in which tents were made'.[109] Mommsen, too, went on the assumption that 'though an experienced craftsman, he belonged to a respectable middle-class family', since only 'prominent municipal figures' were singled out for Roman citizenship.[110] If Paul came from a family of freedmen, some of these hypotheses can be eliminated, but it is even less possible to infer from the apostle's later remarks about his poverty and laborious manual labour that he originated from a proletarian family without possessions, attractive though these notions may seem to some exegetes today.[111] By contrast we have quite a number of accounts of very rich freedmen from the period of the early Principate. Perhaps the most flamboyant example, one of many others, is the host in book 15 of Petronius's *Satyricon* (Trimalchio's Feast). A former Syrian slave, after being set free Trimalchio had become rich by speculating in shipping merchandise.[112] Ramsay had already referred to a further possibility, namely that the change in the young scribe's life possibly resulted in a break with his family and had the inevitable financial consequences.[113] One might, however, equally assume that after his call Paul gave away his possessions for missionary work and then later had to earn his own living. Furthermore his craft as σκηνοποιός, which is again attested only by Luke,[114] need not necessarily of itself indicate poverty: the meaning of the term was already interpreted in different ways in the early church. Even now, many owners of major businesses are proud of having learned 'on the shop floor', i.e. having begin their professional career by learning a job.

In the second century the rabbis required fathers to teach their sons a craft, a practice which – contrary to the view of R.F.Hock – probably goes back to the early Pharisaic period in the first century BCE; for the Pharisaic scribes in the period before 70 also needed a secure way of earning their bread, and at that time crafts already were 'golden opportunities'.[115] Moreover work as an independent craftsman left a person free to arrange the day and, given the stress on the importance of study, made it possible to order one's own life. It was the economic independence provided by practising a craft which enabled scribes to take pupils without charging them, in contrast to the pupils of Greek teachers of rhetoric or philosophy.[116] This 'ideal' of independence could still have influenced Paul, in his deliberate renunciation of the right to support as a missionary (I Thess.2.9; I Cor.9; II Cor.11.7-11; 12.13f.). Contemporary Judaism was evidently no longer familiar with the widespread contempt for manual labour which is still evident in Ben Sira.[117] The Pharisees were certainly no aristocratic movement of the rich; as a lay movement they were closer to the ordinary people and in some opposition to the priestly aristocracy and the rich landowners from among the lay nobility or the Herodians. It is precisely for that reason that they continued to be concerned for the education of the whole people in the law, and had also changed their attitude to manual work since the time of Koheleth and Ben Sira. Some great teachers and pious men from the early period like Hillel and Shammai, the legendary Abba Hilkia and the miracle-worker Hanina b.Dosa, and indeed Akiba, were said to have suffered great poverty in their youth and to have found it hard to earn a living.[118] Shemaiah, Hillel's teacher, is said to have demanded: 'Love manual work and hate being a master and seek no acquaintance with the authorities.'[119] Accordingly Paul need not have learned his craft in Tarsus; he *could* also have taken it up in connection with his studies as a scribe or even later as a Christian, in order to be independent as a missionary. In emphatically putting forward in his informative study the view that Paul learned his trade from his father and underwent a period of apprenticeship of two to three years between the ages of thirteen and fifteen, R.F.Hock is claiming to know rather too much. We cannot simply draw conclusions from apprentice's articles in papyri, where the trade of tentmaker does not appear, to Paul's education in a trade, and we know too little about family conditions to be able to draw sufficiently probable conclusions about his training and his social status.[120]

In his trade Paul was evidently very mobile and not bound to expensive tools. Some strong cutting tools and needles, and a large table of the kind one could find anywhere, might have been enough. Therefore it was possible for him later to find a place to work in any great city without too much trouble. Presumably as a 'tentmaker' he primarily worked in leather, and the material in which he worked perhaps also included the famous cilicium for which Tarsus was known: a thick, coarse material from Cilician goat hair which among other things could be used for military purposes; as a protection against shots; to guard buildings against rain and wind; and as clothing for seamen.[121] The main purchaser of leather tents was the Roman army, but it is hardly probable that Paul's family was given Roman citizenship because of its high-class army supplies.[122] We should not understand the designation 'tentmaker' in too narrow a sense. The goods produced in this trade may have included a variety of leather articles or comparable products, just as a 'saddler' does not produce only saddles.

That despite this craft Paul was not just a simple proletarian is evident from the old traditions of his family which had been carefully preserved, and of which it was evidently proud. Only a few families could clearly derive their origin from a particular tribe which had an eminent place in the history of the people of God. Here we may with justification speak of 'lay nobility by birth', even if his family was not very rich. Paul's remarkable Graeco-Jewish education also indicates an above-average social origin. In antiquity a better education – above all a Greek education – was not to be had for nothing; as a rule it presupposed some material support. One had to pay to go to the *grammatistes*, the Greek elementary teacher. In other words, at the least Paul will have come from a family of that 'petty-bourgeois' middle class which was of decisive significance for the origin and expansion of Christianity. In the same way, we cannot rule out the possibility that he came from a well-to-do family of freedmen: this is supported by the facts not only that they had citizenship of Tarsus, which was obtained by purchase (assuming that the considerations set out above are correct), but also that Paul was sent as a plaintiff to Rome. The material needs for financing higher education were presumably the same in Jerusalem as in Tarsus.

II Upbringing and Education: Tarsus or Jerusalem?

This brings us to a further point of dispute. Where did Paul get his solid elementary education, or, to put it more simply: where did he go to school – in the metropolis of Cilicia or in the Holy City? Here we come to a point where, in addition to the texts in Luke which have been used so far, Paul's own evidence, which hitherto has been neglected, is taking on increasing significance. For with it at the same time we come to the heart of the question of the 'pre-Christian Paul', to the problem of the Jewish theologian. The first, truly fundamental, Christian theologian must already have been a reflective theological thinker as a Pharisaic Jew before the change in his life. This fact is completely overlooked in the most recent account by A.J.Saldarini, who argues in a superficial way. 'Paul,' he comments, 'seems to have been a member of the lower classes with some links to the governing classes. His membership in the Pharisees may have been such a link. However, it is not clear that Paul, as a Pharisee, had gained any particular education or standing in the community.'[123] This comment leaves unexplained all the questions which are important for Paul's historical activity. We do not do him justice if we completely pass over his intellectual contribution, which has been a motive force in world history down to the present day. Precisely as an intellectual and religious figure – why not just say a theologian? – he also belongs in Judaism, since he did not first learn to reflect on God's word and its effect and God's revelation in history to his people in judgment and grace when he became a Christian; it is already part of the fundamental Jewish presuppositions of his life.[124] In the face of this question the problems of Paul's native city, his citizenship and the social status of his family, which have been discussed so far and still remain so popular, become secondary, even if they are not insignificant. To put it more pointedly: the letters of Paul are not only the earliest and most important source for the origin of earliest Christianity, but are also a significant source for the religious thought of a great 'Jewish outsider' in the first century CE.

On the other hand it is quite difficult to draw conclusions from the apostle's comments in his letters, which were written twenty years or more after the change in his life, to the Jewish theologoumena which dominated the thought of the Jewish scribe who at that time was relatively young, especially as we have hardly any direct evidence about Jewish Pharisaic thought from the first half of the first century of our era. The rabbinic accounts of the controversies between Hillel and Shammai and the outbreak of the Jewish War are sparse and, at least in part, historically problematical, and Josephus, too, is silent about the Pharisees in the time of the procurators between Archelaus and 66 CE. We know from him only that they were a religious Jewish-Palestinian 'party' of great influence. The source about the Pharisees of that period which is nearest to them in time is essentially the New Testament, above all Mark, Luke (with Acts) and Paul himself.[125] As far as Paul's later thought as a Christian thinker is concerned, hardly one stone will have been left on another in these more than twenty years between the time of the change in his life and the great letters. His life had taken another, unhoped-for direction in too radical a way. On the other hand, he adopted the individual elements of his new thought from the rich Jewish tradition, and used them to describe the new overwhelming experience which had struck him. So we will do well first to 'feel our way forward' by means of Paul's own testimonies about himself, in which he speaks directly about his past, and at the same time consider the Lukan accounts, the content of which corresponds with these testimonies in an amazing way. These parallels between Luke and the letters of Paul on the apostle's Jewish past are all the more striking since in Luke/Acts, which was written around 75-80, Luke evidently was not yet aware of the collection of Paul's letters.

The mistrust of the *auctor ad Theophilum* which has now become almost a universal fashion hardly takes us any further here, especially as the radical critics of Luke are all too fond of suppressing how much they know *only* from Luke, and their selection of what they accept and reject of Paul, often at whim, is in fact partly based on ignorance.

Paul himself is certainly the main source, but we can add Luke as long as there are no really serious objections to him; the bias of which he is constantly accused, a tendency consciously to falsify the true historical situation and thus to invent new 'facts', has proved questionable.

The starting point for our attempt at an approach must be the statements about Paul's education. Here we have a hotly disputed tradition in Luke and some testimonies by Paul which basically confirm and supplement it.

1 Luke's accounts (Acts 22.3; 26.4f.; 23.6) and Paul's own testimony

The first passage comes at the beginning of a speech which Luke attributes to the apostle at his arrest in Jerusalem, and which he is have said to have made in Aramaic (τῇ Ἑβραΐδι διαλέκτῳ) to the excited crowd in Jerusalem:

> I am a Jew, born at Tarsus in Cilicia, but brought up in this city at the feet of Gamaliel, educated according to the strict matter of the laws of our fathers, being zealous for God as you all are this day.[126]

In the introduction to the speech before Agrippa II and Berenice Luke makes Paul say very much the same thing but more briefly:

> My manner of life from my youth, spent from the beginning among my own nation and in Jerusalem, is known by all the Jews. They have known for a long time, if they are willing to testify, that according to the strictest party of our religion I have lived as a Pharisee.[127]

To the Sanhedrin in Jerusalem Luke makes him also confess:

> Brethren, I am a Pharisee, a son of Pharisees; with respect to the hope and the resurrection of the dead I am on trial.[128]

Philippians 3.4-6, by contrast, is addressed to Jewish-Christian opponents on whom in the paragraph immediately preceding Paul had cast scorn in bitter polemic.

If any other man thinks he has reason for confidence in the flesh, I have more; circumcised on the eighth day, of the people of Israel, of the tribe of Benjamin, a Hebrew born of Hebrews, as to the law a Pharisee, as to zeal a persecutor of the church, as to righteousness under the law blameless.[129]

Even if for the sake of stressing continuity one sought to interpret Luke's Paul in terms of the situation of gradually more threatening persecution at the time of the composition of Luke-Acts under the Flavians,[130] and conversely to find in Paul's own words the sometimes exaggerated polemical sharpness which is characteristic of him, the contrast in the *intention* of these relatively similar biographical notes remains unbridgeable. Luke wants to depict Paul in his continuity with Judaism, while Paul himself wants to express the radical break with all that had once been dear to him as a Pharisaic Jew faithful to the law. That this Pauline 'look back in anger' shows clearly the degree to which even when he was old (Philippians was presumably written in Rome) the apostle continued to dwell on his Jewish past is a rather different matter. It is all the more striking that despite this contrary intention, the *information* provided by Luke, who does not know the letters of Paul, and Paul's own testimony, are very close together in content.

The Philippians passage is supplemented by three further texts from the letters, first a short passage from polemic against Jewish-Christian opponents, who are causing trouble in Corinth and could be representatives of Peter's mission:

But whatever any one dares to boast of – I am speaking as a fool – I also dare to boast of that. Are they Hebrews? So am I. Are they Israelites? So am I. Are they descendants of Abraham? So am I.[131]

In other words, the apostle is here aware of his equal rights with his opponents, who either came from the mother country of Palestine or were closely associated with it.

The second text comes from that part of Romans in which the apostle has the salvation of his people in view in a special way:

I ask then, has God rejected his people? By no means! I myself am an Israelite, a descendant of Abraham, a member of the tribe of Benjamin.[132]

The degree to which Paul was (and remained) a Jew is clear, thirdly, at the beginning of the passage which enumerates the saving benefits of Israel, and which follows the reference to his constant and passionate intercession for his own people:

> For the sake of my brethren, my kinsmen by race. They are Israelites, and to them belong the sonship, the glory, the covenants, the giving of the law, the worship, and the promises; to them belong the patriarchs, and of their race, according to the flesh, is the Messiah...[133]

1.1 The thesis of W.C.van Unnik

If we survey all the evidence, the problem of the pre-Christian Paul focusses on the question: where principally did Paul get the Jewish (and Greek) education that moulded him, in Tarsus or in Jerusalem (or in both cities successively)? W.C.van Unnik expresses this problem as a pure alternative in the title of his fundamental study *Tarsus or Jerusalem*. On the basis of a painstaking philological investigation of Acts 22.3 – 'to put the matter under the microscope' – he came down clearly for Jerusalem.

In this passage, with the three participles γεγεννημένος, ἀνατεθραμμένος and πεπαιδευμένος, Luke uses a biographical scheme which says:

> Paul was born in Tarsus, it was in Jerusalem that he received his upbringing in the parental home, just as it was in Jerusalem that he received his later schooling for the rabbinate.

In other words, van Unnik assumes that Paul's parents returned to Jerusalem with him when he was still a small child:

> This removal took place quite early in Paul's life, apparently before he could peep round the corner of the door and certainly before he went roaming on the street.[134]

Thus according to van Unnik, the pagan Hellenistic milieu of the great city could not have 'corrupted' him later. A further conclusion is that his mother tongue was Aramaic, not Greek: 'It can safely be said, that Aramaic was his earliest and principal tongue.'[135] To begin with, we must take the arguments of van Unnik's impressive investigation very seriously, since in Acts 26.4f. in Paul's speech before Agrippa Luke put considerable stress on the statement in 22.3, piling up in an over-loaded style biographical stylistic elements like 'from my youth up, from the beginning' (ἐκ νεότητος, ἀπ'ἀρχῆς) to serve apologetic purposes.[136] At this point Luke seems to have been very sure of his case, but on the other hand one can ask whether perhaps above all in 26.4 as a good rhetorician he has not somewhat exaggerated (as he was sometimes fond of doing) with his 'is known by all the Jews who knew me formerly'.

1.2 Galatians 1.22 and the objections to an early stay by Paul in Jerusalem

True, since Mommsen's article 'The Legal Proceedings over the Apostle Paul',[137] Gal.1.22 has been constantly quoted against any stay of the pre-Christian Paul in Jerusalem, but in my view this is incorrect. In a completely false interpretation Mommsen himself understands the ἐν τῷ γένει μου ('among my people', Gal.1.14) not in terms of the Jewish people but in terms of the Jews of Tarsus, and also wants to locate the activity of Paul the persecutor in Tarsus. How he could read this out of the account by Paul in Gal.1.13ff. remains incomprehensible, since in 1.17 there is suddenly a mention of a return to Damascus. He does not say a word to indicate that his 'former life in Judaism' or his progress in it (1.13f.) took place in Tarsus. In II Cor.11.26 κινδύνοις ἐκ γένους ('dangers from my own people') and Phil.3.5 ἐκ γένους Ἰσραήλ ('of the people of Israel'), Paul is quite naturally using γένος of his own people. In addition, Mommsen – like a large proportion of present-day exegetes – attached too little importance to the fact that Paul termed himself a 'Hebrew of the Hebrews' and 'as to the law a Pharisee'. How and why the Pharisee Paul, 'in whose case according to Gal.1 it is *very* uncertain whether he stayed in Jerusalem before his Damascus experience',[138] came from Tarsus to Arabia (Gal.1.17) – and strictly avoided Jerusalem (one has only to look at the map) – is neither considered nor explained. Strecker therefore wanted to strengthen this questionable reference to Gal.1.22 by arguing from the smallness of the population of Jerusalem, which Jeremias had estimated at 25,000.

This verse is historically free from doubt only if Paul had not in fact been in Jerusalem before the 'apostolic council' (Gal.2.11), with the exception of a short visit to Cephas (Gal.1.18).[139]

But here – evidently without realizing it – Strecker is on particularly thin ice. The estimates range between 10,000 and 150,000, and the most recent investigations by J.Wilkinson and M.Broshi assume that the number of inhabitants grew between the Hasmonaeans and 66 CE from around 32,000 to around 80,000.[140] Certainly Jerusalem was not a village in which everyone knew everyone else. My own city of Tübingen has 60,000 inhabitants, and I myself know only a very few of them; indeed I know only a tiny proportion of the teaching staff of the university 'by sight' (thus Gal.1.22, κατὰ πρόσωπον), and vice versa the same thing may apply.

1.3 The role of Jerusalem in Paul[141]

Acts 22.3 was certainly formulated by Luke, but it is based on older information, as is the information about the existence of a young nephew of Paul in the Holy City[142] and Paul's Pharisaic origin (Acts 23.6). Here Luke is relying on good and trustworthy tradition, which ultimately finds some support in Paul himself. One might refer first in this connection to Rom.15.19, a text which is normally overlooked, where Paul outlines the span of his missionary work so far:

> So that from Jerusalem and in a circle round to Illyricum I have fully preached the gospel of Christ.[143]

The subject here, expressed by the accusative of the first person, με, in an accusative I clause, may not simply be suppressed in favour of 'the overall movement of the gospel' that 'began with the preaching of the very first apostles in Jerusalem', which is how U.Wilckens takes it;[144] rather, this is exclusively the missionary work of the apostle himself – which was very much under attack – and the reference to Jerusalem as a starting point for his missionary work shows how closely he personally is connected with the Holy City. It played a unique role in his career, and despite the threat to his life he wants to return there again before he goes to the distant West. Nor will Paul have spoken any explosive untruths to the Romans who, while unknown to him, were all too well informed about him. We *could* look at the course of his missionary activity as follows. We already saw the role played in his letters by Jerusalem (and the primitive community) in contrast to Antioch and Damascus or Ephesus and Corinth (which are mentioned more by chance), or even Tarsus, which he keeps from us completely. So we must assume that 'from Jerusalem' is to be related strictly to his person: his missionary career began from the Holy City.[145] He left Jerusalem and was called to become a messenger of the gospel by his vision of Christ on the road, shortly before he reached Damascus. The ἐν κύκλῳ ('in a circle') may indicate the roundabout way he took via Damascus and 'Arabia'. However, Jerusalem remained his starting point. Damascus and probably also the territory of Nabataea were his first mission stations. But in mentioning them we have got well ahead of ourselves.

2 Paul's own testimony about his origins

2.1 A Hebrew of the tribe of Benjamin

The sequences of privileges are another striking feature: 'Hebrews', 'Israelites', 'descendants of Abraham' (II Cor.11.22); 'Israelite', 'descendant of Abraham', 'of the tribe of Benjamin' (Rom.11.1); and more emphatically Phil.3.4b-6: 'circumcised on the eighth day', 'of the people of Israel', 'of the tribe of Benjamin', 'Hebrew of Hebrews', 'Pharisee'. Neither in II Cor.11.22 nor in Phil.3.5 can Hebrew mean anything other than someone speaking Ἑβραϊστί, i.e. a Palestinian Jew speaking the sacred language or Aramaic, or a Diaspora Jew, who in origin and education had extremely close connections with the mother country and who therefore also understood Hebrew.[146] In this context the term certainly does not mean 'Jew' as opposed to Gentile, since that is already expressed by the belonging to Israel, and here as in similar sequences in Paul we do not have an accumulation of synonyms. The first list goes from the more special to the broader; in the second and third it is the other way round: there it is striking that 'Hebrew' comes immediately before 'Pharisee'. Evidently the rival missionaries attached special importance to their pure Judaism and their origin from the Aramaic-speaking mother country. The decisive comments on this sequence can already be found in J.B.Light-foot:[147]

> The four clauses at the beginning of the fifth verse, which describe the privileges inherited by the Apostle apart from his own act of will, are arranged in an ascending scale.

> 1. The circumcision on the eighth day shows that neither Paul himself nor his parents were Gentiles, but rather have to be regarded as Jews who observed the law strictly. Evidently despite Gen.17.12 and Lev.12.3 it was not taken for granted in the Diaspora that 'as far as circumcision went one was an eighth-dayer'. Perhaps this ὀκταήμερος (Phil.3.5) was even a special distinction.[148]

> 2. Nor was Paul a descendant of proselytes; his parents had belonged to the people of Israel from birth.

> 3. His forebears belonged to the tribe of Benjamin which had remained faithful to the Temple on Mount Zion and to Judah.

> 4. He is not a Diaspora Jew alienated from the Holy Land and speaking a foreign language; he and his forebears regard themselves as really true Israelites, as inhabitants of Eretz Israel.

To the four privileges which were given him without his wanting them are added three others which rest on his own decision: that he belonged to the Pharisaic community; that he was active as a persecutor; and that he was completely obedient to the law.

The closest parallel to this designation related to the Eretz Israel, and his language is the contrast depicted in Acts 6.1 between the 'Hellenists' and the 'Hebrews'.[149] Presumably – in an analogous way to his travelling companion Barnabas – Paul could have also counted himself among the 'Hebrews' in Jerusalem by virtue of the origin of his family and his knowledge of languages; in other words, as a 'wanderer between two worlds' he would have had a choice between the two groups. The reference to the tribe of Benjamin (cf.Rom.11.1) at the same time shows that Paul's family was proud of its antiquity, going back to the early period of the Bible, and the precision of its genealogy. The book of Chronicles, which was composed in the fourth century BCE, still lists Benjaminite families (7.6-11; 8; 9.7-9). Mordecai from the book of Esther was a prominent 'fellow tribesman', as was the patriarch Jehuda ha-Nāsī, the redactor of the Mishnah, who according to an authentic account claimed Benjamin as a tribal ancestor. That would also apply to Jehuda's great-great grandfather Gamaliel I, who according to Luke was Paul's teacher.[150] Another prominent Jerusalem family, which provided wood for the sacrifices on 10 Ab, claimed descent from the tribe of Benjamin.[151] So Paul was in the best possible company. Though it is late, a rabbinic tradition calls the tribe of Benjamin the 'most prominent' of all the tribes, since of all the tribal ancestors Benjamin alone was born in Eretz Israel.[152] Nowhere do we have comparable information from the Greek-speaking Diaspora. This fact alone, together with the Palestinian name Saul, which is unusual in the Diaspora, should prevent us from forcibly making Paul a 'pure' Hellenistic Diaspora Jew, who was 'unsullied' by Palestinian tradition.

2.2 The Pharisee

Finally, the 'as to the law a Pharisee' in all probability also indicates Paul's mother country. Before 70 CE the education described in Gal.1.13f., which was distinguished by the 'advance in Jewish teaching' in which Paul surpassed 'his contemporaries among his people' and which made him 'so extremely zealous for the traditions of the fathers', leading him to become a Pharisaic scholar, hardly took place anywhere else than in Jerusalem. Before the destruction of the Temple, that was the only proper place for *strict* Jews – and Paul came from a strict Jewish family and was himself one – to study the Torah.[153] Far too little notice is taken, in German scholarship, in particular of this fact that Paul was a Pharisaic *talmid ḥakham*. If we did not by chance have these three words, κατὰ νόμον Φαρισαῖος, from Paul's pen, historical criticism would dismiss Luke's similar reports, e.g. 'a Pharisee of the Pharisees',[154] as an invention of the *auctor ad Theophilum*. The same is true of the remarks about the Lord's Supper in I Cor.10 and 11 which we have only because of the disturbances in Corinth. Without them scholars would not have allowed Acts 20.11, the account of the 'breaking of bread' in Troas, all by itself. These circumstances should warn us against a misuse of the *argumentum e silentio* which has been particularly popular in New Testament exegesis. We need always to be cautious where we know so little.

It is also more than probable that Paul studied under Gamaliel I, who was at that time the leading Pharisaic teacher. The gifted student will always go to hear the most famous authority in a

place. Those who studied theology in Marburg between 1920 and
1950 went above all to Rudolf Bultmann's lectures, even those
students whose disposition was more 'conservative'. I do not
understand why this point in particular is disputed so doggedly in
the name of 'historical criticism', when it is already suggested by
common sense. Unfortunately we know all too little about Gamaliel
(as about most Pharisaic teachers before 70);[155] it is at least
questionable whether he was the grandson of the great Hillel, and
it is by no means certain that he belonged to Hillel's school. After
70 his son Simon, mentioned occasionally by Josephus,[156] was a
leader of the moderate conservative war party, which resisted the
Zealots. His grandson Gamaliel II, the first 'patriarch' (*nāsī*) and
the real founder of the dynasty of patriarchs, followed the views of
the house of Hillel in his teaching. It is possible, indeed probable,
that there is an older relationship here, but that cannot be
demonstrated with any certainty. Gamaliel I was possibly a man
of compromise, who attempted to stand above the schools. So the
argument as to whether Paul was a Hillelite or Shammaite is also
an idle one.[157] We know hardly anything about the Haggada of the
two schools. The seven *middoth* attributed to Hillel may have been
introduced by him for the first time, but their use was not limited
to his school. They represent a form of argumentation in Hellenistic
rhetoric or exegesis, and to some degree they were common
property.[158] Interest in Jewish mission and the influence of Greek
thought could connect Paul more with Hillel, the 'zealot for the
law' more with Shammai. We have no idea whether the dispute
beween the schools was the decisive factor in the Jerusalem
establishments frequented by the Saul/Paul who was born in
Tarsus. Again, I know a number of theologians who in Marburg
liked to go to Rudolf Otto's lectures as well as to Bultmann's.

The argument that as a Hellenistic Jew Paul could not have
become a 'rabbinic pupil' and aimed at ordination as a 'rabbi' is
completely misguided. In fact before 70 there was still no rabbinate
and no ordination of scholars who then were given the right to
bear the title 'rabbi'.[159] But the scribal *beth-hammidrash* (Sir.51.23
= LXX οἶκος παιδείας) had existed for a long time, and there
were several of them. It had a firm footing in Eretz Israel and there
primarily in the Holy City. Later rabbinic texts enthuse almost
excessively about the 'great house of learning' or the 'numerous

houses of learning' in Jerusalem.[160] The Pharisaic Torah school in the first half of the first century may have had an essentially different stamp – presumably less institutionalized and freer – from that of the second-century Tannaites, who prepared for the establishment of the Mishnah after their victory in Israel.[161] But we should not doubt that the Torah schools in Jerusalem before 70 had enormous significance for Palestinian Judaism and beyond. Presumably there is so little information about Gamaliel I, the most significant Pharisaic teacher in the first half of the first century BCE, because he did not fit so well into the traditions of later times as they became rigid.

2.3 The problem of the Diaspora Pharisee

However, all this has taken us far beyond the still controversial basic question whether Paul studied in Jerusalem. We could follow Strecker and others and judge:

> In view of the intensive Jewish school activity in the Diaspora it is very improbable that Paul could not have received a Pharisaic education outside Jerusalem.[162]

Here Strecker refers to Matt.23.13, to the conversion of King Izates of Adiabene in Josephus, *Antiquities* 20.38-48, and for 'Diaspora Pharisees generally', to H.J.Schoeps.[163] But this is to list one error after another. Schoeps certainly speculates about Paul as a 'Diaspora Pharisee' in his controversy with C.G.Montefiore, but apart from Paul does not cite any evidence at all for the existence of this genre of Pharisee – nor is there any. Matthew 23.15, the great journeys 'over sea and land to gain a single proselyte', does not refer to Pharisees or scribes who were permanently settled in the Diaspora; they did not have to travel further to come into contact with Gentiles. The statement is made from a Palestinian perspective, and certainly does not indicate a permanent Pharisaic mission in the Diaspora, but specific special instances, which were directed from the mother country.[164] Here one might think of the particularly striking case of the conversion of King Izates, or the proselyte Aquila, who was said to have been related to Hadrian.[165] Significantly, Izates sent ten of his sons to Jerusalem 'at a tender age, so that they could be given a thorough upbringing in our mother tongue (Hebrew) and education (i.e. in

the Torah)'. Later his brothers and sons fought side by side with
their Palestinian fellow believers on the walls of Jerusalem against
the Romans.[166] Nevertheless, Strecker sought to cite the conversion
of Izates[167] to support his theory of the existence of Diaspora
Pharisees as a separate group and their relative independence. I
ask myself whether he has ever read all of the account in Josephus,
since the key word 'Pharisee' does not appear here at all. Izates
had been converted by a Jewish merchant named Ananias who
dissuaded him from circumcision because of the political dangers
associated with it. There is nothing to suggest that he was a
Pharisee. A second Jewish traveller, Eleazar, who came from
Galilee and 'was regarded as particularly scrupulous in observing
the ancestral laws' (πανυ περὶ τὰ πάτρια δοκῶν ἀκριβὴς
εἶναι)[168] may perhaps have been a Pharisee, but he was not a
Diaspora Jew.

In his fine article in *Die Religion in Geschichte und Gegenwart*,
Günther Bornkamm showed considerably more knowledge of the
sources and a historical-critical sense:

> But the report that Paul spent some time in Jerusalem and was
> educated there to become a Pharisee deserves at least some
> trust, simply because the sources at our disposal point to
> Pharisaism as a Palestinian movement and Jerusalem as its
> centre; we know virtually nothing of a Diaspora Pharisaism. So
> the reference to Gal.1.22 is hardly enough to challenge the
> tradition, at least at this point.[169]

It is well known that the Pharisees were a Palestinian lay holiness
movement going back to the Hasidim of the Maccabaean period,
whose aim was above all the ritual sanctification of everyday life
in Eretz Israel, as it was required of priests in the sanctuary. The
whole land promised by God to his elect people was to become the
sanctuary of God. A further motive was connected indirectly with
the temple, the correct offering of the gifts from the harvest in
the Holy Land, which belonged to the sanctuary and its cultic
personnel. This applied above all to the tithes.

Both the agrarian commandments and the ritual regulations for
purity ultimately related to shared meals, i.e. the question how

and with whom one could eat: to this degree they were food laws.[170]

So the ideal, model meal was that of the ritually clean priests, who ate hallowed food (wave offerings and parts of sacrifices) in the holy place.[171] For Paul, the dispute which broke out in Antioch (and certainly not just there) over 'eating together'[172] at the same time amounted to a critical coming to terms with his own past and its Pharisaic stamp. That is why he had to put up such energetic opposition. Since any Gentile area was thought to be as unclean as a dead body, and every Gentile was *ipso facto* unclean, and this also applied to food obtained from Gentiles, which in addition was constantly under suspicion of being associated with idolatry, it was really impossible to observe the Torah strictly in a Gentile environment.[173] When Felix sent some priests to the imperial court in Rome they took figs and nuts with them to eat on the journey so that they did not become unclean.[174] A Pharisee from the time of the Second Temple must have felt the same sort of thing abroad, even if he were not a priest. Besides the purity law, of course we find in Pharisaism other important fields of legal interest: festivals, worship, criminal, private and family law, not to mention charity and ethical wisdom (see the discussion between Neusner and Sanders, n.170). But in all their legal teaching they were the successors of the priests (and Levites), who had been the leading teachers of the law up to the Maccabaean revolution.

For the pre-eminent ritual holiness of the land of Israel, especially as it is so eloquently expressed in the later rabbinic tradition, in this connection I would just like to quote some points from the instructive summary by Günter Stemberger:[175]

The accent in the rabbinic statements about the land lies... on the holiness of the land and its consequences; at the beginning of a ten-runged ladder of holy spheres the Mishnah says: 'The land of Israel is holier than all lands' (Kel.I.6)... The land is 'holy' because it belongs to God and therefore must be cultically pure... Therefore the statement about the purity of the land of Israel stands on the same level as that of its holiness: 'The land of Israel is pure' (Miqv.VIII.1). By contrast the other lands are unclean: 'The land of the nations makes unclean... by touching and bearing' (Oh.II.3); 'Anyone who goes on mountains or

rocks in the lands of the peoples is unclean; anyone who goes on
the lake or the shore (which are not directly part of the land) is
clean' (Oh.XVIII.6)... The land is holy and pure, in so far as
it is the land of God that he has chosen as the seat of his
Shekinah... The holiness of the Land of Israel is expressed in
the fact that a whole series of commands of the Torah is
associated directly with the land. Only in the land is one fully
subjected to the commands of the Torah, so one can be a full
Jew only in the land.[176]

The privilege of Israel, that Semikha, the ordination of rabbis,
is possible only in the land, ... could be connected with another
motive, namely the limitation of prophecy to Israel. 'As long as
the land of Israel had not been chosen, all the lands were fit for
the words (of God); as soon as the land of Israel had been
chosen, all the other lands were excluded' (Mek.Pischa 1,
Horovitz-Rabin 2)... From Jonah 1.3, 'And Jonah rose up to
flee to Tarshish from the presence of God', the Mekhilta argues:
'Know that the Shekhinah does not reveal itself outside the land'
(loc.cit). We can also understand the statement by R.Acha (on
a question of the law of inheritance) in the same light: 'Our
brothers abroad are uneducated (*hediotot*) and falsify the
Halakah' (jBB VIII.1.16a). If God reveals himself only in the
land of Israel, in which alone one can fulfil his Torah completely,
it is only logical to conclude that one can be a Jew in the true
sense only in the land.[177]

Although these rabbinic traditions are of course only to be found
at a later period, we may suppose that the concept of election and
the higher worth of Eretz Israel, which was thus also ritually
significant, along with questions about the commandments related
to the land, were present at least in embryo for the time of
the Second Temple, especially in Pharisaic circles which were
concerned for ritual purity.

Because it was possible to observe the Torah in the strict sense
only in the Holy Land, one could therefore only really study it
seriously, i.e. at the same time constantly put it into practice, there.
If 'the Torah goes forth from Zion' (Isa.2.3), then the Temple
mount was the best place to learn it. In the name of R.Meir, a
teacher from the middle of the second century, when even rabbinic

teachers had to go abroad because of the Bar Kokhba revolt, we have the saying: 'Everyone who lives permanently in the land of Israel, who eats the fruits (of the land) in purity and recites *sh^ema* morning and evening, is certain that he is a son of the world to come.'[178]

Abroad there was the threat not only of ritual impurity and contact with the abominations of idolatry, but also – even worse – of false teaching. According to Aboth 1.11, Abtalyon, Hillel's teacher, who was probably active under the late Hasmonaeans and in the early period of Herod, is said to have admonished:

Wise men, take heed to your words, that you do not incur the punishment of exile [from the government, against whom Abtalyon's colleague Shemaiah warned] and *are banished to a place of bad water*, and the pupils who come to you drink and die, and the name of heaven is desecrated.[179]

There is a series of examples under the late Hasmonaeans and Herod of Pharisees and priests having to flee from Judaea for political reasons, for example to Alexandria. As a rule such flight was a religious catastrophe for those involved, and rabbinic legends have vividly elaborated on the way in which rabbinic schools were corrupted in godless Alexandria.[180] It went without saying that after his release or after a change in political circumstances a Pharisee would strive to return to the Holy Land. At around 6,000, the number of 'fellow' Pharisees at the time of Herod was not so large that we would have to assume that there was a substantial number of 'Diaspora Pharisees' as an independent group, and special schools with their own significance.[181] The sources give no indication of any specifically Pharisaic schools outside Palestine at the time of the Second Temple. It is more than questionable whether there was a distinctive school under Jehuda ben Bathyra in Nisibis in Mesopotamia before 70 CE.[182] His grandson of the same name later studied in Eretz Israel. Even Todos (short form of Theodotus) of Rome was not active until after 70 CE, and a school was founded there by Mattiah ben Heresh only after the Bar Kokhba revolt, when a number of rabbis were forced to leave the country.[183] All in all – leaving aside Babylonia in the Amoraean period, from the third century on – the foundation of schools and the activity of rabbis outside Eretz Israel was very rare. Galatians

1.22, along with the biographical information about Paul, does not give us the right to postulate such Pharisaic schools against the sources. It seems to me that before 70 the influence of Diaspora Judaism on the mother country, and especially on the international pilgrimage centre of Jerusalem, was at least as great as *vice versa*.

Finally, at the turn of the century – leaving aside Alexandria and the Therapeutae – we know nothing of G.Strecker's 'intensive Jewish school activity in the Diaspora'. Certainly there may have been Jewish(-Hellenistic) wisdom schools in other major cities like Antioch or Rome, but we have no information about them, and we may not suppose that they had any great effect – in comparison with the mother country. People even came from Babylon to learn the Torah there. We get our first partly obscure information about Torah schools outside Judaea of a Pharisaic (or better, a rabbinic) stamp only some time after the destruction of the temple, in the second century: their foundation was a consequence of the catastrophes of 70 and 132-135 CE and, apart from Babylon, up to the Arab invasion they had only a quite marginal significance.[184]

3 A 'Hebrew of the Hebrews' who writes Greek: the problem of Paul's 'Greek education'

We must therefore take very seriously Paul's report that he was a 'Hebrew of the Hebrews', i.e. a Palestinian Jew, and moreover a Pharisee and pupil of the scribes, and follow van Unnik in accepting that Luke is right in associating Paul with Jerusalem from his early youth. However, that does not mean that we must go to the other extreme and make the later apostle the purest kind of Palestinian Jew, comparable, for example, to James the brother of the Lord. Historical reality is always more complex and more complicated than our attempted solutions – which as a rule are too simple.

First of all it is not as certain as van Unnik supposes on the basis of what Luke says that Paul came to Jerusalem *in his earliest childhood*. Luke himself quite deliberately sets Paul's skills in speaking Greek *and* Aramaic side by side,[185] in the same way as he does his being a citizen of Tarsus *and* growing up in Jerusalem.[186] In so doing he demonstrates the bi-lingual and bi-cultural character of his hero, in my view quite correctly, first mentioning Paul's ability to speak Greek.

We may know about the periods in Paul's life only very roughly, but when it comes to his childhood we can hardly get further than guesses. He may have been born in the first decade of our era. In Philemon, shortly before or after 60, he refers to himself as an 'old man'; according to Acts 7.58, however, at the stoning of Stephen, shortly before his conversion, i.e. at the latest in 32-35 CE, he is still a 'young man'.[187]

Against putting Paul's move to Jerusalem so early is the fact that Paul speaks Greek in an idiosyncratic way, but at the same time has such a masterly control of the language that he is hardly likely to have learned it as a second language.[188] His treatment of the text of the Greek Bible is also so sovereign that we may assume that he grew up with it, using later versions revised on the basis of the original Hebrew text in Isaiah, Job and I Kings.[189] As the revised scroll of the Twelve Prophets from Naḥal Ḥever and the later work of Aquila and Theodotion show, there was particular interest in such revisions of the text in Jewish Palestine.[190] Especially in Isaiah, Job and the books of Samuel and Kings, the LXX translation differed markedly from the Hebrew text and it is unjustified to suppose 'that Paul was not even aware of the differences between his revised text of Isaiah, Job and III King-doms and the unrevised version of these books'.[191] Any attentive reader of the Bible knows the differences between various trans-lations. We may not make the apostle a dilettante and ignoramus. And in going on to concede to Paul 'only a certain knowledge of scripture communicated in the Hellenistic synagogue'[192] and assuming that because of a lack of knowledge of the text – as in the case of professors today – Paul was dependent on written material, Koch fails to recognize that Paul's use of scripture developed out of constant oral teaching. For Paul the decisive thing was argumentation with the text of scripture in teaching which will certainly often have gone on for hours. His letters were only a chance by-product, indispensable though they later became for the coming-to-be, indeed the existence, of the church.

It is more than questionable whether Paul regularly took very cumbersome Jewish scrolls of scripture around with him on his journeys. The revised texts could very well in part also derive from his own work as a scribe. Like a strict orthodox Muslim today, numerous orthodox Jews and quite a few Swabian pietists, Paul knew large parts of his Holy Scripture off by heart. This would be true above all of the Greek psalter, the prayer book of Judaism. In many respects his language is shaped by that of the psalms. But this sovereign knowledge of the Greek Bible was a basic presupposition of his regular oral teaching, as this is attested in Acts 19.9 for a period of two years in the school of Tyrannus. The frequent debates with Jews in the synagogue, but in some circumstances also with Gentiles,[193] presupposed that the teacher had an effortless control of scripture. Paul did not give lectures as we do today, nor could he interrupt the flow of his argument to look up the quotation he wanted in an arsenal of various scriptural scrolls. There was not yet a handy edition of the Septuagint comparable to our Rahlfs or Swete. Like truly great theological teachers of the recent past, Schlatter, Holl, von Harnack, Loofs, Lightfoot and others, he spoke completely without notes. That was also true of a contemporary Jewish teacher like Philo and then later of Origen. Paul was in a position to quote texts of scripture quite literally, to abbreviate them, to combine them, or to adapt his interpretation of them to the situation, as in the Targum.[194] When Koch also admonishes us that in Phil.3.6 Paul did not claim 'that he also is or has been a γραμματεύς' (93), he overlooks the fact that the ordinary Greek reader would necessarily have understood this term to mean copyist, secretary or minor official. Philo uses it only once (*ad Flaccum* 3), in precisely this sense. It also almost always has this sense in Josephus. We first find γραμματεύς in the association of 'scribes' and 'Pharisees' in the Synoptic Gospels, but in Mark and Luke it is still used with clear distinctions. Q still also knows the parallel term νομικός;[195] the completely stereotyped association 'scribes and Pharisees' (γραμματεῖς καὶ Φαρισαῖοι) first arose in the Gospel of Matthew. It is a typically Palestinian coinage.[196] At the same time it becomes clear that Koch is familiar neither with the particular institution of the Jewish Palestinian *sopherim* nor with the Jewish school which centred on learning the Torah by heart.[197] Both Josephus and Luke stress the special scrupulousness (ἀκρίβεια) of the Pharisees in the exegesis of scripture and the observation of the Law. How could Paul say of himself in retrospect as a former Pharisee that he was 'blameless as to the righteousness which is in the law' if, as

Professor Koch assumes, he had only a superficial knowledge of the Torah?

There is no doubt about it: Paul was at home in the Greek Bible because he had used it – presumably from his earliest childhood. He probably had not read any classical Greek literature worth mentioning apart from the Greek (and Hebrew) Bible and Jewish pseudepigrapha like the Wisdom of Solomon. Eduard Norden went against a tendency of scholarship in his time which is again in vogue today when he pointed out:

> I would not venture to dispute the assertion that Paul could have read some of Plato, for example (much as my subjective feeling rebels against that), but what can we make of such problematic judgments?
>
> I would ask anyone who wants to prove anything with certainty to provide convincing proof, and so far this has not been produced, or rather no one has even demonstrated any echoes of either Plato or any other Greek author, for what are usually claimed to be proofs or echoes prove on only a cursory examination to be absolutely nothing.[198]

Norden finally acknowledged that he found it 'very difficult' to understand Paul as a writer, first of all because he was arguing in a strange way, and 'secondly, his style, taken as a whole, is also un-Greek', in contrast to Hebrews, I Clement or Barnabas (499f.). On the other hand his language is substantially different from the simple Greek of a Mark or of the Johannine writings, including Revelation, which in part has Semitic colouring. Here too he again proves to be a 'wanderer between two worlds'. Norden himself points out that the apostle could have used the means of Greek rhetoric in an idiosyncratic way.[199] We shall have to discuss how he arrived at this 'rhetoric of the heart'[200] in a later section, on the higher Jewish-Greek education of 'Sha'ul, who is also called Paul'.

4 Summary hypotheses

What biographical explanation are we to give of these sometimes almost confusing phenomena? On the basis of what has been said so far, the following conjectures suggest themselves:

1. Paul was born in Tarsus and grew up in a strictly Jewish

family of a Pharisaic stamp which had connections with the mother country of Palestine. On the other hand, his father was a Roman citizen (or freedman) and probably also a citizen of Tarsus with a relatively high social status. Therefore in this family, Greek was probably the main language. Greek was Paul's mother tongue, but he also had a command of Hebrew, the 'holy language' of scripture and liturgy, and Aramaic, the vernacular of Jewish Palestine. A Pharisee who was faithful to the law and a 'Hebrew of Hebrews' who spoke only Greek would be a strange mixture. For a man like Philo the situation was completely different. A deep divide separates Paul and the Alexandrian here.

2. Paul seems to have gone to a good Greek elementary school, which was a *Jewish* school – because the literature from Homer to Euripides used in regular teaching was quite alien to him. The literature that he knows – as is also suggested by his vocabulary – is that of the Septuagint and related religious writings. This point distinguishes him from the majority of other Jewish authors who wrote Greek, since their 'vocabulary' is literary. This is also true – with a few exceptions, like Luke and Hebrews – for the very earliest Christian literature. He could have spent at least part of his schooldays in Tarsus. He also learned the Jewish Bible primarily in the form of the LXX. He is at home in it.

3. If Greek was the dominant language in the family, we might also conjecture that the family had had to spend at least a generation in the Diaspora, and perhaps even longer. How Paul's parents or earlier forebears came to Tarsus we do not know. In all probability this way led through slavery as the result of hostilities, which were frequent in Jewish Palestine after 63 BCE, and by a subsequent bestowing of freedom which gave the family Roman citizenship.

4. Acts 22.3; 26.4f. and Paul's own testimony, orientated on Palestinian Judaism, make it very likely that Paul returned to Jerusalem as an adolescent. Acts 23.16, the note that he was warned in Jerusalem by a nephew, strengthens the possibility of a close family tie to the Holy City. However, it remains questionable when and how this happened. Van Unnik's assumption that Paul must have returned to Jerusalem with his parents in earliest childhood cannot be proved any more than the conjecture by Zahn,[201] which he rejects as 'pure phantasy', that 'Paul's parents

perhaps sent their son to Jerusalem to grow up there with his kinsfolk, perhaps from the time when he was eight or ten years old, and perhaps even in the house of his married sister there'.[202] Nor are we helped much here by the well-known remark of the otherwise unknown Jehuda ben Tema,[203] which follows the Greek stages of growing up: 'To scripture at five, to the Mishnah at ten, to the commandments at thirteen, to the Talmud at fifteen and to the bridal chamber at eighteen...'(mAboth 5.21). In my view, both Paul's excellent command of his Greek mother tongue and his sovereign treatment of the Greek Bible suggest that Tarsus cannot be pushed completely into the background, even if it must take second place to Jerusalem in Paul's growth. However, there was also a good Greek school in Jerusalem. Finally, we cannot rule out the possibility that he regularly moved to and fro between Tarsus and Jerusalem. His return according to Acts 9.30; 11.25 shows that even after his time in Jerusalem he maintained links with his birthplace (and perhaps also with the Jewish members of his family there). As we simply do not know enough, we can leave the details of the question open, though we must remember that van Unnik has Luke on his side.

III Pharisaic Study of the Law in Judaism

1 The Pharisaic house of learning

In Acts 22.3d, Luke indicates a second stage of education, to be clearly distinguished from childhood and elementary schooldays, a stage which began about the age of fifteen: 'at the feet of Gamaliel, educated according to the strict manner of the law of our fathers.' This is a reference to study of the law in the school of the best-known Pharisaic head during the second quarter of the first century CE. Luke seems to know the manner of instruction in the school: the highly-respected teacher sits on a chair, and his pupils sit on the floor 'at his feet': 'He (Aqiba) came and sat at the feet of Rabbi Eliezer.'[204] Luke's formula κατὰ ἀκρίβειαν τοῦ πατρῴου νόμου, 'according to the strict manner of the law of our fathers', shows that he was familiar with the Pharisaic-scribal milieu. But it is amazing that the much-reviled Luke can express these circumstances so exactly. He gives the most accurate and positive accounts of Jewish situations of any non-Jew in the ancient world. Josephus, too, constantly uses words beginning ἀκριβ- as a special designation of the Pharisees. Thus he describes Simon, the son of our Gamaliel: 'This man of Jerusalem came from a very famous family, and from the party of the Pharisees, who have the reputation of surpassing the others in the realm of ancestral laws by their precise knowledge (ἀκριβείᾳ)'.[205] This passage is the best illustration of the κατὰ νόμον Φαρισαῖος ('as to the law a Pharisee') and the concluding κατὰ δικαιοσύνην τὴν ἐν νόμῳ ('as to righteousness under the law') from Phil.3.6 and shows that in the case of the Pharisee Sha'ul we must presuppose the study of scribal knowledge in connection with Gal.1.14 (see below). The ἀκρίβεια stressed here can only be acquired in this way. The 'Pharisee, son of Pharisees' thus took advantage of that possibility which had presumably still been closed to his ancestors since they were slaves or freedmen and thus dependent on their masters, being completely or partially unfree: he was able to study the Torah in Jerusalem, the place of origin of all true wisdom,[206] in order to become a teacher of that law and thus take a leading role in his 'religious party', indeed in his people.

Paul himself mentions this part of his autobiography in Gal.1.13f.:

> For you have heard of my former life in Judaism, how I persecuted the church of God violently and tried to destroy it; and *I made constant progress in Judaism beyond many of my own age among my people, so extremely zealous was I for the traditions of my fathers.*[207]

The basis for this autobiographical report *can* only refer to the study of the law as practised by the Pharisees, a study which is extremely improbable in this form in a Jewish-Hellenistic school in Tarsus or elsewhere in the Diaspora. In no way can we follow Mommsen in translating ἐν τῷ γένει μου as 'in my homeland' (i.e. in Tarsus);[208] in accordance with Paul's usage elsewhere it means 'in my people' (see above 23 and n.137). Moreover, that the zeal for the law which is equally attested by Paul and Luke was a typically Palestinian phenomenon between the time of the Maccabees and 70 CE is also attested in our sources only for Jewish Palestine – where it was very strong.[209] Just as nowadays a gifted and ambitious student will want to study at a first-class college and with the best teachers, so given Paul's exceptional intelligence and the ambition which keeps breaking out time and again in the letters – a danger of which he was constantly aware (II Cor.12.7; I Cor.9.15; 15.10, etc.) – we may presuppose that his zeal for study could find fulfilment only where the most famous authorities were teaching and where according to God's commandment the Torah was at home, i.e. in Jerusalem. One could paraphrase 'in Judaism' with 'in the law': the durative imperfect προέκοπτον ('made constant progress') of the young Saul is a reference to his progress in the study of the Torah, the real heart of Judaism, on which, as Josephus finely shows in his apology for Judaism against Apion, all expressions of Jewish life and indeed the whole of Jewish existence were founded. And this progress relates not just to an introductory instruction in some Diaspora synagogue in Tarsus or elsewhere, but to 'graduate study' at the central place where Torah was taught, in the holy city. A little later, in Gal.2.14, Paul uses the verb ἰουδαΐζειν to describe 'living according to the law'.

The numerous contemporaries whom the brilliant young *talmid ḥakham* surpassed in the study of the law were his fellow students.[210]

Ancient study, in the Hellenistic world as in Judaism, was always structured to include a degree of competition: we find this competitive ideal both in the Eastern wisdom of the Hellenistic period and in Greek *paideia*.[211] In my view I Cor.1.20 sheds brief light on this spiritual milieu of the Pharisaic school which Paul himself experienced, with the following 'triad': σοφός (*ḥākām*), γραμματεύς (*sopēr*), συζητής (*dāršān, dōreš*): wise man, scribe, debater. These are designations from the Pharisaic *bet midrash*. The Corinthians understand these terms, which are hardly comprehensible to a pagan Greek in their real – Jewish – significance, because of course during his eighteenth-month stay there Paul will have told them of his former study of the law and thus at the same time of his mistaken way (cf. I Cor. 15.9). In other words, I Cor.1.20 has an autobiographical background. What was formerly the aim of his own profession here becomes the embodiment of the wisdom of this world, because Paul once himself took offence at the cross, as his contemporary representatives did (and, apart from him, still do).

2 The problem of 'Pharisaic teaching' before 70

The great unknown is the question what Pharisaic study of the law looked like in the first half of the second century in Jerusalem, and what knowledge or, more precisely, what 'theology', 'soteriology' and 'anthropology' was taught there at that time. This unknown factor is what makes it so difficult to discuss the complex theme of 'Paul and Palestinian Judaism' really convincingly.[212] One thing is certain here: we cannot transfer the reports about the Tannaitic teachers, the 'rabbis', which have been handed down to us in written sources beginning in the third century, directly and without further reflection to the Pharisaic school in Jerusalem at the start of our era. On this point earlier generations of scholars were too generous. On the other hand we may not adopt what nowadays often seems to be the most convenient solution and simply declare them to be irrelevant. Both these statements follow from an examination of the sources themselves. For it is amazing how little we learn in rabbinic sources about Pharisaic teachers before 70, their views and traditions. That holds true not least for Gamaliel I and his son Simon, who could have been perhaps the same age as Paul. This reduction of the tradition, for all the continuity, indicates a certain distance. The later 'rabbinic sages' did not much like the designation *perushim*, 'the separated ones': subsequently it could almost become a taunt and acquire the connotation of 'pious sectarian';[213] they did not use at all the more popular Aramaic *p'rishayya*, from which Φαρισαῖος was formed. Rather, the new elite, shaped by years, indeed decades, of study in the school, identified themselves and their spiritual forebears, in solidarity over against all the 'uneducated', with the proud name *hakhamim*, 'the wise'.[214] The so-called rabbinate and the institutions associated with it, the firmly ordered study ending in ordination which was a qualification for the office of judge and gave a person the right to use the title rabbi, came into being only in the decades after 70; in a self-glorifying and completely unhistorical way the later teachers dated their institutions back into the earlier periods, as far as Moses and Joshua.[215] Probably at the same time there was also a suppression of the older traditions, lasting over a lengthy period and sometimes rigorous; this was probably connected with the catastrophes of the two Jewish wars, and among other things resulted in very little being preserved of the views of, say, Gamaliel I, 'the old', and almost nothing at all of those of his son Simon,[216] who in his old age had been caught up in the Jewish revolt. It is a piece of good fortune that the latter (and therefore also his father) is mentioned by Josephus; otherwise 'critical scholarship' would merely see the first Gamaliel as a Lukan anachronism, or a projection back into Jerusalem before the destruction of the Temple of his very much better known grandson Gamaliel II from the period around 90/100. The halakic traditions, which are primarily orientated on the controversies of Hillel and Shammai, predominantly contain discussions of questions of purity and food laws, from which a one-sided picture can easily arise. The haggada, which is of particular interest to us, is preserved only in a very fragmentary way, and is primarily limited to the sentences in the Sayings of the Fathers and more or less legendary anecdotes.[217]

In the light of this development it should be noted that in contrast to the progressive 'unification' of Palestinian Judaism under the leadership of the rabbinic scribes after 70, the spiritual face of Jerusalem before its destruction was a markedly 'pluralistic' one.[218] Alongside the Pharisees and the groups of scribes who led them was the aristocratic-conservative party of the Sadducees with the leading men of the priestly nobility and the well-to-do laity: the Boethusians, close to the high-priestly clan of Boethus, whose son Simon had been summoned from Alexandria by Herod as high priest were a special group.[219] They had a positive relationship to the Herodians, the descendants or clientèle of the old royal family.[220] The Essenes, too, had a settlement in Jerusalem which was certainly flourishing; it probably acted as a spiritual centre, as later did the Christian monasteries.[221] In addition there were political and religious 'radicals',[222] members of the baptist movement,[223] apocalyptic enthusiasts[224] and quite a number of Greek speakers who had returned from the Diaspora and met in synagogues of their own.[225] Jerusalem and its environs must have presented the contemporary visitor with a confusingly varied picture.

Here, however, we should not forget that despite this plurality, by the end of the second century BCE the Pharisees were already the leading spiritual group and had the largest following. Despite the recent hypotheses of Morton Smith and Neusner, we may not underestimate their significance.[226] They had probably already formed the anti-Hasmonaean, political-religious opposition at the end of the reign of John Hyrcanus and had then risen against Alexander Jannaeus and sparked off a bloody civil war. After his death, under his widow Salome Alexandra, for a short time between 76 and 67 BCE they even held political power in the land, and took a bloody vengeance on their former persecutors. These beginnings, shaped by the political struggle for power, allow us to conclude that there was a strong theocratic element in early Pharisaism; here the harsh experiences of the Maccabaean fight for freedom, which lasted for around three hundred years, still stand in the background. Anyone who wanted to impose God's will as laid down in the Torah also by political means could not be too squeamish when it came to using force. Real pacifism was probably extremely rare in pre-70 Jewish Palestine. The Old Testament scriptures were not pacifist at all, at least as long as there was pagan foreign rule. After the Roman conquest in 63 and the thirty-three year rule of Herod from 37 to 4 BCE there was necessarily a degree of depoliticization and probably also spiritualization; on the other hand the theocratic element continued to have an effect in a messianic-eschatological form and, as Josephus reports to Nicolaus of Damascus, introduced disturbances even into the Herodian family.[227] At the latest at the time of the transformation of Judaea into a Roman province in 6 CE, a certain division becomes visible. Zadduk, who along with Judas the Galilean founded the freedom movement, is explicitly said by Josephus to have been a Pharisee (*Antt.*18.4-10). By contrast we find the 'leading Pharisees' along with the most influential priests in a coalition which sought to keep peace with Rome after the cessation of the *tamid* offering for the emperor in July 66 (*BJ* 2.411) and after the failure of this last attempt later reunited Simon son of Gamaliel with the Sadducean leaders in the fight against the threat of a preponderance of radicals (*BJ* 4.159; *Vita* 190ff.).[228] In other words, between 6 and 66 CE the Pharisees were split politically, and this division is probably also connected with the controversies between the schools of Hillel and Shammai. Rabbinic legend reports bloody clashes between the two groups at the beginning of the Jewish war,[229] and a complaint attributed to Rabban Johanan ben Zakkai, but formulated at a later time, runs: 'Since those who are of a proud heart increased in Israel, the divisions multiplied in Israel and two Toroth came into being. Since the disciples of Shammai and Hillel multiplied, who had not served all the needs of their teachers, the divisions multiplied in Israel and two Toroth came into being.'[230] The attempts at union by the scholars in Jabneh were aimed, among other things, at overcoming these 'divisions'.[231] I have already pointed out that it does not make much sense to attach Paul to one of the two schools. The 'zeal for the law' and the readiness to use force associated with it puts him more on the side of the radical wing, but his close connection with the Greek-speaking Diaspora and his interest in gaining proselytes, which is probably also to be presupposed, put him more on the liberal wing.

3 Pauline theology and rabbinic literature[232]

Despite these substantial differences between the rabbinic teachers of the second century and the Pharisaic houses of learning in Jerusalem in the first half of the first century, which are so hard for us to envisage, there are a surprisingly large number of points of contact between Pauline theology, the foundations of which Paul acquired during his study in Jerusalem, and later rabbinic literature.

In polemic against a remark of mine, Georg Strecker asserts that it is a 'fact that a rabbinic school tradition in the strict sense of the word can be recognized only towards the end of the first century' and 'literary evidence for it begins very much later and for this reason can be utilized for New Testament exegesis only with considerable qualification'.[233] Quite apart from the fact that *all* history of religions parallels to the New Testament 'can be utilized only with considerable qualification', here again we find the usual unhistorical cliché which cannot be eradicated from the works of a number of German New Testament scholars. The Mishnah was fixed in writing around 200 and the Tosephta and the Tannaitic Midrashim in the third century. They had preliminary written stages (like the Gospels) which can be traced back to the time of Aqiba: however, it goes without saying that an intrinsic connection can be made between the rabbinic schools after 70 (Johanan ben Zakkai and after him Gamaliel II in Jabneh) and pre-70 Pharisaic schools in Jerusalem. Gamaliel II, the first *nāsī'* in Jabneh, was the son of Simon ben Gamaliel I, the head of a leading Pharisaic school in Jerusalem, i.e. the grandson of Paul's teacher. The earlier schools with their scribes did not yet have a clear and absolute majority; in addition, other groups had 'schools'. Strecker contradicts himself when on the one hand in general terms he rejects the possibility of 'learned studies in rabbinic fashion' for the time of Jesus but on the other hand a page earlier refers quite anachronistically to 'Rabbi Hillel'. Hillel was not a rabbi in the later sense of the word, but rather was active as a head and founder in Herod's time of the Pharisaic school which was most influential at a later period.

Within the limits of this short book I can give only a few basically random references. The first 640 pages of Billerbeck, Vol.III, offer overwhelming evidence of the great variety of relationships that there are between Paul and later rabbinic theology. Even if nowadays it has sometimes become almost good form to revile this great scholar, who was an ordinary pastor, and whom none of us theologians can emulate in knowledge of rabbinic sources, his work is still unsurpassed – and, as I look round the landscape of New Testament study, will continue to remain so. We should not forget that he died on 23 December 1932 (!) at the age of eighty; his monumental work was composed between 1906 and 1922, and he contributed more towards a positive understanding of early Judaism in the sphere of theology than any New Testament scholar of his time and indeed down to the present day. We should not disparage his great achievement because of the wrong use of his work by some imprudent theologians, and at the same time we should remember that he was still working with the methods of his time.[234]

This is not the place to enumerate all the ingredients in Pauline theology which may – presumably – come from the Pharisaic school in particular and from Jewish Palestinian thought in general. My view is that they relate to by far the greater part of Pauline theology – even if they are presented in excellent Greek. Despite all the parallels,[235] the difference from the *typically* Hellenistic-Jewish literature composed outside Palestine, mostly with a marked philosophical stamp – from Aristobulus and the Letter of Aristeas through II-IV Maccabees to the Sibylline Oracles, Philo and even Josephus – is evident. The Wisdom of Solomon, the Jewish-Hellenistic work which is perhaps closest to Paul, combines Palestinian with Hellenistic tradition, as does Paul himself; here Wisdom, which presumably comes from Egypt, has more marked 'Hellenistic'-syncretistic features.[236]

We could begin with the completely un-Greek greeting in Paul's letters, which is orientated on the Palestinian form of greeting by wishing a person peace,[237] and continue with the judgment on the sin of the Gentiles in Rom.1.20ff., the description of God as judge of the world and the Jewish self-awareness in Rom.2; here it is striking how much Palestinian and Jewish-Hellenistic elements fuse together in both chapters into a seamless unity.[238] The Abraham midrash in Rom.4 and Gal.3 largely corresponds to rabbinic exegesis, and the same is true of Rom.9-11; I Cor.7.1-12

or 10.1-13. The Adam-Christ typology in Rom.5.12ff. should also
be mentioned here, and freedom from the obligation of the law
through death (Rom.6.7) or from the marriage tie through the
death of the spouse (7.2f.). In Rom.7.7ff. one could see a conversion
of the rabbinic doctrine of the victorious battle of the good impulse
against the evil impulse (*jeṣer*) with the help of the law. One might
say generally that in fact the apostle sought to refute the teaching
which was once an obligation on him with the methods that he
had learned in the Pharisaic school. Here the positive parallels are
as numerous as the obvious antitheses. mSanh 10.1, 'all Israel has
a share in the world to come', has an analogy in Rom.11.26; I
Cor.10.6-10 recalls mSanh 10.3f.: 'The generation of the wilderness
has no share in the world to come'; the compromise of the house
of Shammai (tSanh 13.3), which in connection with Dan.12.2
forms a middle group between the righteous and the 'completely
godless' that according to Zech.13.9 will only be purified in
Gehenna, sheds light on the enigmatic statement in I Cor.3.15 (cf.
5.5). On the other hand, for Paul – completely against all rabbinic
tradition, but in accord with IV Ezra – *all* descendants of Adam
are *rāsā' gāmūr*, 'complete evildoers', because of the power of sin
which is at work in them; for that very reason salvation is received
only in faith in God who justifies the impious (Rom.4.5; cf.5.6).
For Paul God is not just someone who 'inclines to grace' (*maṭṭeh
lᵉpī ḥesed*) his verdict when he makes a decision in judgment – like
a pair of scales, according to his being as described in Ex.34.6 (*rab-
ḥesed*); rather, this judgment rests exclusively on grace, for he is the
one who justifies the impious, δικαιῶν τὸν ἀσεβῆ (in Delitzsch's
Hebrew translation, *maṣdīq 'et-hārāšā'*) without any achievement
as a precondition. The righteous who are saved are those who are
justified *sola gratia*. It is interesting that the house of Hillel – like
Paul in Rom.4.3-8 – quoted David with a song of thanksgiving of
the redeemed (Ps.116) after the Torah passage Ex.34.6 (tSanh
13.3). Mention should also be made here of the considerable
number of formulae and phrases in Paul which we meet again
similarly in rabbinic texts. Paul's juridical language, which is
orientated on the 'justification of the sinner without the works of
the law', should therefore not be treated as a secondary theologou-
menon of the first Christian theologian, which is what tends to
happen today, precisely because the linguistic forms and categories

of thought go back to his time of study in the Pharisaic school in Jerualem and, as Gal.1-3 and Phil.3 show, had a determinative influence on the change in his life. They accompanied him throughout his life.

4 Parallels from apocalyptic and the Essenes

However, it would be completely wrong to look for analogies to the letters of Paul one-sidedly and predominantly in later rabbinic writings, since at the same time we must remember the spiritual plurality in Jerusalem in the period before 70 CE. A mere glance through Billerbeck brings out the numerous and sometimes astonishing parallels to apocalyptic texts, primarily to IV Ezra and Syrian Baruch, which come from the Pharisaic sphere (cf.II Cor.12.1ff.; also 4.8; I Cor.13.1). They provide the link to the Hekhalot texts which have now preserved a preliminary stage of the Essenes through the heavenly liturgies of the sabbath sacrifice hymns from Cave 4Q.[239]

Here we come up against another trend in Jewish Palestinian thought which influenced the young student at the Pharisaic school in Jerusalem. The Essenes actually had settlements in Jerusalem itself – which were presumably flourishing and influential – by the Essene gate in the south of the city,[240] and there can be no doubt that this elitist, austere, esoteric, predominantly priestly movement (though it also had an apocalyptic stamp) exercised a great spiritual power of attraction with its rigorous ideas of purity. As Josephus, Philo, Pliny the Elder and Dio Chrysostom show, this extended far beyond the frontiers of Palestinian Judaism and – through an *interpretatio graeca* – even into the Hellenistic world.[241] At fourteen Josephus wanted to study not only the teachings of the Pharisees and Sadducees, but also those of the Essenes; in addition, for a while he attached himself to the baptist ascetic Bannus: his report may be exaggerated and stylized, but it certainly has a historical nucleus.[242] The spiritual interests of the young and ambitious Paul were certainly no less varied than those of Josephus, who came from the priestly nobility of Jerusalem.

Presumably Pharisees and Essenes, who in the last resort in fact go back to a common 'hasidic' root,[243] were essentially nearer to one another, despite the rough anti-Pharisaic polemic in the Essene

writings, which criticize them as 'seekers of smooth things', than
rabbinic literature from some centuries later indicates when it
rejects all 'heretics'.

Paul's relations to Qumran have often been discussed recently,
and at times there have been arguments over them.[244] Here too I
can be brief. Paul is linked to the Qumran writings by his basic
eschatological-dualistic attitude, his sense of an imminent end to
this aeon and of the presence of salvation, concealed from non-
believers (though in a quite different form, which in Paul is
qualified by the coming of the Messiah): the eschatological gift of
the Spirit, which among other things makes it possible to interpret
scripture 'congenially' in terms of the eschatological present, the
predestination bound up with God's sovereign election and the
associated inability of human beings to attain salvation by themselves through a free decision of the will – a feature which according
to Josephus was controversial in contemporary Judaism. By
contrast, human freedom of the will is stressed more from Sirach
through the Sadducees and to a moderate degree the Pharisees up
to Rabbi Aqiba and later rabbinic teachers: 'All is foreseen (by
God), and nevertheless there is freedom of decision; humankind
(*hakkōl*) is guided by kindness, (but) according to the mass of
actions' (mAb 3.15; cf. Josephus, *Antt.* 18.12-15; PsSal.9.4; 14.8;
IV Ezra 7.21-25, 72ff.; 9.11 etc.; SyrBar 85.7). The parable of
the merchant with his account book which follows immediately
afterwards shows how in contrast to Essene and Pauline thought,
in Aqiba strict account is taken of God – to use Paul's words in
Rom.4.4 κατὰ ὀφείλημα ('as due').[245] Possibly the intensified
demand for complete obedience to the Torah without qualification
(Gal.3.10,12; 5.3; cf. Rom.2.25; I Cor.7.19) is also connected with
Essene Torah rigorism, which calls for perfection. In that case, as
a young Pharisee, according to Phil.3.6 Paul will have thought
such obedience possible.

The contacts with Essene theology even extend to details of
terminology like 'God's righteousness', 'children of light', 'sinful
flesh',[246] the association of justification with purification,[247] the
present 'evil time'[248] or the new creation.[249] Whereas we have so
far found no parallels for the central concept ἔργα νόμου, works of
the law, in rabbinic literature, it is interesting that *miqṣat maᵃśē
hātōrā* appears in a letter about to be published which presumably

comes from the Teacher of Righteousness, addressed to the Wicked Priest, and the formula *maᵃśē hātōrā* occurs twice. Even more frequent are formulations like 'his' or 'your works in the Torah'. The letter ends with the statement (according to the translation by H.Stegemann): 'and may this be reckoned to you (by God) as righteousness, if you do what is right and good before him[250] for your own good and for the good of Israel.' Without an article, as a literal equivalent of ἔργα νόμου (= *maᵃśē tōrā*), the formula appears in 4QFlor I.7, presumably referring to the action of the Essene community as an eschatological fulfilment of Ex.15.17f.: '...and he said, they were to build him a sanctuary among men, in which they would offer works of the law to him as incense offerings'. For Paul, the *maᵃśē tōrā* as *human* works find their end in the eschatological community of salvation. Even if we wish to deny Pauline authorship of the remarkable dualistic textual insertion in II Cor.6.14-7.1, in which there are obvious links with Qumran (I myself am not convinced by this attempt),[251] there are such varied influences of Essene thought that one can begin from the presupposition that they were not mediated secondarily through earliest Christianity but that the pre-Christian Paul was already influenced by this terminology and conceptuality in Jerusalem.

5 The character of Pharisaism before 70

What can be said about Paul and earliest Christianity also applies generally to the Pharisaism of the period before 70 CE: taking into account its considerable plurality, it presumably had an essentially stronger eschatological, theocratic-political and dualistic stamp than is suggested by its later development in the rabbinic texts. Between it and these texts stands the 'censorship' of the 'academy' of Jabneh which renewed Palestinian Judaism. Before the catastrophe, prophetic prediction was more related to the present, the apocalyptic and mystical element came more strongly to the fore (though of course even at a later stage it continued to be a constant undercurrent), and there was more openness towards charismatic and enthusiastic movements like that of John the Baptist or Jesus' own activity. The spiritual awakening of the Maccabaean period and the internal struggles which followed, over the true theocratic form of the people of God, had a still more marked effect: the consequence was a tendency towards a rigorous accentuation of the Torah, for example among the Essenes, and also among the radical groups dependent on Judas the Galilean, right down to the school of Shammai. One indication of this accentuation is the rigorous implementation of the prohibition of images and pressure towards forcible circumcision of Gentiles in Eretz Israel.[252]

That this charismatic eschatological ferment was stronger even in Pharisaic circles is indicated, for example, by the quotation of Amos 8.11 which tEduyot 1.1 attributes to the 'wise men in the vineyard of Jabneh'. The word of Yahweh, which is sought throughout the land and not found, is described as 'prophecy' (*nebū'āh*), as knowledge about 'the end' (*hāqēṣ*), and finally it is stressed that 'no one of the words of the Torah is identical with another word of the Torah'; in other words, in the preceding period of high eschatological and political tension, when the 'prophecies' and the revelations about 'the end' were accumulating, all criteria for the right exegesis of the Torah had been lost, since, as the introduction to the text has it, even the 'words of the scribes' (during and after the catastrophe) were no longer available. Therefore they resolved first of all to return to the basic definitions of the halakah and with them lay the foundation for the new beginning.[253]

Another highly remarkable statement is attributed to Hillel, falling outside the framework of rabbinic literature, about the possession of the Spirit by all Israelites in connection with the overcoming of the dilemma caused by the clash between the sabbath commandment and the individual pesach offering. This indicates that before 70 the question of the activity of the Spirit in Israel in inspiration was not decided upon completely negatively, in the sense that the Spirit had ceased. After arguments on a number of different levels, from mere analogy through scriptural proof by *gezera shawa*, scriptural proof *qal wa-ḥomer* and reference to the tradition which had been handed down, Hillel had rejected the last objection, that the Israelites might not bring any sacrificial knife into the temple on Pesach sabbath, with the argument: 'Leave them be, the Holy Spirit is upon them. If they are not prophets, then they are at least sons of prophets.' The Holy Spirit promptly gave the people the solution to the dilemma: they attached the knives to the sacrificial animals and had them transported into the temple that way. The later tradition of this legend in the Jerusalem Talmud omits the clause about the people possessing the Spirit – presumably because it was found offensive, which makes the whole passage lose its point.[254] We also find comparable sets of arguments at different levels on ethical questions in Paul – perhaps again a reminiscence from the Pharisaic school: for example I Cor.9.7-14 from general experience to scriptural proof and sacrifice in the temple and then at least to the supreme authority, the saying of the Lord; and, less consistently and convincingly, in I Cor.11.7ff.,13ff.: here the last argument is general usage in the communities.

These two rabbinic examples may illustrate that the spiritual climate in Jerusalem was still different from that in Jabneh, Usha or Tiberias. Hope for the imminent reign of God and a possible new activity of the Spirit moved the people and many scribes, even more strongly than after the fearful catastrophes, to which these very hopes, albeit mistaken ones, had contributed. Only on the presupposition of such a multiform yet 'international' milieu, which affected even the most important religious group, the Pharisees, can we conceive of the rise of popular movements extending through all strata, like that of John the Baptist or the Jesus community, which according to Luke was also joined by priests and Pharisees – and Hellenists (Acts 6.1,7; 15.5; cf.21.20f.).

IV Greek-speaking Jerusalem and Greek Synagogue Education

1 Jerusalem as a 'Greek city'

So far, though, I have been describing only one of the 'worlds' of the 'wanderer between two worlds': autochtonous, Palestinian-Jewish Jerusalem. The Holy City had become a cosmopolitan city, not least as a result of Herod, and while it might not be able to stand comparison with the chief cities of the Roman empire in size, it certainly could in splendour and renown. It proved extremely attractive to many Greek-speaking Jews of the Diaspora, especially if they were faithful to the law: after all, it was 'the city of the great king' (Matt.5.35), the place which God himself had chosen to dwell in, the place of the perpetual worship of God and the great festivals of Israel which were obligatory for all the people, so that there they could 'rejoice before the Lord' – festivals which were also well known to the Christian communities and which in some circumstances even Paul could take seriously.[255] Probably at that time Jerusalem was the great pilgrimage centre of antiquity, which year by year attracted hundreds of thousands of visitors. At the same time it was the eschatological centre of the world, the destination of the homecoming Diaspora and of the pilgrimages of the nations, the place of the coming of the messiah (Rom.11.26; cf. Acts 1.11), the place of judgment in Gehinnom and the metropolis of his coming kingdom. That was reason enough for returning there if one could manage to do so, to spend the evening of one's life there, to study the Torah there in the Holy Place, to be buried there and to await the resurrection and the coming of the messiah there.[256]

I have described elsewhere at length the social and religious milieu of the Greek-speaking 'Hellenists' in Jerusalem.[257] Alongside the Acts of the Apostles and Josephus, here the numerous inscriptions are the main source of information – all in all around 33% of the roughly 250 inscriptions found in and around Jerusalem from the time of the Second Temple are in Greek and about 7% are bilingual.[258] Even if we take into account the fact that ossuary inscriptions come predominantly from members of the middle and upper classes, we may assume that around 10-15% of the then inhabitants of Jerusalem spoke Greek as their mother tongue; these would have been predominantly people who had returned to Jerusalem, or their descendants. In a population of about 100,000 in Jerusalem and its surroundings that would give a population group of around 10,000 to 15,000. To this should be added the Greek-speaking pilgrims from the Hellenistic cities in Palestine and from the Syrian, Egyptian and Western Diaspora who streamed into Jerusalem in their tens, indeed hundreds, of thousands at the time of the great festivals. The annual transfer of the didrachm tax and the sacrifices and gifts of the pilgrims brought considerable riches into the country, which benefited at least the population of Jerusalem, the majority of which therefore distanced themselves from the eschatologically motivated attempts at rebellion. The farmers and craftsmen from Judaea may also have profited from this, but in the country prejudice against the city and foreigners (and at the same time against the rich landlords and merchants) was stronger. Here the rebel movement found more support.[259]

In addition to Jews who spoke Greek as their mother tongue and who (like Saul/Paul) also understood Aramaic and Hebrew, there were a large number of 'Hebrews' with a very good command of Greek. Their most significant representative is Josephus. We also find these bilingual 'Graeco-Palestinians' in the New Testament', for example John Mark or Silas (*šʾîlā*)/ Silvanus; in individual instances, as for example with Barnabas from Cyprus or Mnason (Acts 21.16), we may hesitate over which group to put a person in: that applies in Paul's own case. Greek education was also given in Galilean cities like Sepphoris (three miles from Nazareth), Tiberias – where Josephus praises the admirable Greek schooling of Justus of Tiberias (*Vita* 40.336) – and probably even in Julias Bethsaida. It was impossible to found a new 'Hellenistic' city without a Greek school. Therefore I believe that even some of Jesus' disciples knew Greek, above all Philip and Andrew, who had Greek names; we may suppose that Simon Peter and James the brother of Jesus also had command of the world language.[260] Presumably the linguistic situation was similar to that in Jerusalem today. Just as now more Jewish inhabitants there speak English than American Jews who have settled there speak Hebrew, so then more 'Hebrews' will have understood Greek than 'Hellenists'' Aramaic. So at a very early stage the earliest Christian community came to be divided: the 'Hellenists' from the Greek-speaking Diaspora – or at least a considerable proportion of them – could not understand the Hebrew/Aramaic worship in the Jerusalem synagogues. For that reason the Jewish 'Hellenists' organized themselves into a multitude of synagogue communities which brought together compatriots and were organized on that basis, like the synagogue of the 'Libertinoi', the freedmen from Rome, and alongside it the synagogues of the Cyreneans, the Alexandrians, the Cilicians and the Jews from the province of Asia (Acts 6.9). The Tosephta (tMegillla 3.6) mentions a synagogue of the Alexandrians, the Talmud Babli (26a) one of the 'Tarsians'(?).[261] Greek inscriptions mention Jews from Alexandria, Cyrenaica (Mark 15.21), from Capua in Campania (CIJ no.1284), Chalcis in Antilebanon (CIJ no.1233),[262] and also from places in Palestine like Bethel (CIJ no.1283) or Scythopolis (CIJ nos.1372-4). Acts 6.7 also mentions the proselyte Nicolaos from Antioch, characteristically at the end of the list of the seven. However, indications of places are very rare in the inscriptions and therefore more or less fortuitous. A διδάσκαλος ('teacher') appears three times on ossuary inscriptions (CIJ nos.1266, 1268f.) and once on the long side there is the Hebraized Greek name tdtywn, i.e. Theodotion (no.1266).[263] Presumably at least some of these synagogues had their own teaching staff.[264]

Most illuminating is the only synagogue inscription from Jerusalem that we possess, which is at the same time the earliest of any kind that we have from Palestine. This is the Greek inscription which I have already mentioned, by Theodotus,[265] son of Vettenus, who was presumably descended from someone who returned from Rome; he was himself a priest and was ruler of the synagogue in the third generation. The beginning of the building of the extensive synagogue that he completed, which also had a hospice for pilgrims to festivals, went back to his 'fathers' (probably his father and grandfather) and therefore was begun as early as the Herodian period. As the institution of the synagogue, which is attested substantially later in Palestine than in Egypt, Delos or Rome, i.e. only from the first century CE, spread in the mother country above all as a result of Pharisaic initiatives[266] – the priestly nobility had no interest in creating competition for the temple – I assume that this foundation, too, had a Pharisaic background.[267] In my view this becomes clear from the special aim of the synagogue, which is explicitly mentioned in the inscription: the reading of the law and the teaching of the commandments: εἰς ἀνάγνωσιν νόμου καὶ εἰς διδαχὴν ἐντολῶν.

The reading of the law was supplemented by the teaching of the commandments. As the oral Torah of the Pharisees went far beyond the simple wording of the Torah as recognized only by the priestly Sadducees, for the Pharisaic teacher instruction in the specific individual commandments was necessary alongside a reading of the words of the law, and at all events this was more important to them than to the average Jew. If it was the aim of the Pharisees to educate the people in the law, and if, as many indications suggest, for this reason, from around the first century (BCE or CE) they encouraged the extension of the institution of the synagogue and the Jewish elementary school,[268] they must also have been interested in instructing the festival pilgrims from the Diaspora precisely in the law as they understood it, i.e. in the διδαχὴν ἐντολῶν. This would have been especially the case, since it was particularly in Eretz Israel, in the holy city and the temple, that many commandments of the Torah first took on real significance. Here things were quite different from the Diaspora, among the Gentiles, where it was impossible to observe the law correctly because numerous commandments did not apply there. Above all, pilgrims 'from abroad' had to be taught the regulations relating to the cult which went beyond the written Torah.

2 Possibilities for higher Jewish-Greek education in Jerusalem

It is natural to suppose that the young Paul was at home in this environment of Pharisaic Hellenists; he studied the Torah in the school on the temple mount and at the same time improved his Jewish-Greek education, since as a Greek-speaking *talmid ḥakham* he must have felt it important to instruct Jews who came to Jerusalem from the Diaspora in the true – Pharisaic – understanding of the law. Nowhere did so many Greek-speaking Jews and Gentile sympathizers from all over the empire gather together so constantly as in Jerusalem. Anyone who wanted to influence them had to attempt to do so from there. The significance of Jerusalem as the metropolis of world Judaism between Herod and 70 CE can hardly be overestimated.

A convincing 'teaching of the commandments' in Greek, which included preaching in the synagogue, also called for linguistic competence. For that very reason a Jewish Hellenistic school established for effective teaching and proclamation also had to pass on a certain basic training in rhetoric, though this did not correspond to the Attic-style school rhetoric of the time, the ideals of which can be studied a generation before Paul in Dionysius of Halicarnassus. This basically un-literary rhetorical training, focussed on speaking publicly in the synagogue, probably gave rise to the contrast in Paul's style which was observed by Eduard Norden: 'that despite his sovereign contempt for beautiful form, the apostle often enough made use of the means of elegant rhetoric which are absent from the Gospels, but... not of such as he appropriated from the reading of Greek writers'. What can be found, rather, are echoes of 'Asian sophistry', the representatives of which 'were ignorant of the literature of the past', with its short sentences, often put together in whole series, and sharp antitheses. 'In contrast to contemporary orators, for Paul external rhetorical artifice was merely incidental'; one could even say that it was a means to an end: 'it served only to express the δεινότης and σεμνότης of his ideas'.[269] The content sought its appropriate 'urgent form'. This included the diatribe, the style of which has often been observed in Paul. Contrary to the latest, very thorough investigation by T.Schmeller on 'Paul and the "Diatribe"', which in conclusion only arrives at the sceptical judgment that 'we cannot explain *to what extent* Paul in fact learned this style and *where* he got it from',[270] it seems to me most plausible to suppose that Paul learned the basic insights of his indubitable rhetorical art, which is not orientated on classical literary models, through practical application in the Greek-speaking synagogues in Jerusalem. Here he had broad possibilities of applying it among a large and constantly growing number of Jewish and 'godfearing' pilgrims from the Diaspora, cultivated in the synagogues of Jerusalem. If one wants to use such terms, he 'preached circumcision' there (Gal.5.11). However, we know nothing of particular Jewish missionaries to the Gentiles. The only two Jewish-Hellenistic sermons which have come down to us from antiquity, Pseudo-Philo *de Jona* and *de Sampsone*, provide a rich display of the use of the diatribe in their very lively presentation, although they are sermon texts which at the same time have features of the encomium.[271] There can be no doubt that Paul's art derives from oral teaching; in comparison with the abundance of his oral preaching in more than twenty years of mission, the letters are only *parerga et paralipomena*, however impressive and indeed unique they may seem to us (and seemed to some readers in Corinth, II Cor.10.10). Here I would not deny that Paul *a priori* had a particular gift for rhetorical style; but to use Cicero's words, '*sic esse non eloquentiam ex artificio sed artificium ex eloquentia natum*';[272] to his gift will have been added practical exercise in the art.

That there was Greek rhetorical instruction in Jerusalem is attested in connection with Herod, who was instructed in the science by Nicolaus of Damascus, along with many other sciences; we may also presuppose a sometimes high degree of Greek education among his descendants.[273] The family of the high priest Simon son of Boethus, whom Herod called to Alexandria from Jerusalem, which was supported by a particular group of Sadducees, the Boethusians, and said to have been particularly rich, will have nurtured Greek education.[274] Josephus must have been given at least his basic Greek education in Jerusalem, and despite his emphasis on his training as a Jewish priest must have followed it to such a degree as to be able to lead a delegation to Rome when he was barely twenty-five years old. He gained the favour of the empress Poppaea and was able to carry out his mission successfully. He would hardly have been able to do this had he been a Jew who could speak Greek only haltingly.[275] Finally, the figure of the orator Tertullus whom the high priest Ananias and the members of the Sanhedrin who accompanied him took along to Caesarea from Jerusalem to support their accusation before Felix is an indication of oratorical instruction in Jerusalem.[276] As was usual with orators, he will have earned most of his living by teaching. We do not know whether he was a Jew. If he had his permanent home in Jerusalem, this seems to me to be probable. Whether Paul had such instruction may be left an open question. However, it is beyond question that synagogue preaching in Greek, which sought to preach Jewish faith as true 'philosophy' in the middle and upper classes in the city, presupposed a certain basic practical training in oratory, if it was really to hold and convince the audience. As the pilgrims from the Diaspora usually did not come from the proletariat and also had some interest in education, I would prefer to assume that there was a concern for an equivalent oratorical level in the leading synagogues of the Hellenists in Jerusalem.[277] Would this have been a matter of indifference to so ambitious a young scholar and rising teacher and preacher as Paul? The Jewish-Christian 'Hellenists' expelled from Jerusalem, who later carried on their mission in Phoenicia and Syria as far as Antioch, came from this milieu, and perhaps some of them had had a similar education. That is true even of Paul's opponents in II Corinthians, who claimed to be 'Hebrews', and seemed to be superior to Paul in appearance and rhetoric (II Cor.10.10; 11.5f.,22). The charge against Paul that he was ἰδιώτης τῷ λόγῳ, unskilled in speaking, shows that rhetorical skills were expected of religious propagandists and preachers and that despite his impressive letters, in comparison with his opponents Paul did not live up to such expectations.

In addition to that we have a series of indications of literary activity among Palestinian Jews – some presumably of a Pharisaic stamp – in Palestine. This includes the correcting of the earlier Greek translations of Old Testament writings by the original text, above all where the original text and translation were relatively far apart, for example in the prophetic books or in Job. One indication of this is the Greek scroll of the Twelve Prophets from Wadi Murabaat. If Paul used such a recension in Isaiah, Job and I Kings, this could go back to his earlier activity in Jerusalem (see above, 35f.). The latest translations of books of the 'Septuagint' like Song of Songs, Ezra-Nehemiah (II Esdras) and Koheleth – the latter already in the style of Aquila – were probably made in Palestine by Jews close to Pharisaism. In addition, there are renderings of the Apocrypha and Pseudepigrapha, for example Jewish apocalypses, not all of which were translated into Greek in Alexandria and Antioch. In the case of the Greek book of Esther we know through a colophon that the translation and expansion took place either towards the end of the second or the beginning of the first century in Jerusalem. Greek fragments of the apocryphal *Epistula Jeremiae* were found in Qumran, which may similarly be supposed to have originated in Judaea, as has now also a Greek paraphrase of Exodus (see n.257). Edifying writings in the original Greek were also composed in the mother country, like the writings of the Jewish historian Eupolemus in the second century BCE; the Testaments of the Twelve Patriarchs or the *Vitae Prophetarum* also seem to have originated there: the latter perhaps as information for festival pilgrims about the fates and tombs of the prophets.[278] Not only the pilgrims of the Greek Diaspora but also the 'Hellenists' living in Jerusalem needed religious books in their mother tongue. When in Acts 8.30ff. Luke describes the Ethiopian finance minister reading the Greek Isaiah scroll in his carriage travelling back to his homeland, he lets the reader suppose that this scroll was bought in Jerusalem. In pilgrimage centres edifying religious literature still sells very well even today.

3 Summary hypotheses

Taking all this together, we can attach more importance to 'Jewish Greek education in Jerusalem' in the period after Herod and up to the first Jewish War than has usually been assumed. This must have consequences for our understanding of the pre-Christian Paul: on the one hand he studied Pharisaic scribal learning in the school of Gamaliel and perhaps with some other teachers; on the other he had his spiritual home in some of the Greek-speaking synagogues in Jerusalem (or perhaps there was only one), where he may have seen his task as being that of a teacher communicating the Pharisaic understanding of the law to the Diaspora Jews who streamed to Jerusalem in large numbers. Therefore he acquired there the basic knowledge of a Jewish-Greek rhetoric aimed at synagogue preaching which was essentially different from the literary style of the Greek schools.

This background best explains that complex of events which led to his sharp conflict with the Christian group of 'Hellenists' in the early period of the primitive community, a conflict which turned

him into a persecutor and was the presupposition for the change
in his life.

V   The Persecutor

1 The question of chronology

Pauline chronology and that of early Christianity have recently (but to my mind wrongly) become very controversial questions.[279] However, I see no really convincing reasons for departing from the broad consensus. This puts Paul's first stay in Corinth around 50/51 CE as a result of the Gallio inscription and therefore puts the Apostolic Council around 48/49. If we count back between fifteen and seventeen years from the Apostolic Council, we arrive at 34-31 CE for Paul's conversion. The crucifixion of Jesus is still best dated at the Passover of 30 CE. So I myself incline towards an early date for the Damascus event; indeed even Harnack's conjecture that the roughly eighteen months during which according to *Ascensio Jesajae* 9.16, and according to Irenaeus among the Gnostics (and now in the *Epistula Jacobi* of Nag Hammadi),[280] the disciples were instructed by the risen Jesus, represented a reminiscence of the timespan between the primal events and Paul's conversion before Damascus, cannot be completely dismissed out of hand.[281] I Corinthians 15.4-8 makes an interval of many years improbable, even if the 'and to me, as one born out of due time' (ὡσπερεὶ τῷ ἐκτρώματι ὤφθη κἀμοί) indicates some distance in time from the earlier appearances. Evidently Paul's own vision of the Risen Christ is definitively the last one: it took place 'last of all'.[282] This relatively brief interval of between eighteen months and three years makes speculations about chronologically 'pre-Pauline' community tradition in the letters difficult – everything was still coming to be.[283] We can look only in Jerusalem for a 'pre-Pauline Hellenistic community', and it is very possible, indeed almost probable, that the young Saul even witnessed Jesus' death – perhaps from the distance of the Greek-speaking Jews. Whether

one can allow II Cor.5.16 as evidence for this is an open question.
There the emphasis lies on the 'know after the flesh', i.e. on the
manner of knowing and not on the object. He, Paul, had known
Christ in a 'fleshly' way, i.e. in a way corresponding to the sinful,
old Adam. That *could* – also – refer to a brief encounter with Jesus
in Jerusalem, but is far more likely to refer to the rejection of the
crucified (pseudo-)messiah as one accursed by God (Gal.3.13).
That the crucified Messiah (Χριστὸς ἐσταυρωμένος, I Cor.1.23),
Jesus of Nazareth, was a σκάνδαλον, a serious religious stumbling
block, for the Jews did not rest only on the experience of the
Christian missionary Paul; it had first been his own innermost
conviction as the Pharisaic teacher Sha'ul. The themes of the false
prophet, the deceiver of the people, the desecrator of the temple
and the blasphemer of God could have been combined in the
accusation brought against Jesus.[284] All these motives may already
have played a part in the trial of Jesus, which lay only a very short
time back in the past. Through the execution of this criminal on
the tree of shame, God's just judgment on him had become manifest
to all. The assertion of his former followers that God had raised him
from the dead, had exalted him to himself 'in power' (Rom.1.3f.) to
the right hand of God and appointed him Messiah, Son of God
and coming judge of the world,[285] had to be opposed with all
resolution. Like many responsible and learned men in Jerusalem,
Sha'ul too will have shared this view – and in so doing have
completely misjudged the crucified Messiah of Israel, as he himself
later confesses, 'in a fleshly way'. However, this fundamental,
indeed embittered rejection of Jesus, which probably linked Paul
with most of the leading figures in Jerusalem, did not yet amount
to the violent persecution of Jesus' followers. According to Luke
the old man Gamaliel, the head of the Pharisaic school, was of the
opinion that this new and strange messianic sect should not be
proceeded against by compulsion, through measures taken by the
authorities, but left to God's judgment, i.e. to later developments
(Acts 5.34-40). That the Pharisees did not react as sharply as the
Sadducean priestly authorities against the Jewish Christians who
were less faithful to the law is evident from their protest against
the execution by Annas II of James the brother of the Lord and
other leading Christians in 62 CE.[286]

We cannot rule out the possibility that here as elsewhere Luke is using an 'old' reliable tradition in his special way of writing 'early Christian history': between the first community in Jerusalem and the composition of his work lies a period of about fifty years. In the year 1990 I can still remember, sometimes very accurately, the portentous events of the years 1933-45, which I experienced between the ages of six and eighteen, and I know a good deal more from eye-witness reports. Can we completely deny Luke the use of such old reminiscences by eye-witnesses, even if he has reshaped them in a literary way to suit his bias? This brings us to our last question: *why* did Sha'ul/Paul in particular, as he himself confesses, become the inexorable persecutor of this new movement or at least part of it?

2 The biography of the persecutor[287]

Before we attempt to answer that question, there is another 'chronological' biographical question: how old was Sha'ul and what was his official position or function when he became a persecutor of the Christ who then radically changed his life? We have already touched on this problem (see above, 35), but we need to consider it further. In the texts which have already been cited several times Paul stresses only his own initiative (and thus his guilt) and mentions the basic reason: '... as to the law a Pharisee, as to zeal a persecutor of the church, as to righteousness under the law blameless' (Phil.3.6). He persecuted the community as a Pharisee, in the firm conviction that in so doing he was acting according to God's law and will, in zeal for this law. Galatians 1.13f. also goes in a similar direction: the Galatians know his earlier conduct 'in Judaism' – one could also say in obedience to the law, that he (persistently) 'persecuted the church of God violently and tried to destroy it',[288] and that (at the same time) he surpassed many of his contemporaries among his people, i.e. his fellow students, in his progress in the study of the law and his obedience to it (the two cannot be separated). There is not a word of others who were involved or who were also to blame. He alone is 'not fit to be called an apostle because I persecuted the community of God' (I Cor.15.9).[289] After his conversion, which was at the same time a calling, the communities in Judaea learned

that 'our persecutor now proclaims the faith that he once sought
to destroy; and they praised God because of me' (Gal.1.23f.).

So Paul must himself have played a decisive role in this persecution. Here in Galatians he had no reason to exaggerate; on the
contrary, with the stress on his activity as a persecutor he is putting
himself in a negative light in the face of the threatening situation
in Galatia: he is handicapped in every respect. Evidently he had
told the Galatians about this dark part of his biography at an
earlier stage (1.13): 'For you have heard of my former life' means
that they had already heard about it from him in detail. Now he
can summarize the earlier information harshly and briefly – all too
briefly for us. Paul probably told all the communities which he
founded about his activity as a persecutor and about his call.[290]
He shows in I Corinthians how much this burden troubled him:
in order to make up for his heavy guilt, he is proclaiming the gospel
without recompense, a task which is laid on him as a divine
compulsion. If he wanted to break out from it, he would have to
expect the punishment of the divine judge (I Cor.9.16). Evidently
– in obedience and zeal for the law – he had here taken an initiative
of his own, or had vigorously and somewhat independently carried
forward measures introduced by others with the aim of clearing
the decks. But that means that he no longer had a completely
subordinate position, that he was no longer just a young student,
but already had some authority as one who had 'progressed'
(προέκοπτον). My conjecture is that he already had a acknowledged teaching function in a Greek-speaking synagogue in Jerusalem (or perhaps several of them).

Luke's evidence is ambiguous at this point. On the one hand he
gives the νεανίας, the young man Saul, only a subordinate role at
the stoning of Stephen, that of looking after the garments of the
witnesses who had to begin the execution.[291] In the persecution
which follows directly afterwards, however, Paul then immediately
plays the decisive role, which could in essence be completely in
accord with the references in the letters.[292] He arrests Christians
in their homes and has them carried off to prison (Acts 8.3) or
flogged in the synagogues (Acts 22.19), indeed he himself is the
driving force behind their condemnation, in that as the judge
authorized by the high priests he votes for the death penalty (22.4:
'persecuted to the death'; 26.10b; cf. 9.1: 'breathing threats and

murder'). Here Paul is even given a decisive function in the supreme organs of Jewish justice, and at the same time – probably contrary to historical reality – it is presupposed that Jerusalem courts could impose and carry out death penalties without further ado. The mild advice of Gamaliel (Acts 5.34ff.), Paul's teacher (Acts 22.31), seems to have been completely forgotten. Luke is evidently exaggerating somewhat here to heighten the drama in his account, a practice of which he is also fond elsewhere. The activity of the thirteenth witness as a persecutor is depicted in vivid colours in order to make the later Christian missionary shine out all the more clearly against the dark background.[293] Quite certainly in doing this Luke is not seeking to produce polemic against Paul and lower his status. Rather, according to Luke, 'the nonsense of Jewish hostility to Christians generally is evident from the activity of the resolute Jewish persecutor Paul, which is doomed to failure'.[294] Possibly here Luke is also projecting later events like the execution of the sons of Zebedee and James the brother of Jesus into the early period. Modern conjectures are mistaken when they seek to take up Luke's description, which becomes more intense by stages, and because of his function as judge make Sha'ul/Paul an ordained rabbi, a member of the supreme court or even, in a further train of thought, a widower, because ordained rabbis had to be married. Here – as I said earlier[295] – later conditions are being introduced. In the light of Gal.1.13f. Luke's νεανίας, 'young man'(Acts 7.58),[296] is to be taken seriously. Sha'ul may have been between twenty-five and thirty-five years old at that time; he was no longer just a *talmid*, but already had some responsibility in the sphere of the Greek-speaking synagogues of Jerusalem, presumably as a teacher, when he was torn from a promising and ambitious career and his life took on a completely new direction. According to the Damascus Document (10.4-8), among the Essenes the ten chosen 'judges of the community' had to be between twenty-five and sixty and be 'instructed in the book HHGW and in the principles of the community'. According to the addition to the community rule 1QSa 1.12ff., an age of twenty-five was the presupposition 'for taking a place' among the leading members of the community, and of thirty 'for hearing a case and passing judgment'. By that time Sha'ul will have attained that age.

3 The persecutor and his opponents

3.1 The Greek-speaking Jewish Christians in Jerusalem

A further contradiction in Luke's account is that on the one hand
he intensifies the terrors of the persecution to the point of execution,
but on the other has the leaders of the Christian community, the
twelve apostles, unaffected by it. Despite the blazing persecution,
which is said to affect the whole community, they remain in
Jerusalem as though nothing had happened there, a feature which
contradicts the persecutions which Luke himself depicts earlier
and later, and also sounds intrinsically highly improbable.[297] The
solution to this riddle has widely been recognized by scholars:[298]
contrary to the account by Luke, which seeks as far as possible to
avoid any appearance of a division of the community in Jerusalem,
depicted in ideal terms (though it cannot completely succeed in
doing so, as already becomes evident in 5.1ff.; 6.1ff.), our starting
point must be that from the very beginnings of the apostolic
preaching there were two groups of communities which held
separate services for linguistic reasons: the Aramaic speaking
'Hebrews', who were in the majority, and the 'Hellenist' minority.
The two groups reflect the *linguistic* division of the Jerusalem
population which had become unavoidable as a result of the need
for separate services, one in Aramaic/Hebrew and the other in
Greek. For at least some of the Greek-speaking Christians found
prayer and worship in the Aramaic vernacular incomprehensible.[299] The 'Seven' of Acts 6.5, all of whom have Greek names,
which for the most part were unusual in Jewish Palestine, were
not just entrusted by the apostles with the problems of providing
for widows, but formed the charismatic leadership of this group in
the community in an analogous way to that of the 'Twelve' among
the Hebrews. According to Luke, their first two representatives,
Stephen and Philip, were in no way concerned with economic
questions, but were missionaries impelled by the Spirit. Luke
avoids the difficulty that for him previously only the Twelve had
been the authorized proclaimers of the message by at first making
Stephen, 'full of grace and power', do only 'wonders and great
signs among the people' (6.8), which (abruptly and without
reasons) provoked bitter opposition from members of the syna-

gogue (or more probably the synagogues) 'of the Libertines' (perhaps identical with the synagogue of Theodotus), 'the Alexandrians and the Cyreneans', and moreover from Jews from Cilicia and Asia Minor.[300]

In the debate (συζητοῦντες, Acts 6.9), they cannot cope with 'the wisdom and the spirit' with which Stephen advocates the cause of Jesus (according to Luke, how could things be otherwise?). The fact that here Jews appear from 'Cilicia', which in contrast to Cyrene, Egypt, Asia and Rome is absent from the great listing of the Diaspora in Acts 2.9-11, is a first indication that the *auctor ad Theophilum* is cautiously moving towards the person of the most important hero, Saul/Paul, who appears for the first time in a relatively insignificant subsidiary role right at the end of the Stephen drama in 7.58. For Luke, the martyrdom of Stephen is the introduction to the appearance of Paul. And historically speaking, he may even have been right.

3.2 Problems in Luke's account of Stephen and parallels with Paul

Despite all the differences between Luke's contradictory account of the persecution in Acts 6.8-8.3 (cf.9.1f.) and Paul's own testimonies, there is also a series of astonishing points of contact:

1. Stephen's charismatic activity and the bitter resistance to him occur – leaving aside the disruptive introduction of the Sanhedrin in 6.12 and of the high priest in 7.1 – in the very milieu in which, according to our conjecture, Paul was also working as a scribal student or a young teacher. Only the 'Hellenists' appear as those who are really affected by the following pogrom of Christians in 8.4f.; 11.19ff.: first Philip and then the Jewish Christians from Cyprus and Cyrenaica who are driven out of Jerusalem.[301] Would not Paul the persecutor have been connected with these events?

2. In Luke the charge is of blasphemous attacks on the basic elements of Israel's salvation, the temple and the Torah.[302] These accusations (which according to Luke are false) stir up the people and bring about the intervention of the supreme authority; however, the trial ends (after a speech by the accused, most of the content of which is out of place, and which does not even begin to answer the serious charges laid against him but presents a rather long-winded survey of salvation history),[303] in tumult and with an

execution which has more the characteristics of irregular lynch law. This suggests that the original account of the martyrdom did not speak of an orderly trial before the Sanhedrin; rather, the whole process may have been played out within the context of one of the Hellenistic synagogue communities in Jerusalem, with the victim being stoned by its enraged members. Although after 6 CE the Jews in Judaea had been deprived of the right to inflict the death penalty or at least to execute the condemned person, there were examples of lynch law for religious reasons. The restraint with which Saul/Paul is introduced in 7.58 may therefore well rest on a historical reminiscence.[304]

3. Paul certainly stresses the fact of his massive activity as a persecutor, but gives no details. He mentions only the motive that we already know, that he persecuted the community out of zeal. This κατὰ ζῆλος in Phil.3.6 is framed by two references to the law. It does not mean so much individual emotion as the concrete fact of 'zeal for the law'. In Galatians 1.13, too, there is a connection between the 'violent persecution' and the 'zealot for ancestral traditions' who surpassed his colleagues. This κατὰ ζῆλος does not primarily stress the subjective and emotional character of what he is doing (though this is what Luke means in Acts 9.1), as does the English 'zealously', but the objective fact of 'zeal for the law'.[305] In Gal.1.13f., too, in the characterization of Paul's past 'in Judaism' there is an objective connection between 'the boundless' persecution of the community and the 'zeal for his ancestral traditions' which surpassed that of his ancestors. Here we have the zeal for the law of which Phinehas (Num.25) and Elijah (I Kings 18) were the model, and which in particular had been part of the ideal of radical groups since the time of the Maccabees. Such a 'zealot' was unconditionally prepared to use force in order to turn God's wrath away from Israel, giving his own life to protect sanctuary and law against the serious lawbreaker. Such zeal could appeal to the covenant of priesthood which Phinehas received as a reward for his heroic action (Num.25.10-13):

> Then Phinehas stood up and interposed, and the plague was stayed. And that has been reckoned to him a righteousness from generation to generation for ever (Ps.106.30,31).[306]

Even Luke, who in Acts 21.38 rejects a connection between

Paul, the Egyptian rebel and the 'Sicarii', cannot avoid describing Paul a little later as 'zealous' (ζηλωτής) for God (22.39). Of course that does not mean that the Pharisaic Jew was closely connected with the 'Zealot' movement of a Judas of Galilee, but it does mean that for God's cause and for the hallowing of the law he was prepared to use force if necessary, even to the point of killing the lawbreaker. This was an attitude which was very popular in contemporary Judaism and, as Luke rightly indicates with the addition 'as all of you are today' (23.2d), also provoked the mob organized against Paul. It is amazing how accurately Luke portrays the religious and political atmosphere (as in present-day Islam, the two factors cannot be separated) of the time of the procurator Felix towards the end of the 50s.[307] The best modern paradigm for this atmosphere is present-day Islamic fundamentalism with its theocratic ideals, which cause us so much concern today.

Paul's 'zeal', which made him a persecutor, is thus directed against what in his eyes were severe transgressions of the law, of which Stephen, too, was accused. So there are unmistakable factual connections between Luke's account and Paul's own testimony.

3.3 The meaning of πορθεῖν in Paul and Luke

Paul himself twice emphasizes that he 'tried to destroy' the community or the new faith: in Gal.1.13 he says 'I persecuted the church of God violently and tried to destroy it' and in 1.22f., in commenting on a third party, namely 'the community in Judaea' which he does not know personally, he says that they had only heard that 'he who once persecuted us is now preaching the faith he once tried to destroy' (ἐπόρθει). Luke uses the same verb πορθεῖν in Acts 9.21: when after Paul's conversion he began to proclaim Jesus as the Son of God in the synagogues of Damascus, 'all who heard him were beside themselves and said, "Is not this the man who destroyed (ὁ πορθήσας) those in Jerusalem who call on this name..."' Whereas the imperfect ἐδίωκον in Gal.1.13 has a durative aspect ('persistently persecuted'), in 1.13,23, ἐπόρθει, the conative aspect is determinative: the persecutor *attempted* to destroy the Christian communities. The verb πορθεῖν has a very harsh ring and denotes violent action.[308] In Josephus, *BJ* 4.534, it denotes the burning of the villages and towns of Idumaea by Simon bar Giora and is used synonymously with λυμαίνεσθαι (Acts 8.3:

'Saul laid waste [ἐλυμαίνετο] to the church...). 'It implies the idea of physical or moral violence against people.'[309] Menoud[310] conjectures that Paul attacked the faith of Christians more than their persons, but we cannot read that out of Paul's terminology, which corresponds in an amazing way to that of Luke. Together with πορθεῖν, διώκειν means much more than a sharp polemical discussion. Presumably only the legal situation, which put executions under the jurisdiction of the prefect, prevented there being any executions. After the death of Stephen it is possible that there were also other cases of illegitimate 'zealous' lynch law. Zeal for the law after the model of Phinehas also included spontaneous action which by-passed the regular course of law. Later rabbinic exegesis of Num.25 discussed this point at length.[311] The 'as to zeal' in Phil.3.6 and the twofold πορθεῖν in Gal.1.13, 23 thus belong closely together. This is the use of brute force. Even if Luke may be exaggerating, in accord with the dramatic and rhetorical style of his historical account which belongs to the genre of dramatic historiography, when he speaks of Paul's death sentences as a 'special judge' (Acts 26.10; cf. 22.4; 9.1), there is a good deal of room for all kinds of threats, constraints and force against people, including the synagogue punishment of thirty-nine strokes, which Paul himself suffered five times and which in some circumstances could cost the delinquent his life. Even individual instances of lynch law cannot be excluded.[312]

3.4 The place of the persecution: the problem of Gal.1.22f.

But which community was Paul seeking to annihilate? He does not mention any particular place, and presupposes that the Galatians know. And indeed they already did know his whole previous history, as is shown by the 'you have heard' at the beginning of his autobiographical report in Gal.1.13: in other words, they were already better informed than we are. Probably they had information from two sides: from Paul himself and from the Judaists who had come among them.

The 'I persecuted the church of God and tried to destroy it' at first sight suggests the whole of the 'primitive church' and not just a particular individual community. If this 'attempt at annihilation' took place primarily in Jerusalem and then threatened to spread to other places, the general term would be more comprehensible than in the case of one single peripheral community.[313] Elsewhere, in I Thess.2.14, Paul says that the young Christians in Thessalonica are 'imitators of the communities of God in Christ Jesus which are in Judaea' (cf.Gal.1.13,21), because 'you suffered the same things from your own countrymen as they did from the Jews'. At first sight, one might think here of the persecution under Agrippa I, but could Paul also not have had in mind the persecution which he himself carried out? We do not hear anything else from *him* about pogroms against the Christians outside Judaea, in Syria. In II Cor.11.32, in contrast to Acts 9.24f., which speaks of an attack by the Jews of Damascus, he speaks only of the machinations of the 'ethnarch' of the Nabataean king Aretas IV in Damascus.[314] Here there is probably a certain intrinsic link between these events in Damascus which followed Paul's conversion and the subsequent journey to Jerusalem (Gal.1.17f.). Probably after his flight from Damascus Paul visited Peter in Jerusalem – a place which in my view he knew all too well, but had avoided for three years. If we look at one of the many maps of the journeys of the apostle Paul, we see how close Damascus is to Jerusalem. The rich and famous oasis at the foot of the Antilebanon was the closest major city of Syria to Jewish Palestine with a large Jewish community. Both places belong firmly together in Paul's biography (cf. Gal.1.17f.), and so in Rom.15.19 he can pass over the less important Damascus in favour of Jerusalem. Although in Gal.1 for all too understandable reasons he has to stress his distance from the community in Jerusalem led by Peter and James, from the beginning and essentially all his life he had links with this city: the place of his youth, his study and his first encounter with the sect of Christians would not let him go.

But does not Gal.1.22f., which I have already cited several times, tell against any activity of Paul as persecutor in the Holy City? That Paul, the 'Hellenist' and pupil of the scribes, was not personally known to what were still very young communities in *Judaea* (not Jerusalem – this is commonly overlooked in the literature) which had hardly been consolidated, does not need further defence, since our starting point must be that in accordance with widespread usage 'Judaea' here includes the whole of Jewish Palestine. Paul uses 'the wider understanding of Judaea in the Hellenistic and Roman sphere as the land of the Jews'[315] – as

Luke also does often. He can therefore dispense completely with
mentioning Galilee or Samaria. For those to whom he was writing,
in Galatia (and Thessalonica), Jewish Palestine as a whole was
the famous 'Judaea', the homeland of the new faith, far in the
south-east. Paul cannot presuppose the exact knowledge of the
Holy Land now so easily available to us through maps in
Bibles and elsewhere. Not even the predominant majority of the
inhabitants of Jerusalem can have known this 'student' or young
teacher 'personally'. His activity as persecutor in Jerusalem is
more problematical. If, as Luke reports, he dragged Christian men
and women from their houses and threw them into prison and sat
over them in judgment, he cannot have been unknown to them.

Here we *could* conjecture that the young 'Hellenist' was still
restrained when he was in Jerusalem, but was then sent to
Damascus, there to devote himself entirely to the persecution of
the community which was still small and only beginning to grow.
At all events, Saul and his like-minded friends were concerned to
stand on principle. It is also clear from the 'and again I returned
to Damascus' (Gal.1.17) that the change in his life is geographically
connected with Damascus. As Gal.1 shows, Paul presupposes an
exact knowledge of the stages of his life among his readers; he can
therefore mention or omit places at will because the readers –
unlike us – are already aware of the basic data of his life. In the
apologetic context of the letter he is concerned above all to stress
his freedom from those in Jerusalem; he wants to have as little as
possible to do with the apostles there. It is understandable that in
Gal.1 he mentions Jerusalem only where it is absolutely necessary.
The mention of the geographical stages *before* the change in his life
can thus be completely omitted anyway: all that matters is his
activity afterwards. Moreover, the assertion in Gal.1.20, 'In what
I am writing to you, before God, I do not lie!', makes it clear that
in Galatia other biographical details about Paul had been put into
circulation, presumably by the Judaists who had infiltrated there.
Certainly they presented Paul's link to Jerusalem as being more
close – perhaps on the basis of his pre-Christian past. Paul has to
defend himself against them and limits himself to his stays in the
Holy City after his conversion. Neither Luke nor Paul produce
entirely unbiassed reports here. Even if Paul is telling the truth,

he need not be telling 'the *whole* truth'; he may be keeping quiet about vital matters.

What tells against Damascus as the place of persecution here is primarily the threefold account by Luke which is firm on this point – for all the other differences: the encounter with the risen Christ took place on the way to Damascus (Acts 9.2f.; 22.5f.; 16.12), quite near to the city (9.3; 22.6). What reason would Luke or his source have for changing the tradition to such an extent? Would not a conversion of the persecutor in the very act, in the place of his atrocities, have been more effective? But according to the account in Acts it did not happen after intensive activity of persecution there, but immediately before a planned pogrom in this city. At that time Paul already came to Damascus as a 'changed man'. Why should Luke have falsified or invented it all? I cannot find a special Lukan bias here.

Moreover, I can hardly imagine that the rabid persecutor would immediately have been welcomed by his victims with open arms and after a stay in 'Arabia', which was probably not all that long, would have wanted to return to the place of his misdeeds to spend further time there. Furthermore, as an 'apostate', would he not necessarily have been afraid of the hatred, indeed the retribution of his former friends (and employers), whose particularly aggressive instrument he had been? All this tells against a persecution in Damascus with Sha'ul as an instigator. By contrast, we can understand all too well why after the radical change in his life he did not immediately, and with pleasure, return to Jerusalem, if the Holy City had been the place of his violent zeal against the new messianic sect.

But is it not best to understand Gal.1.23 as a report from the persecuted community, i.e. the community in Damascus? That is the question. For it is by no means obvious that a mere two or three years after the passover at which Jesus was crucified Damascus should already have had a significant independent community which Paul then tried to destroy (having been sent from Jerusalem, since there is nothing to indicate that he had had a stay of any length in Damascus before the christophany to him), a community which then went on to report to the churches in Judaea the miracle of his conversion. Nor is it clear why it in particular should cause such offence and not other Christian conventicles in Palestine and Syria. Or were delegates also sent to other cities, of whom no details have come down to us? Strangely enough, Luke uses ἐκκλησία only for the Christians in Jerusalem or Judaea in Acts 8.3 and 9.31; in Damascus he speaks only of Ananias and 'the disciples' (9.10-19.25). Was it not quite a different community that Paul not only *tried* to destroy but really did 'smite' in its original place, Jerusalem, namely the group of 'Hellenists', which was quite small in comparison to the 'Hebrews'? Following the killing of Stephen this group was driven out of Jerusalem by the persecution carried on by the young Sha'ul/Paul and became even more successful missionaries, something that the persecutor could not have reckoned with: 'Now those who were scattered went about preaching the word...' (Acts 8.4). There was Philip in Samaria and in the cities of the coastal region which were independent of Jerusalem, and others even in Phoenicia and as far as Cyprus and Antioch (Acts 11.19ff.).

Was the 'zealot for the law' then sent to Damascus because 'Hellenists' driven out of Jerusalem were continuing their mission-ary drive intensively there? Could not some 'Hellenists' have deliberately settled in the famous trading metropolis, which had long since been a Greek *polis*, with its large Jewish community and many godfearers?[316] Here Luke speaks – certainly with historical accuracy – of 'synagogues' in Damascus in the plural (Acts 9.2,20). Might not even a decisive role have been played by an instruction of the Spirit in the style of CD 6.5[317] and Amos 5.26 (cf.CD 7.15-19)? In the rabbinic texts Damascus belongs in the frontier region of Eretz Israel and is to become a part of it, above all in the messianic time.[318] The flight of the Hellenists to Damascus in particular could therefore be connected with messianic expec-tations.[319] Be this as it may, Damascus had stronger ties with the Holy Land than Antioch and Northern Syria. We cannot establish a connection between Tarsus and Damascus, but those between Jerusalem and Damascus were relatively close. However, no historical arguments avail against colleagues who think that Luke must always be wrong. It is also striking that the Christians in Damascus are the first to be mentioned in Luke outside 'Judaea' (in the wider sense). Given Luke's tendency to exaggerate and introduce the highest Jewish authorities as often as possible, the high priest need not necessarily have been involved in the persecution in Jerusalem. He may have approved the proceedings against the new messianic sect which he also hated, but it would be enough had Sha'ul/Paul been sent to Damascus by one or more synagogues of the Jewish 'Hellenists', possibly with a letter of commendation from the high priest. According to Acts 9.1f. the *initiative* to persecute the Christians in Damascus here clearly begins with Paul.[320] In that case the later conflict in Jerusalem reported in Acts 9.29, which was a threat to Paul's life, would have been a controversy with his former friends and like-minded people, who were rightly bitter at his 'apostasy' to the opposition and sought the apostate's life.[321] That would again explain the fact that he remained in Jerusalem for only fourteen days and, moreover, got to know only Cephas/Peter and James (Gal.1.17).

The earliest Christian 'Hebrews' in Jerusalem, not to mention those in Jewish Palestine, remained relatively unaffected by these 'internal' controversies within the Greek-speaking synagogues of Jerusalem. The persecution within the synagogue initiated by Sha'ul did not concern them directly, and so they did not get to know Paul himself personally at all. Then they later heard of the 'Hellenists' who had been driven out at that time: 'He who once persecuted us now proclaims the faith that at that time he sought to destroy.' That they too, though not directly involved, and perhaps already distinct from the Christian 'Hellenists' by virtue of some theological ideas about law, temple and christology, were moved by the miracle of the conversion of the one who had persecuted their brethren, shows their praise of God: even if they had not known Paul personally and had not directly suffered under his zeal for the law, they were aware of a bond between them and their brothers of the other community and their former suffering. At the same time their reaction shows that at this early period 'Hebrews' and 'Hellenists' may not be thought already to have been separated by an unbridgeable chasm. This is also indicated by the fact that the 'Hellenists' took over Aramaic cries in prayer like *abba* and *maranatha* from the 'Hebrews' for their liturgical usage. So we should not without further ado read the conflicts of Gal.2 into the time when Paul was a persecutor, which lay around seventeen years in the past. The reason why after the shattering experience of his change of career Sha'ul/Paul did not return to

Jerusalem immediately, but went into Nabataean Arabia, was not an already existing aversion to 'the apostles before me'.

How could one who had only just been converted have developed such an aversion? Indeed according to his own account he had not discussed his further career with anyone even in Damascus. Rather, he was no longer certain whether he was safe in Jerusalem as an apostate and traitor who had gone over to the other side. When he did 'go up to Jerusalem' (Gal.1.18) after 'three years' – presumably because, having fled from Damascus, he believed that the matter was now buried and he could get to know Peter without danger – he again found himself risking his life (Acts 9.29): 'zeal for the law' was now also directed against him. This is probably one of the main reasons why, from that point, for fourteen years he avoided the Holy City. He does not say that there was a conflict with Peter and James already at that time, and we need not interpret the fact that he did not see any of the other apostles as meaning that he did not want to see them; rather, these earliest Jewish missionaries will not have been in Jerusalem at that time and the interval before his flight to Tarsus was too short (9.30). But the Lukan account that there were 'disciples' who were still 'afraid' of this doubtful convert (9.26) is also within the bounds of possibility, and the same is true of Barnabas' role as mediator. However, in that case Barnabas will have taken Paul only to Peter and James, and not to the 'apostles' who were probably absent, so that he saw 'none of the other apostles' (Gal.1.18). Perhaps the Judaists from Jerusalem had put forward a version of these events in Galatia which is closer to that of Luke, and Paul can repudiate it because it is not correct (Acts 9.27). Paul's assertion, almost amounting to an oath, which immediately follows, shows that here he is resolutely determined to reject false information. On the other hand, he does not have to say everything that happened at that time. At all events, the visit to Jerusalem three years after the change in his life would have been sensible timing. The remarkable verse Acts 9.29 also indicates a controversy. Perhaps here Luke is opposing a tradition that Paul could not appear publicly in Jerusalem but had to hide – which would have been quite understandable. Nevertheless, during this 'briefing visit' – which was not a short one – he will have learned much from Peter that interested him. It must have been a high point in the history of earliest Christianity.[322] Another reason why Paul now avoided Jerusalem for a long time was that he had been given quite a different commission, 'to preach him among the Gentiles', and that could happen only outside Judaea.

4 The theological reasons for the persecution

This last point is certainly the most interesting, but also the most difficult and most disputed in our considerations. The change in Paul's career itself, the vision of the Risen Christ in his glory bestowed by God and the 'shining forth' of the glory of Christ in his heart which made him missionary to the Gentiles (II Cor.4.6), ceases to be part of the theme of the 'pre-Christian Paul', for with it begins a completely new and radically different period of his life. At the same time a psychological interpretation of Paul's conversion must be ruled out. Paul gives no indications in this direction. We do not learn that at the bottom of his heart he had been influenced by the crucified Messiah or the Christians whom he persecuted, nor do we know anything of discontent with the law and its strict demands or of inner struggles which prepared the way – on the contrary, he knew that he was 'as to the righteousness of the law blameless', as is shown by the last decisive statement in the climactic chain in Phil.3.6, which shows the firm basis of his former self-confidence. No one who is afflicted by depressions talks like that.[323] This unique confession shows that the young scribe Paul believed that he could live up to the high demands of perfect observance of the Torah of a Pharisaic kind, without any qualifications.[324]

The appearance of the risen and crucified messiah struck him like lightning, and the change which turned his previous life upside down was grounded for him solely in God's unfathomable saving counsel: ὅτε δὲ εὐδόκησεν ('when it pleased...') corresponds to the Old Testament *rāṣāh* and God's unfathomable action of electing grace works like the word of creation in Gen.1.1: 'The God who said "Let light shine out of darkness" has shone in our hearts to give the light of the knowledge of the glory of God in the face of Christ.'[325] This radical conversion at the same time represents a fundamental reversal of all previous values which determined his life; immediately after the famous enumeration in Phil.3.5f. he confesses, 'but what for me was gain I regarded as loss for Christ's sake...'[326] We just do not know enough to begin on the psychological sounding which is omnipresent today, and it is good that that is the case. At the same time it becomes abundantly clear that Paul's theological thought was governed by this change and the radical reversal of previous 'values' associated with it. The Pauline theology of the cross, the question of the law as a way to salvation and justification at the judgment, are not 'subsidiary craters'[327] which formed on the basis of later conflicts in the communities; from the beginning they directed the course of the former Pharisaic scribe – and we should reflect on what that means.[328] Even in asking the hypothetical question about the theological motives of the persecutor, we can begin from those 'values' which according to his own testimony were essential to the young Pharisee and scribal pupil. And in principle we can say: he persecuted the Jewish Christian Hellenists in Jerusalem because he saw what was most holy in Israel threatened by their proclamation and their conduct.

However, the first beginnings of a conflict probably lie in a more harmless fact of a sociological nature – that area which is so popular today. A synagogue community formed a fixed social group which depended for its existence on the cohesion of its members and their readiness to support it. If 'enthusiastic sectarians' had invaded such a relatively closed group and sought to alter the old, sound order, there must have been bad blood. The description of the Pauline mission in Acts gives us as much material to illustrate this as the letters of Paul or the later polemic against heretics from the Pastorals to Irenaeus.[329]

One could perhaps guard against such sectarians only by a rigorous 'banning from the house' or exclusion from the community. We find such defensive measures in, among others, the letters of John and the letters to the seven churches in Revelation; indeed Paul himself already commanded the Corinthians in his first, lost, letter not to have any communion with the doers of iniquity; later he intensified this to relate to open, serious sins of all kinds, for which eucharistic communion was to be broken (I Cor.5.9,13). Precisely in times of a struggle for the survival of the truth handed down, which now seems to us to be intolerant, the church proved to be an offshoot of Judaism. Things were very dangerous if trouble-makers at the same time persistently disseminated fatal heresies and made people question the foundation of their religious identity because they carried on active, successful mission for their own conventicle, without being oppressed by all the attempts at self-defence, and in so doing basically threatened the traditional conception of Jewish theocracy. But that seems to have been the case with the 'Hellenists' in the circles around Stephen. Faced with the misleading 'blasphemous words against this holy place and the law', the 'orthodox' Jew could only react with 'zeal for the law' and defend God's honour, if need be with force. When Christians came to power later, they hardly acted any differently. Among those Greek-speaking Jews who had returned to the Holy City for religious reasons, could be found on the one hand the tendency towards some criticism of the commercial practices of the pilgrimage city and the secularized temple hier-archy and a stress on the predominance of the ritual command-ments over the ethical ones; on the other hand, however, there was also a particular sensitivity towards the Temple of God and his holy commandments.[330] In some circumstances the two tendencies could come into conflict. With the Pharisee Sha'ul/Paul the latter attitude seems to have been the stronger.

The motives which led to the stoning of Stephen and those which shortly afterwards made the young Sha'ul a persecutor cannot therefore have been very different. But we should beware of excessively radical theses. We may not assume that either Stephen or the victims of the persecution of the Christian Hellenists, in which the young teacher played a crucial role, in principle disputed the significance of the Torah for salvation and carried on an active mission to the Gentiles apart from the law, as is later reported by Luke of the mission of the Hellenists in Antioch.[331] This not only went against the situation of the new eschatological community which had hardly been consolidated, a community which one, two or three years after the death and resurrection had hardly penetrated beyond Jewish Palestine, but was *a priori* an impossi-bility in both Jewish Galilee and in Jerusalem. Moreover, it would anticipate both Paul's new revolutionary theological insight and later developments in Antioch during the obscure fourteen years. Speculations of this kind are possible only if we fail to observe the chronology (which is a popular course nowadays) and overlook the situation in Palestinian and Syrian Judaism. If we leave aside

the unique case of Paul, about whose early missionary activity we
have no concrete knowledge, the earliest church was led step by
step to a mission to the Gentiles without the law. Here too (if we
leave out Paul), Luke's stylized account seems to me by and large
to be right, though we should see events in Caesarea (Acts 10.1-
11.18) and in Antioch (11.19-26) as taking place alongside each
other rather than one after the other. This development also applies
to the pioneers here, the 'Hellenists'. The first beginnings in this
direction may have consisted in the fact that, as was usual in the
Jewish Diaspora, godfearers who were seized with the new faith
were not forced to undergo circumcision under the threat of
exclusion from salvation. But that was hardly the point that
aroused wrath against Stephen and zeal for the Torah in Paul.
Rather, we should note how close in time we still are to the activity
of Jesus. As some New Testament scholars are hardly aware of the
fact that the history of earliest Christianity is played out in often
quite brief periods which are easily surveyed, this *fundamental*
chronological problem is also readily overlooked. Scholars sometimes argue about the earliest church as though Jesus had never
lived or as if he had been rapidly forgotten. The 'Hellenists''
criticism of Torah and temple must have developed starting points
in the preaching of Jesus, which was only between one and three
years in the past and remembered quite directly, whether in the
concentration of the commandments on the love command or in
the antitheses of the Sermon on the Mount, the rejection of the
Pharisaic 'tradition of the elders' or the questioning of ritual
commands relating to purity (Mark 7.5ff., 15ff.; Luke 10.7f.).
Because of the controversy with the pagan environment, for the
Diaspora Jews the law had a more marked universal and ethical
character; with them what is undoubtedly Jesus' own criticism of
the law could therefore fall on particularly fertile ground. However,
this criticism was still not a matter of principle, but related more
to specific individual points, for example arising out of the ritual
laws.[332]

The same is even more true of criticism of the temple. A threat
against the temple – spoken with messianic authority – played an
essential part in the trial of Jesus (Mark 14.58; Matt.26.51; cf.
John 2.19), and in the light of Zech.14.21b the 'cleansing of the
temple' is also to be understood as a messianic act. Jesus' saying

about the temple in Mark 11.17 with its combination of Isa.56.7
and Jer.7.11, which describes the temple as no longer a place of
sacrifice but a universal place of prayer, could perhaps be an
expression of the critical attitude of the Hellenists towards the
temple cult. The execution of Jesus, for which the high-priestly
leaders of the people were partly responsible, caused further
offence. From the beginning, his death 'for the many' (Mark 10.45;
14.24) put in question the expiatory effect of temple worship: with
it the sacrificial cult in the sanctuary seemed to have become
obsolete.[333] In my view, Stephen's speech, which is essentially
different in style from the other speeches which were composed by
Luke himself, usually on the basis of earlier traditions, represents
the remnants of a Jewish-Christian Hellenistic sermon from an
earlier period which has been stylistically improved by Luke.
Though it fits so badly in the framework of the trial of Stephen, its
tendency to be critical of the cult is unmistakable. With this
attitude, the 'Hellenists' were evidently more radical than the
'Hebrews', who tended to be more conservative towards the
preaching of Jesus. The leadership of this latter group was later
taken over by James the brother of Jesus after the persecution of
the community by Agrippa I in 42 or 43.

Further offence was caused by the proclamation of the crucified
Messiah. Deuteronomy 21.22f. puts 'the one who is hanged upon
the tree' under a divine curse (LXX: κεκατηραμένος ὑπὸ τοῦ
θεοῦ πᾶς κρεμάμενος ἐπὶ ξύλου). The Temple Scroll from 11Q
also applies this curse to those executed by crucifixion.[334] Against
this background, did not the proclamation that a crucified blasphemer who led the people astray was the Messiah of Israel itself
inevitably look like blasphemy? When Paul explicitly stresses
around twenty years later that the crucified Christ – here one could
almost speak of the crucified Messiah – is a stumbling block to the
Jews (I Cor.1.23), he is describing not only his present experience
of mission but the personal offence which he had taken to the
message of the crucified Messiah as a Pharisaic scribe on the basis
of his understanding of the Torah, when he still knew Christ 'after
the flesh'. His interpretation of Gal.3.13[335] can best be explained
against this background. At that time he really did see the crucified
Jesus of Nazareth, the blasphemer who had led the people astray,
as the one who had been rightly 'accursed' by God, just as he could

counter the Hellenists' criticism of the Torah which limited the significance of individual commandments and groups of commandments with full conviction, using the text from Deut.27.26 (cf.28.58; 29.20,27) which he quotes in Galatians 3.10: 'Cursed be every one who does not abide by all things written in the book of the law, and do them.' The Torah puts under God's curse anyone who does not observe all its commandments and prohibitions. To the young Pharisaic student the agitators seemed to be accursed lawbreakers, and followers and proclaimers of an accursed deceiver who had led the people astray – was that not reason enough, like Phinehas, to enter the breach in 'zeal for the Torah', to bring down a just punishment on their enemies or to drive them out? Who would blame the passionate hothead for such zeal for God's cause? After all, even twenty-five years later, as an older man, he could say of himself, 'Who is offended and I do not burn?' (II Cor. 11.29). In the same letter to the Corinthians (11.2) he exclaims, 'I feel a divine zeal for you' (ζηλῶ γὰρ ὑμᾶς θεοῦ ζήλῳ). The 'zeal' of the young Pharisee in Jerusalem was certainly no less than that of the apostle who had grown older. That was what *had* to be done.

Yet then everything was turned upside down: the crucified Messiah who according to Luke's account met him just before Damascus with the question 'Saul, Saul, why do you persecute me?' became the ground and content of his life. The one who according to Deut.21.22f. was 'accursed', who had been put to death on the tree of shame, encountered him in the splendour of divine glory. Exalted to the right hand of God, i.e. to share God's throne on the Merkaba,[336] he revealed himself to Paul as Son of God, as messiah of Israel *and* redeemer of all who believe. What had previously been a stumbling block came to occupy the centre of his new existence, and his Pharisaic theology orientated on the gift of the Torah and its demands now became the theology of the cross, the message of the Messiah who had already come, who 'died for us while we were still sinners' (Rom.5.8) and who reconciles his 'enemies' with God through his death (5.10). In Paul's vision of Christ, which called him to become apostle to the Gentiles, he – the former enemy – was entrusted with the gospel that proclaims the God of Israel *and* of the Gentiles who is gracious 'in Christ', the Father of Jesus Christ, who justifies the godless.

5 Summary: Paul the persecutor

It seems to me to be quite possible, by taking seriously both the main sources, Paul *and* Luke, and weighing them up critically, in broad outline to arrive at something like an overall picture of the 'pre-Christian Paul'. In it, the apostle's own testimonies indeed have priority over Luke, but despite his contrary tendency Luke's accounts, some of which correspond with Paul in an amazing way, may not just be swept away as being fictitious and utterly incredible. To end with, we must attempt to reconstruct the last dramatic events before the great change in Paul's life. Here, as often in our discipline, I can offer only a hypothetical reconstruction, but it is one which seems to me to be relatively plausible on the basis of all the evidence in the sources and after weighing up all the other hypotheses.

As the result of the agitation of the new messianic Jesus movement, or more precisely the Jewish Christian 'Hellenists', in the Greek-speaking synagogues of Jerusalem, considerable unrest developed there and there was an energetic reaction. The proclamation of the Greek-speaking followers of the messiah Jesus of Nazareth, crucified a short time earlier, which was critical of the ritual parts of the Torah and the cult, was a provocation to the majority who were loyal to the law. The most active spokesman of the new group, Stephen, was stoned to death after a tumultuous gathering in one of these synagogues. On this occasion Sha'ul/Paul, the scribal student and young teacher, played only a subsidiary role. But when the representatives of this enthusiastic group which was hostile to the law did not lie low, but continued to agitate, he took the initiative and brought about a 'pogrom' within the limited sphere of the 'Hellenistic' synagogues of Jerusalem against these sectarians. Here he followed the example of Phinehas in his 'zeal for the law' and did not shrink from the use of brute force. Presumably 'Hellenists' were arrested as they discussed in the synagogues, and condemned to the usual punishment of thirty-nine lashes; some may even have suffered more serious physical hurt and even have been killed. In this way the relatively small community of the 'Hellenists' was largely destroyed and fled from Jerusalem to neighbouring territories and cities. Sha'ul/Paul accepted a mission from these synagogues in Jerusalem to Damas-

cus, to take proceedings against the agitators who had fled there
and their local supporters. When he was almost at his destination
he had that vision of the risen Christ which shattered his old life
and opened up a completely new and unexpected future for him.

For the most part Pauline theology rests on the radical reversal
of former values and aims which came about through the encounter
with the crucified and risen Jesus of Nazareth. The Jewish teacher
becomes the missionary to the Gentiles; the 'zeal for the law' is
replaced by the proclamation of the gospel without the law;
justification of the righteous on the basis of their 'works of the law'
is replaced by justification of the 'godless' through faith alone; the
free will is replaced by the faith which is given by grace alone as
the creation of the word; and hatred of the crucified and accursed
pseudo-messiah is replaced by a theology of the cross which
grounds the salvation of all men and women in the representative
accursed death of the messiah on the cross.

Although people nowadays are fond of asserting otherwise, no
one understood the real essence of Pauline theology, the salvation
given *sola gratia*, by faith alone, better than Augustine and Martin
Luther. Despite this rigorous reversal of all previous values and
ideals (Phil.3.7-11), Pauline theology – and therefore also Christian
theology – remains very closely bound up with Jewish theology.
Its individual elements and thought-structure derive almost
exclusively from Judaism. This revolutionary change becomes
visible precisely in the fact that its previous theological views
remain present even in their critical reversal as a negative foil, and
help to determine the location of the new position. Paul first learned
his theological thinking in no other place than a Jewish house of
learning, and before he proclaimed Christ to the Gentiles, he had
interpreted the law in the synagogue – very probably in Jerusalem
itself – to Jews from the Diaspora. Only against this background
can we understand that formula which is fundamental to him: 'For
Christ is the end of the law, that everyone who has faith in him
may be justified' (Rom.10.4) It describes the revolutionary shift
in his life, and he experienced its truth personally – in a more
radical way than anyone else.

Notes

In the notes, books are cited in chronological order; commentaries are cited by author and details of series.

1. General literature: T.Zahn, 'Zur Lebensgeschichte des Apostels Paulus', *NKZ* 15, 1904, 23-41, 189-200; A.Steinmann, 'Zum Werdegang des Paulus. Die Jugendzeit in Tarsus', *Verzeichnis der Vorlesungen an der Staatlichen Akademie zu Braunsberg*, Braunsberg 1928, 1-39; E.Barnikol, *Die vorchristliche und frühchristliche Zeit des Paulus. Nach seinen geschichtlichen und geographischen Selbstzeugnissen in Galaterbrief*, FEUC 1, Kiel 1929; A.Oepke, 'Probleme der vorchristlichen Zeit des Paulus', *ThStKr* 105, 1933, 387-424 (reprinted in *Das Paulusbild in der neueren deutschen Forschung*, WdF 24, ed. K.H.Rengstorf with U.Luck, Darmstadt ³1982, 410-46); K.Adam, 'Der junge Paulus', in *Paulus-Hellas-Oikumene*. *1900th Anniversary of the Coming of St Paul to Greece*, Athens 1951, 9-21.

2. M.Dibelius/W.G.Kümmel, *Paul*, London 1953, 15-45, does not discuss the pre-Christian Paul separately, but within the chapters 'The Jewish and Greek Worlds', 'Paul the Man' and 'Paul Turns to Christ'; G.Bornkamm, *Paul*, London and New York 1971, 3-12: 'Paul's Descent and Environment before his Conversion'; 13-25: 'Paul's Persecution of the Church and his Conversion and Call'; O.Kuss, *Paulus*, Regensburg 1971, 37-44: the beginnings of Paul up to his activity as an active persecutor of believers in Jesus (brief but informative); J.Becker, *Paulus. Der Apostel der Völker*, Tübingen 1989, 34-59: Paul as a Pharisee from Tarsus; 60-87: the call to be apostle to the Gentiles, in which there is also a discussion of Paul as persecutor. Even D.Hildebrandt, *Saulus Paulus. Ein Doppelleben*, Munich and Vienna 1989, devotes only a few pages (55-65) to the young Paul in his novellistic portrait written with much understanding and great empathy towards the biographical and historical details of Paul's life. This is surely a reflection of the present situation in research, which is concerned *ad nauseam* with Paul's understanding of the law but reflects very little on Paul the Pharisee in this connection. We cannot understand the former if we do not take the latter into account.

3. Justin, *Dial*.2.3-8.2: for Justin as teacher cf. now U.Neymeyr, *Die christlichen Lehrer im zweiten Jahrhundert. Ihre Lehrtätigkeit, ihr Selbstverständnis und ihre Geschichte*, VigChrSuppl 4, Leiden 1989, 16-35; in *Vis*. I, 1.1f (the so-called 'bathing of Rhoda'), Hermas also contains a brief section the autobiographical character of which is disputed. For this and 'the problem of the autobiographical in the *Shepherd*', see M.Leutzsch, *Die Wahrnehmung sozialer Wirklichkeit im 'Hirten des Hermas'*, FRLANT 150, Göttingen 1989, 20-49. Compare the introductions to the other Visions and Similitudes, in all of which there are biographical echoes.

4. Gal.1.13-17; I Cor.15.8f.; II Cor.11.22; Rom.11.1; Phil.3.4-6.

5. On this see A.Deissmann, *Paul*, London 1926, 'Paul the Jew', 83-110; W.D.Davies, *Paul and Rabbinic Judaism. Some Rabbinic Elements in Pauline Theology*, London ²1955, especially the conclusion, 321-4; D.Flusser, 'Die jüdische und griechische Bildung des Paulus', in *Paulus*, ed. E.Lessing, Freiburg 1980, 11-39: 16ff. There is a survey of scholarship up to his own day in H.J.Schoeps, *Paul. The Theology of the Apostle in the Light of Jewish Religious History*, London 1961, 37-42, 'The Palestinian-Judaic Approach'. Relatively little space remains in Bultmann's work for the Jewish heritage of Paul, cf. R.Bultmann, 'Zur Geschichte des Paulus-Forschung'. *ThR* 1, 1929, 26-59 (reprinted in WdF 24 [see n.1], 304-37); he enthusiastically celebrates the works of the history of religions school with their completely one-sided stress on Hellenistic influence (322f.); cf. also section 16 of his *Theology of the New Testament*, Vol.1, London and New York 1951: 'The Historical Position of Paul'. K.H.Schelkle, *Paulus. Leben-Briefe-Theologie*, EdF 152, takes too little account of the Jewish character of Pauline theology: after a short section on Hellenism (42-5) the historically questionable chapter on 'Gnosis' follows, taking up more room than that on the Jewish roots of Paul.

6. In particular the commentaries on Acts by E.Haenchen, H.Conzelmann and G.Schille are marked by a radical scepticism towards the historical value of Luke's accounts. The following quotation from Schille is typical: 'When it depicts the actions of the leading figures and their convincing speeches, Acts reproduces the picture that the second Christian generation created of its most important men. It is concerned neither with historical circumstances, about which Luke was never very bothered, nor even with indicating a psychological development in the modern sense; Luke sets down the picture of the apostles circulating in his own day, which had become wreathed in a first halo! Therefore we best do justice to Luke and Acts by taking their statements as a contribution not to the persons of the apostles but to the formation of the tradition about them, i.e. to the picture of Peter and Paul that was unfolding', ThHK 5, Berlin 1983, 50. For the history of scholarship cf.W.W.Gasque, *A History*

of the Criticism of the Acts of the Apostles, BGBE 17, Tübingen 1975 (for Haenchen see 235-47; for Conzelmann see 247-50); id., 'Recent Commentaries on the Acts of the Apostles', *Themelios* 14, 1988/9, 21-33, see 30f.: a review of the English translation of Conzelmann's commentary. By contrast the works of G.Lüdemann attempt a link between radical criticism and the discovery of historically reliable traditions, cf. *Paul: Apostle to the Gentiles*, 1. *Studies on Chronology*, Philadelphia and London 1984, 21-5; *Early Christianity according to the Traditions in Acts. A Commentary*, London and Philadelphia 1989, 1-18.

7. L.Baeck, 'The Faith of Paul', *JJS* 3, 1952, 93-110. This disparagement of Luke the historian has its parallels in the tendency criticism of the nineteenth-century Tübingen school, which made the mistake of denying Luke any historical reliability because of his manifest 'tendencies'. This approach was rightly attacked already by the great ancient historian E.Meyer, *Ursprung und Anfänge des Christentums* III, Stuttgart and Berlin 1923, 64: 'The Tübingen school, F.C.Baur and his followers, were quite right in asserting that Acts is dominated by a tendency and is therefore one-sided... But it would be a misconception to conclude from this that it is a late book, which falsifies the original material and therefore is hardly usable historically. Rather, what we find here is the view of a contemporary who was involved in the events: we see how Luke, Paul's pupil and companion, himself a Gentile by birth, who studied the Jewish revelation zealously and became convinced of the certainty of salvation, dealt with the great problem which concerned the growing church and led it to hard internal struggles, under the influence of the teaching of his master. That necessarily leads to a shift in the conception of individual events and to the attempt to bridge over the oppositions. But the basic lines of development have nevertheless been drawn rightly.'

8. It is to be doubted whether there is ever historical writing, of whatever kind, which can fulfil the alleged postulate of absolute objectivity. Thus H.-G.Gadamer (*Truth and Method*, London and New York [2]1989, 204-12, 'Ranke's historical worldview') can also speak of his method in terms of 'naivete' (208) which, influenced by Hegel's philosophy, begins from the complete 'self-transparency of being' (212). Moreover it is precisely Ranke who shows the abiding relatedness of historian and poet (216).

9. It is to the credit of Claus-Jürgen Thornton that in his 1990 Tübingen dissertation *Der Zeuge des Zeugen. Lukas als Historiker der Paulusreisen* (to be published in WUNT, first series) he has demonstrated this convincingly; cf. also E.Plümacher, *Lukas als hellenistischer Schriftsteller*, StUNT 9, Göttingen 1972; M.Hengel, *Acts and the History of Earliest Christianity*, London and Philadelphia 1979, esp. 59-68; id., 'Luke the Historian and the Geography of Palestine in the Acts of the Apostles', in *Between Jesus and*

Paul, London and Philadelphia 1983, 97-127; C.J.Hemer, *The Book of Acts in the Setting of Hellenistic History*, WUNT 49, Tübingen 1989.

10. For citizenship of Tarsus see Acts 21.39; cf. 22.3; 9.11,30 (cf.11.25); for Roman citizenship see Acts 16.37f.; 22.25; 23.27.

11. I. Ancient sources on Tarsus: Strabo, *Geog.* 14.5.9-15: the description of Cilicia begins in 14.5.1; 2 describes the slave trade of the Cilician pirates and 3ff. is a description of the smaller Cilician cities; 8 describes the Rhodian settlement of Soloi from the eighth century BCE, the old rival of Tarsus, which had, however, completely lagged behind Tarsus since the first century BCE. Soloi was the place from which Chrysippus, head of the Stoic school (third century BCE), came; his father had moved here from Tarsus, and his pupil and successor Zeno also came from there. So, too, did the comic poets Philemon (fourth to third century BCE) and Aratus, the author of the famous *Phainomena* (Acts 17.28); for the foundation inscription of Sardanapalus in Anchiale, which recalls the foundation of this city along with Tarsus on the same day, reported by Strabo, cf. I Cor.15.32b, where Paul quotes Isa.22.13 (LXX). The inscription reads: 'Eat, drink, play, for other things are not worth a snap of the fingers.'

Dio of Prusa (= Dio Chrysostom, c.40-115 CE), *Or.*33; 34. The following passages are particularly interesting. 33.5: an allusion to the numerous famous teachers who were already active in the city; this is at the same time a reference to the omnipresence of orators; 33.28: the decadence of the city is attacked – more cities perish from decadence than from wars; 33.45 enumerates the pantheon of Tarsus, cf. also 33.47: Heracles visits the place of his sacrifices in Tarsus; 33.48 mentions the veiling of women as a sign of their virtue, cf. I Cor.11.1ff. (for this see Steinmann, 'Werdegang des Paulus' [n.1], 10; C.B.Welles, 'Hellenistic Tarsus', *MUSJ* 38, 1962, 67; W.Ramsay, *The Cities of St Paul*, London 1907, 202-5); 33.62-64: vigorous attacks on the fashion in Tarsus according to which the men shave off all their hair and on the tendency to become a hermaphrodite; 34.7f.: the city received special favours of a political kind from Augustus (which is certainly also where the generous bestowal of Roman citizenship belongs, since at the time of Augustus the number of Roman citizens in the empire grew by 900,000 between the two censuses which he carried out in 18 BCE and 14 CE; thus of the fifty million inhabitants of the Roman empire [including slaves], about five million possessed Roman citizenship, cf. *Res Gestae* 8 and M.Giebel, *Augustus*, Reinbek bei Hamburg 1984, 74f., see also n.54 below); 34.21-23: on the citizenship of the linen weavers (see n.54 below). For Dio's information about Tarsus see T.Callandar, 'The Tarsian Orations of Dio Chrysostom', *JHS* 24, 1904, 58-69; Welles, 'Hellenistic Tarsus', 62-75; D.Kienast and H.Castritius, 'Ein vernachlässigtes Zeugnis für die Reichspolitik Trajans: Die 2. tarsische Rede des Dion von Prusa', *Historia* 20, 1971, 62-83.

Philostratus, *Apollonios-Vita* I.7: Apollonius was taken from Tyana in Cappadocia to the north side of the Taurus to be educated in Tarsus: 'When he was fourteen years old, his father took him to Tarsus, to the house of Euthydemus, who was from Phoenicia. Euthydemus was a good rhetorician, and began to teach him; for his part, he was attached to his tutor, but he found the nature of the city unpleasant, and not conducive to studying philosophy: for more than anywhere else it is a place where there are mocking and immoral men who seize upon luxury, and devote themselves more to fine linen cloths than the Athenians do to wisdom. With his father's permission, therefore, he transferred his teacher to Aegae nearby, in which there was the peacefulness that is helpful for philosophizing, and activities more suitable for young men, and a temple of Asclepius, and Asclepius himself manifest to mortals.' For 1.12 cf. Rom.1.26f.; VI.34 refers to Jews in Tarsus.

In 51/50 BCE Cicero was governor of Cilicia in Tarsus, and he reports on it in numerous letters, for example in those to Atticus and Caelius and in Book 3 of the collection *ad familias*, cf. M.Fuhrmann, *Cicero und die römische Republik*, Munich and Zurich 1989, 173-85 on his governorship in Cilicia (175 has a list of his letters from this period).

II. Secondary literature on Tarsus: W.Ramsay, *The Cities of St Paul*, London 1907, 85-224; H.Böhlig, *Die Geisteskultur von Tarsos im augusteischen Zeitalter mit Berücksichtigung der paulinischen Schriften*, FRLANT 9, Göttingen 1913; Steinmann, 'Werdegang' (n.1); W.Ruge, 'Tarsus', *PW* IV A 2, 1932, cols.2413-39; W.C.van Unnik, *Tarsus or Jerusalem. The City of Paul's Youth*, in id., *Sparsa Collecta I*, NT.S 29, Leiden 1973, 259-320; id., 'Once again Tarsus or Jerusalem', ibid., 321-7; H.Goldman (ed.), *Excavations at Gözlü Kule, Tarsus*, three double volumes, New Jersey 1950-63; C.B.Welles, 'Hellenistic Tarsus', *MUSJ* 38, 1962, 41-75; C.J.Hemer, 'Tarsus', *ISBE* IV, 1988, 734-6. For the geographical and climatic situation of this area and for the further development of Tarsus up to modern times, see L.Rother, *Die Städte der Cukurova: Adana – Mersin – Tarsus. Ein Beitrag zum Gestalt-, Struktur- und Funktionswandel türkischer Städte*, Tübinger Geographische Studien 42, Tübingen 1971; for the Pauline period see 36f.: 'The Hey-day of Cilician Cities in the Hellenistic-Roman Period'.

III. For the history of Roman rule in Asia Minor or Cilicia cf. A.H.M.Jones, *The Cities of the Eastern Roman Provinces*, Oxford 1937; id., 'The Economic Life of the Towns of the Roman Empire', *RSJB* 7, 1955, 161-94 (also in id., *The Roman Economy. Studies in Ancient Economic and Administrative History*, ed. P.A.Brunt, Oxford 1974, 35-60); id., *The Greek*

City from Alexander to Justinian, Oxford ²1966; E.Gren, *Kleinasien und der Ostbalkan in der wirtschaftlichen Entwicklung der römischen Kaiserzeit*, Uppsala dissertation 1941; D.Magie, *Roman Rule in Asia Minor* II, New Jersey 1950; C.Préaux, 'Institutions économiques et sociales des villes héllénistiques, principalement en Orient', *RSJB* 7, 1955, 80-135; G.W.Bowersock, *Augustus and the Greek World*, Oxford 1965; B.Levick, *Roman Colonies in Southern Asia Minor*, London 1967; T.Pekary, 'Kleinasien unter römischer Herrschaft', *ANRW* II 7.2, Berlin and New York 1980, 595-675.

12. Cf. R.Riesner, *Die Frühzeit des Paulus. Studien zur Chronologie, Missionsstrategie und Theologie des Apostels Paulus bis zum ersten Thessalonicherbrief*, Tübingen Habilitationsschrift 1990 (to be published in WUNT first series), 128, 201-4 (on Rom.15.19), 213f. (literature in notes 100-3); also J.L.Kelso, 'Key Cities in Paul's Missionary Program', *BS* 79, 1922, 481-6; Deissmann, *Paul* (n.5), 174ff.; W.A.Meeks, *The First Urban Christians*, New Haven and London 1983, 9-13, 40-50; M.H.Conn, 'Lucan Perspective and the Cities', *Missiology* 13, 1985, 409-28.

13. Sepphoris, only three miles away from Nazareth, is not mentioned at all, and Tiberias appears as a geographical feature only in John 6.1,23; 21.1. Tyre and Sidon, the Decapolis and Caesarea Philippi are mentioned only in connection with their territory.

14. Acts 22.3; cf. 9.11,30; 11.25; 21.39; C.Burchard, *Der dreizehnte Zeuge*, FRLANT 103, Göttingen 1970, 34f. n.42, thinks his origin from Tarsus 'not indubitable'. According to Burchard, an earlier tradition taken over by Luke underlies only the statement in Acts 22.3, while there is nothing comparable for any origin from Tarsus. Barnikol, 'Vorchristliche Zeit' (n.1), 12f., already expressed doubt here.

15. But see Deissmann, *Paul* (n.5), 70ff.; Pauline imagery reflects 'the civilization of the ancient great city' (71), cf. ibid., 39f.; similarly Steinmann, 'Werdegang' (n.1), 37ff. That Paul's association preferred this particular imagery in the dictation of his letters is possibly a reference to the environment which shaped his youth (but it should never be forgotten that Jerusalem, too, was to some degree a great Hellenistic city, see below 54ff.); the attempt of E.F.Synge to draw conclusions for Paul's theology from his youth in Tarsus is speculative: 'St Paul's Boyhood and Conversion and his Attitude to Race', *ExpT* 94, 1983/4, 260-3.

16. Luke's report also deserves trust because it runs counter to his own 'image' of Paul, which attempts to stress Paul's links with Judaea and Jewish Christianity; cf. Burchard, *Zeuge* (n.14), 34 n.41, who notes that Luke would have 'preferred to indicate a place of birth in Palestine rather than in Tarsus'. Nevertheless he sticks to the historical truth!

17. Cf. Riesner, *Frühzeit* (n.12), 215-18.

18. Rom.15.19, 25f., 31; I Cor.16.3; Gal.1.17f.; 2.1; 4.25f.

19. Rom.15.31; II Cor.1.16; Gal.1.22; I Thess.2.14.

20. I Cor.1.2; II Cor.1.1,23 (cf. also II Cor 6.11; II Tim.4.20).

21. I Cor.15.32; 16.8 (cf. also Eph 1.1; I Tim.1.3; II Tim.1.18; 4.12) or II Cor.11.32; Gal.1.17.

22. Gal.2.11 (cf.also II Tim.3.11).

23. Strabo, *Geography* 14.5,13.

24. Cf. J.B.Lightfoot, 'St Paul's Preparation for the Ministry', in id., *Biblical Essays*, London 1904, 191-211, on Greek education, 205f.; Meyer, *Ursprung* (n.7), III, 314; K.L.Schmidt, 'Paulus und die antike Welt', WdF 24 (n.1), 214-45: 223f. (originally Vorträge der Bibliothek Warburg, Leipzig 1927, 38-64); Flusser, 'Jüdische Bildung' (n.5), 32ff.

25. For this see the only two Jewish Hellenistic synagogue sermons preserved from antiquity, *De Jona* and *De Sampsone*, ed. F.Siegert, *Drei hellenistisch-jüdische Predigten. Ps.Philon, 'Über Jona', 'Über Simson' und 'Über die Gottesbezeichnung "wohltätig verzehrendes Feuer"'*, WUNT I.20, Tübingen 1980. A commentary on both by F.Siegert will appear in WUNT first series. For the relationship between synagogue and school see R.Riesner, *Jesus als Lehrer*, WUNT II.7, Tübingen [3]1988, 151ff.

26. For the content of the cyclical teaching plan of the Hellenistic school up to the first century CE cf. J.Dolch, *Lehrplan des Abendlandes*, Darmstadt 1982, 47-71, 89-95.

27. The conjecture of H.Windisch, KEK 6, [9]1924, new edition by G.Strecker, 1970, 'that Paul himself had seen the mime and heard of it does not seem to me to be impossible' (316) is improbable. Still less was Paul influenced by the role of the foolish braggart in the mime when he talks of speaking as a fool in II Cor.11.21-12.10. The term 'folly' comes from Jewish wisdom. H.D.Betz, *Der Apostel Paulus und die sokratische Tradition*, BHTh 45, Tübingen 1972, 79f., follows Windisch, but conjectures that this literary form, too, came to him by way of popular philosophy. See also C.Wolff, ThHK 8, 1989, 20ff. For the problem see now the criticism of U.Heckel, *Kraft in Schwachheit*, Tübingen theological dissertation, to be published in WUNT in 1991. In my view such an ironically alienating way of talking comes from the rhetorical arsenal of synagogue preaching.

The Jewish evidence on the theatre is collected in Bill.IV.1, 401-5; Josephus, *Antt*.15.268, also calls the theatre an alien custom, in connection with Herod's building activities. Nevertheless the numerous and great theatres in Israel (Sepphoris, Tiberias, the Herodian buildings in Jerusalem, see R.A.Batey, 'Jesus and the Theatre', *NTS* 30, 1984, 563-74) show that quite a large number of people enjoyed them. One might also refer to the Jewish tragedian Ezekiel, who in Alexandria in the second century BCE wrote a tragedy on the Exodus from Egypt influenced by Euripides,

in iambic trimeters, which was conceived of as a stage play (on this
see R.G.Robertson, 'Ezekiel the Tragedian', in J.H.Charlesworth, *Old
Testament Pseudepigrapha* II, Garden City, NY and London 1985, 803-19).
We cannot exclude the possibility that dramas in the style of Ezekiel were
performed or recited in Jerusalem and other Jewish centres. The Jewish
theatre inscription of Miletus (second to third century CE) also suggests
a varied treatment of this question, cf. E.Schürer, *The History of the Jewish
People in the Age of Jesus Christ (175 BC – AD 135)*, III.1, revised and edited
by G.Vermes, F.Millar and M.Goodman, Edinburgh 1986, 24f., 167f. In
addition to this there is the inscription relating to the renovation of an
amphitheatre from Berenice in Cyrenaica (from around the beginning of
our era), in which a Jew and Roman citizen is honoured by the Jewish
politeuma of the city for his services, see G.Lüderitz, *Corpus jüdischer Zeugnisse
aus der Cyrenaika*, TAVO.B 53, Wiesbaden 1983, no.70; R.Tracey, 'Jewish
Renovation of an Amphitheatre', *NewDocs* 4, Macquarie University 1987,
202-9. We certainly cannot rule out the possibility that Paul went to the
theatre, but it is not very probable.

For the attitude of the early church to the theatre cf. W.Weissmann,
*Kirche und Schauspiele. Die Schauspiele im Urteil der lateinischen Kirchenväter
unter besonderer Berücksichtigung von Augustin, Cass.27*, Würzburg 1972;
H.Jürgens, *Pompa Diaboli. Die Bekanntschaft der lateinischen Kirchenväter mit
dem antiken Theaterwesen*, philosophical dissertation (typescript) Tübingen
1969 (see ibid., 192 n.2: in Christian polemic against the theatre Jews
and Manichaeans are often mentioned alongside the pagans). But here
too it should be noted that this rigorism is limited mainly to the West and
the church authors wrote polemic against the theatre only because some
Christians were evidently very fond of going there, and even justified this
with quotations from the Bible, cf. A.von Harnack, *Die Mission und
Ausbreitung des Christentums in den ersten drei Jahrhunderten*, Leipzig [4]1924,
311-15. Cf. also P.Lampe, *Die stadtrömischen Christen in den ersten beiden
Jahrhunderten*, WUNT II.18, Tübingen [2]1989, 107f.

28. Cf. A.Lesky, *Geschichte der Griechischen Literatur*, Berne and Munich
[3]1971, 722. The iambic trimeter quoted by Paul appears as no.218 in
J.M.Edmonds, *The Fragments of Attic Comedy IIIB, Menander*, Leiden 1961
(626f.), as a proverb in Menander, *Monostichoi* 808, ed. S.Jaekel, Leipzig
1964, 79. Probably the best-known proverb from Menander is Caesar's
famous *alea iacta est* ('the die is cast'), a remark which he is supposed to
have made after crossing the Rubicon, cf. Suetonius, *Life of Caesar* 32 (the
Greek text of Menander ran ἀνερρίφθω κύβος and came from the
comedy ΑΡΡΗΦΟΡΟΣ Η ΑΥΛΗΤΡΙΣ, cf. A.Koerte, *Menandri quae
supersunt* II, BSGRT, Leipzig 1959, no.59, in Edmonds, no.65 [pp.568f.]).

We do not know in the case of either Paul or Caesar whether they were aware of the origin of these detached sayings.

29. For the texts, which all come from Christian sources, see A.M.Denis, *Fragmenta Pseudepigraphorum quae supersunt Graeca*, PVTG, Leiden 1970, 161ff.; N.Walter, in *JSHRZ* IV, Göttingen 1983, 244-73. Collections of testimonies from Greek classical writers would in themselves have been helpful for the Jewish missionary Saul (see below, 60) in his concern to describe to his fellow-countrymen from the Diaspora the superiority of Jewish-Pharisaic piety. That they were evidently no longer used in his time may be connected with the growing influence of Palestine, the mother country, in the imperial period, cf. M.Hengel, 'Der alte und der neue "Schürer"', *JSS* 35, 1990, 19-72 (57, 60f.). Nevertheless such anthologies show that there were trends in Judaism which could also take to heart the Pauline principle from I Thess.5.21 for the Greek dramas; this even applies to Euripides, who despite his polytheistic dramas was later cited as a witness for monotheism (Clement of Alexandria, *Protrepticon* 6,68,3; cf. *Stromateis* 5.11.75, where a quotation from Euripides is used as an illustration of Isa.1.11).

30. Strabo, *Geography*, 14.5.13.

31. E.Schwartz, *Charakterköpfe aus der Antike*, ed. J.Stroux, Stuttgart 1943, 208. That Paul the Jew 'thinks and writes in Greek' and that this 'Greek does not have anything to do with any school or any model, but... comes directly from the heart' is also stressed by the great philologian of antiquity, U.von Wilamowitz-Moellendorf, see 'Die griechische Literatur des Altertums', in *Die Kultur der Gegenwart* I 8, Leipzig and Berlin [3]1912, 3-318: 232. Cf. Deissmann, *Paul* (n.5), 42, who associates his linguistic ability with his social status: 'A careful investigation of the vocabulary of Paul's Epistles has proved that Paul does not write literary Greek; if further the relation of his style to Atticism be studied, it is still clearer that he made no attempt to write according to accepted Greek standards. These observations confirm our thesis that both as regards his home circumstances and the place he occupies in history he stands below the educated upper classes. But even though his vocabulary is that of the people and the tone of every-day speech is predominant in his letters, yet his unliterary language is not vulgar to the degree that finds expression in many contemporary papyri. On the ground of his language rather Paul should be assigned to a higher class'; Dibelius/Kümmel, *Paul* (n.2), 27f.; Bornkamm, *Paul* (n.2), 9f. arrive at a similar verdict.

32. Cf. Lucian, *Bis acc.* 27 (= LCL *Lucian* III, 136); he first learned Greek in the elementary school, cf. further *Adv.indoct.* 4 (= LCL III, 180); *Pseudolog.*1 (= LCL V, 372).

33. Cf. Lesky, *Geschichte* (n.28), 937-41, but he stresses that Lucian,

who read and wrote much, had been spared a deeper penetration into the 'problems of great poetry'.

34. *Navig.* 2; K.Kilburn translates: 'He spoke in a slovenly manner, one long, continuous prattle; he spoke Greek, but his accent and intonation pointed to his native land' (LCL *Lucian* VI, 433).

35. Above all S.Ben-Chorin's book on Paul, *Paulus, der Völkerapostel in jüdischer Sicht*, Munich 1970, describes the apostle as a wanderer and mediator between two worlds, but of these the Jewish world often falls by the wayside. His programme of becoming a Jew to the Jews and a Greek to the Greeks makes him suspect to both: 'The Jews felt that he was a dangerous Hellenist and many Christians rejected him as a rabbinic sophist', thus id., 'Paulus – Mittler zwischen Juden und Christen', in his collection *Weil wir Brüder sind*, Gerlingen 1988, 180-94: 192.

36. Böhlig, *Geisteskultur von Tarsos* (n.11), 22-57, collects all the material about Sandon known in his time and interprets this figure in connection with the dying and rising vegetation deities Adonis (Syria), Attis (Phrygia), Osiris (Egypt) and Tammuz (Babylon). In his view mysteries developed from their cults, the binding link in which is the Soter concept. The comparison with Pauline christology is then made on 51-7: 'Just as Paul doubtless coincides with Syrian terminology in the use of the name Kyrios, so too his dying and rising saviour is an undeniable parallel to the Heracles-Sandon apotheosis...' For the further development of this thesis and criticism of it cf. Schoeps, *Paul* (n.5), 17f., who describes Böhlig's remarks as exaggerations (17 n.2) and at best allows 'the associative influence of the apostle's youthful memories', which as a conceptual world influenced his Christ-soteriology. For L.Goppelt see his *Die apostolische und nachapostolische Zeit*, KIG 1A, Göttingen 1962, A48; for criticism see Burchard, *Zeuge* (n.14), 35 n.42. In particular Bultmann and his pupils, referring back to the history of religions school, said that Christianity was a syncretistic religion in which not only Gnosticism but above all the mystery religions were drawn in as the source of important theologoumena (cf. R.Bultmann, *Primitive Christianity in its Contemporary Setting*, London 1956, 156ff., 175f., 184f.; id., *Theology* [n.5], see especially §13, 'The Sacraments', and §33.3, 'The Death and Resurrection of Christ as a Saving Event'). For a comprehensive criticism of the derivation of Pauline theology from the mysteries cf. A.J.M.Wedderburn, *Baptism and Resurrection. Studies in Pauline Theology against its Graeco-Roman Background*, WUNT I.44, Tübingen 1987. W.Burkert, *Antike Mysterien*, Munich 1990, also energetically stresses the fundamental differences between Jewish and Christian religious feeling on the one hand and the piety of the mysteries on the other, cf. e.g. 9ff.,20f., 53ff., etc.

For Sandon cf. further J.Zwicker, 'Sandon', *PW* 2R. I A 2, 1920, 2264-

8; H.Goldman, 'The Sandon Monument of Tarsus', *JAOS* 60, 1940, 544-63; id., *Sandon and Herakles*, Hesp.Suppl. 8, American School of Classical Studies at Athens 1949, 164-74 (it was the Greeks under Alexander who first fused the two figures together); W.Fauth, 'Sandon', *KP* 4, Munich 1972, 1541f. Sandon-Heracles was not a mystery god at all.

For the foundation legends of Tarsus see M.P.Nilsson, *HAW* V.2.2, Munich [4]1988, 57; for the Mithras cult of the Cilician pirates (who were the first to acquaint the Greeks with this cult, see Plutarch, *Pompey* 24.7). Coins from Tarsus depicting the bull sacrifice of Mithras were minted in the third century CE by Gordian III (ibid., 186 n.118); there is a photograph of the coins in Nilsson, plate 16.2.

For the history of religion in this area generally see Böhlig, *Geisteskultur von Tarsos* (n.11), 8-107, 'Die Religion von Tarsus'; Goldman, *Excavations* (n.11) I: this volume lists the finds from the Hellenistic-Roman period which emerged in the excavation of the earlier deeper strata. Goldman stresses in his preface that Tarsus from the time of Augustus and Paul is still not excavated, because of its location under modern Tarsus. Nevertheless the abundance of terra cotta figures of Greek gods and heroes which have been found give an impressive picture of the religious variety of this city: T.S.MacKay, 'The Major Sanctuaries of Pamphylia and Cilicia', *ANRW* II 18.3, Berlin and New York 1990, 2045-129.

37. Cf. Steinmann, *Werdegang* (n.1), 7; Kienast and Castritius, 'Zeugnis' (n.11), 66, 106f. (the beginning of the emperor cult in Asia Minor from 30 BCE; an intensification began only from 9 BCE on), 202-14; H.W.Tajra, *The Trial of St Paul*, WUNT II.35, Tübingen 1989, 39ff., who rightly stresses that the emperor cult was still at a very early stage during the time of Augustus and participation in it was not yet obligatory, see also Schoeps, *Paul* (n.5), 18, and his final evaluation and rejection of attempts exclusively or predominantly to explain Paul in terms of pagan Hellenistic culture: 'Essentially one must rather say – and this consideration qualifies all pagan-Hellenistic interpretations of Paul – that a considered assessment of the spiritual forces of his environment as possible sources or influential factors in his theology must exclude pure Hellenism, however certain it may be that he was directly acquainted with it as a reality of his age. The "Hellenistic" trait in his thought which undeniably exists is not to be explained by direct influence, was obviously not an independent "formative factor" stemming from his youth in Tarsus, but rather the result of a process of assimilation, since Hellenism had long before been penetrated by the spirit of the Jewish Diaspora' (23). This was not seen clearly enough in the account of Paul in R.Reitzenstein, *Die hellenistischen Mysterienreligionen*, Stuttgart [3]1927 (= Darmstadt 1956), 333-93 (Paul as a pneumatic), 417-25 (on the history

of Paul's development), and in turn had such a baneful influence on
Bultmann's understanding of Paul, and Schoeps rightly criticized it, cf.
M.Hengel, *The 'Hellenization' of Judaea in the First Century after Christ*,
London and Philadelphia 1989, 58f. n.4.

38. Acts 21.37-39.

39. On this see e.g. Jones, *Cities* (n.11), 159-62, 172-4, on citizenship in
the Greek *poleis* in the East (Tarsus, 174). In all the cities, in addition to
the full citizens there were 'a number of domiciled aliens (usually called
κάτοικοι) who had some rights, but not full citizenship' (160). In contrast
to the situation in Rome, slaves were not given citizenship immediately
on their emancipation. It is important for Paul's situation that 'Roman
citizenship was under the principate compatible with local citizenship,
whose obligations were unaffected by it' (172). D. Nörr, *'Origo*. Studien
zur Orts-, Stadt- und Reichszugehörigkeit in der Antike', *TRG* 31, 1963,
525-600, points out that from the time of Cicero it is the case that 'the
Roman citizen, who may not hold double *civitas* in the constitutional
sense, can still have a twofold standing in law' (555), cf. 556-64, on dual
citizenship in antiquity: citizenship of a town was sometimes given very
generously, since in this way the city could raise the number of those
liable to taxes and liturgy (558). In addition honorary citizenship was
frequently bestowed (one example is Dio of Prusa, the citizen of Apamaea,
Nicomedia, Nicaea and other cities of the East, cf. *Or*.38, 39,41). The
Romans attempted in vain to control Greek law in this matter. Conflicts
betwen Roman and *peregrinus* citizenship emerge for the first time in the
first century BCE, but the strict maxim 'that Roman citizenship cannot
be reconciled with *peregrinus* citizenship' (Nörr, 562) was got round from
the beginning, and there is no evidence that the Romans took action
against this misuse, so that 'in the period of the empire...the thesis of the
compatibility of citizenships had generally at least found a footing
formally' (563). In the course of the period of the principate the bestowing
of citizenship increased, especially by Greek states to the Roman citizens
living in them, though the legal problems resulting from this cannot be
clarified in detail.

40. Thus according to Dio Cassius, 47.26, Soloi had already been
named Pompeiopolis earlier by Pompey. Here we can see the rivalry
between the two cities: Tarsus, which was friendly to Caesar and
Augustus, and 'republican' Soloi, see n.11.

41. On this see Nörr, *'Origo'* (n.39), 567f.

42. For these events in Tarsus see Dio Cassius, 47.30f.; Appian, *Bellum
civile*, IV. 64; V.7.

43. Dio Chrysostom 34.21-23 reports that in the time of the empire,
citizenship of Tarsus could be bought for 500 drachmae (this corresponds

to the income of an ordinary day labourer for two years), cf. W.Ruge, 'Tarsus', *PW* 2.R.4, 1932, 2431f. (for citizenship of Tarsus generally and that of Paul, 2420f.).

44. On this see the literature listed in Schürer, *History* (n.27), III.1, 126 n.2.

45. W.M.Ramsay, *St Paul the Traveller and the Roman Citizen*, London [10]1908, 31f.

46. See below, 25–29.

47. See Böhlig, *Geisteskultur* (n.11), 128-67, on the Judaism of Tarsus; V.Tcherikover, *Hellenistic Civilization and the Jews*, Philadelphia 1961, 287-9; Welles, 'Hellenistic Tarsus' (n.11), 59-62; Schürer, *History* (n.27), III.1, 33f., and the additional material in H.Bloedhorn, *JSS* 35, 1990, 68. Moreover there seem to have been close connections between Cilicia and Judaea; for example, Josephus mentions Cilician mercenaries which Alexander Jannaeus had hired (*Antt.* 13.374, see A.Schalit, *König Herodes*, SJ 4, Berlin 1969, 168); there were dynastic links between Herod the Great and King Archelaus of Cappadocia (whose realm since 20 BCE had also included rugged Cilicia bordering on Tarsus: Herod's son by Mariamne, Alexander, married Glaphyra, a daughter of Archelaus), on this cf. D.Kienast, *Augustus. Princeps und Monarch*, Darmstadt 1982, 408 n.195 and 279-81; Schalit, *Herodes*, 588f., 597f., 610-13, 620-8. Herod was also active in Cilicia as a benefactor and master-builder, cf. Josephus, *BJ* 1.48 and Schalit, 417,425. So it is not suprising that rabbinic literature records an intensive trade with Cilicia: after agricultural products above all in textiles, cf. Bill.3.611, 665, 746f. and *CIJ* II, no.931, the epitaph of a presbyter Isakis from Tarsus who describes himself as λινοπώλης (cf. Schürer, *History* [n.27], III.1,35). Paul's origin might be sought in this milieu and that also offers the *possibility* that he had citizenship of Tarsus, cf. Böhlig, *Geisteskultur* (n.11), 132f. For Josephus on Tarsus see *Antt.* 1.127; 8.181; Jonah tried to sail there, 9.208. Cf. Isa.66.19 LXX and Bill. 3.621.

48. The word occurs only four times in the New Testament, three times in Luke (Luke 15.15; 19.19; Acts 21.39) and once in Hebrews, 8.11. Outside the Acts passage a political context is never implied, and the two texts from the Gospel show that Luke knows a wider significance, cf. Tajra, *Trial* (n.37), 79.

49. But see Josephus, *Antt.* 12,119; Seleucus Nikator granted the Jews full citizenship of the places in Asia and Syria which he founded, on this see Hemer, *Book of Acts* (n.9), 540, 573, on the 'ethical conception of the *polis*' (Dio Chrysostom, *Or.*32.87) as a place of τάξις and εὐκοσμία. For the terminology in Josephus, Philo and the LXX see Tajra, *Trial* (n.37), 79.

50. Cf. ibid., index, s.v. 'citizenship, Greek, held or desired by Jews' and 'civic status, of Jews' (579), and Schürer, *History* (n.27), III.1, 126-37, 'Civic Rights'.

51. The Jewish struggle for citizenship of Alexandria is particularly well attested, cf. Josephus, *Antt.* 14. 110-18 and the letter of the Emperor Claudius from 41 (P.Lond VI, 1912 = *CPJ* no.153). See E.M.Smallwood, *The Jews under Roman Rule*, SJLA 20, Leiden ²1981, 224-55; Tajra, *Trial* (n.37), 18ff.

52. Smallwood, *Jews* (n.51), 285-8.

53. Ibid., 359-64.

54. *Or.* 34.23, and on this Ruge, 'Tarsus' (n.43), 2432; Préaux, 'Institutions économiques' (n.11), 123 and n.3. For the linen weavers of Tarsus see Kienast and Castritius, 'Zeugnis' (n.11), 65f., 69f.. They conjecture that the low reputation of the linen weavers is connected with the fact that 'above all non-Greeks worked in the linen factories, who were only slightly Hellenized and therefore regarded as foreigners' (66). That does not necessarily mean that they were all without means and belonged to the lower social stratum. This is shown very well by the classification of this group of the population by Jones, which coincides strikingly with that of Deissmann (see above, n.31). In connection with Dio's report he writes: 'He represents them as poor but respectable men, who would enjoy the rights of citizenship if they could afford the registration fee of 500 drachmae. The weavers must therefore have been free men of modest means, not necessarily very poor, for 500 drachmae is a large sum, about two years pay for a legionary. This suggests an organization in small family workshops, with a few apprentices and labourers, slave or free, as in the villages and towns of Egypt' (359, in 'The Cloth Industry under the Roman Empire', in id., *Roman Economy* [n.11], 350-64, originally in *EcHR* 13, 1960, 183-92; for family businesses in the textile industry see 357).

An interesting parallel to conditions in Tarsus is offered by an inscription from Cyrene, cf. Lüderitz, 'Zeugnisse aus der Cyrenaika' (n.27), no.8; on the one hand it shows that there were Jews who had citizenship and on the other it mentions particular crafts which excluded people from citizenship.

55. Cf. the inscription from Dyme in Achaea (in H.Collitz, *Griechische Dialektinschriften* 2, Göttingen 1899, 1614 = no.531 in Dittenberger, *Syll³*): the inscription probably comes from the first half of the third century BCE. It is clear from it that all foreigners were given citizenship provided that they were free and descended from free parents, and paid a talent within a year. Sons up to seventeen and unmarried daughters were given citizenship along with the father or, in the case of a widow, with the

mother. For Byzantium there is a similar report in Ps.Aristotle, *Oecon* 1346b. There is also evidence of the sale of citizenship in Ephesus for 6 minae in the third century BCE, cf. *Syll*[3], no.363, and P.Roussel, 'La vente du droit de Cité (Note sur une Inscription d'Éphèse)', *RevPhil* 37, 1913, 332-4; M.Holleaux, 'Éphèse et les Priéniens *du Charax*', *RÉG* 29, 1916, 29-45, see esp. 38f., 45. There are further instances from Thasos (see C.Picard, *BCH* 45, 1921, 153 no.6; L.Robert, *RevPhil* 3.ser 10, 1936, 131-3) and Tritea (see A.Wilhelm, *Neue Beiträge zur griechischen Inschriftenkunde* I, SAWW.PH 166.1, 1911, 37.1ff), and from the Egyptian Aspendos (see M.Segre, 'Decreto di Aspendos', *Aegyptus* 14, 1934, 253-68, see esp. 267f.; I am indebted for these references to a seminar paper by N.Förster in connection with my seminar on the early Paul in the winter semester of 1989/90).

56. Dio Cassius 54.7, cf. Nörr, '*Origo*' (n.39), 559.

57. The closing verdict of Tajra, *Trial* (n.37), 78-80 (Paul a *polites* of Tarsus) is rather different. He does not see any compelling indication in Acts 21.39 that Paul had citizenship of Tarsus: 'We would like to conclude by saying that Paul's Tarsian citizenship cannot be proved on the basis of Acts XXI,39. The use of the word *polites* in that passage was in a non-juridical sense and most likely refers to Paul's membership in the resident Jewish community at Tarsus rather than to any citizenship in the Greek *polis*. His mention of Tarsus in this verse is a statement of domicile and not a proclamation of citizenship... Paul's statement that he was a *polites* of Tarsus did not – and could not – have the same legal effect on the supreme Roman authority in Jerusalem as did his subsequent proclamation of Roman citizenship' (80). The last statement is possibly false. Citizenship of a *civitas libera* guaranteed its holder free choice of a place of trial. Possibly, therefore, Paul could thank his citizenship of Tarsus among other things for his being brought to Rome, since his Roman citizenship guaranteed him only a hearing before a Roman court, cf. P.Garnsey, 'The *Lex Iulia* and Appeal under the Empire', *JRS* 56, 1966, 167-89, on Paul's case, 182-5; id., *Social Status and Legal Privilege in the Roman Empire*, Oxford 1970: on Paul 75f., 268. Garnsey shows that there were still differences within Roman citizenship which played a part in the granting of an appeal to the emperor.

58. General literature: L.Wenger, 'Bürgerrecht', *RAC* 2, 1954, 778-86; A.N.Sherwin-White, *The Roman Citizenship*, Oxford [2]1974; id, 'The Roman Citizenship. A Survey of its Development into a World Franchise', *ANRW* I.2, 1972, 23-58; E.Ferenczy, 'Rechtshistorische Bemerkungen zur Ausdehnung des römischen Bürgerrechts und zum *ius Italicum* unter dem Prinzipat', *ANRW* II. 14, 1982, 1017-58.

For Paul's Roman citizenship: Zahn, 'Lebensgeschichte' (n.1), 23-34;

Steinmann, *Werdegang* (n.1), 24f.; H.J.Cadbury, 'Roman Law and the Trial of Paul', in F.J.F.Jackson and K.Lake, *The Beginnings of Christianity* V, London 1933, 297-338; R.Schwartz, 'A propos du statut personnel de l'apôtre Paul', *RHPR* 37, 1957, 91-6: in his view Paul had only Roman citizenship, not that of Tarsus. He only acquired this on the basis of a misunderstanding on the part of an Alexandrian redactor of Acts 21, who had transferred his own Alexandrian conditions to Tarsus; W.Seston, 'Tertullian et les Origines de la Citoyenneté romaine de S.Paul', in *Neotestamentica et Patristica. FS O.Cullmann*, NT.S 6, Leiden 1962, 305-12 (the starting point of the investigation is Tertullian, *Scorpiace* 15, where Paul's citizenship is taken as a matter of course without the jurist Tertullian indicating how he could have received it); G.Kehnscherper, *Der Apostel Paulus als römischer Bürger*, TU 87 (= *Studia Evangelica* II, ed. F.L.Cross), Berlin 1964, 411-40 (on this see Kuss, *Paulus* [n.2], 40 n.2); J.Vogt, 'Der Apostel Paulus als römischer Bürger', *Universitas* 36, 1981, 145-52; M.Carrez, 'Note sur les évènements d'Éphèse et l'appel de Paul à sa citoyenneté romaine', in *A Cause de l'Evangile, FS J.Dupont OSB*, LD 123, Paris 1985, 769-77; W.Stegemann, 'War der Apostel Paulus römischer Bürger?', *ZNW* 78, 1987, 200-29; T.Hosaka, 'Lukas und das Imperium Romanum', *AJBI* 14, 1988, 82-134; Lüdemann, *Earliest Christianity* (n.6), 240f.; Tajra, *Trial* (n.37), 81-9.

59. Stegemann in particular attempted to deny the credibility of Luke's description. There is now a detailed refutation of his arguments in Riesner, *Frühzeit* (n.12), 127-35, cf. already Tajra, *Trial* (n.37), 87ff.

60. Cf. H.Windisch, KEK 6, ⁹1924 (new edition by G.Strecker 1970), 356; Hosaka, *Imperium Romanum* (n.58), 115f.; Lampe, *Stadtrömische Christen* (n.27), 66f. and n.189; Nörr, '*Origo*' (n.39), 597, also mentions our relatively slight knowledge of Roman law in the time of the principate. Furthermore it is insufficiently noted that even the appeal to Roman citizenship still left a good deal of freedom to the magistrates, especially as there were also differences among the *cives Romani*, cf. Garnsey, *Social Status* (n.57): on Paul, 75f., 268. Cf. also W.Eisenhut, 'Die römische Gefängnisstrafe', *ANRW* I. 2, Berlin and New York 1972, 268-82, who against the widespread denial of mere imprisonment in Roman law cites a number of instances which make it clear that a limited term of imprisonment was used for lesser crimes. 'It (the punishment of imprisonment) was pronounced for lesser crimes which were hardly punishable with the death penalty, or just for crimes which were not generally covered by the law because they were offences only against morality, respectability and custom, without being a direct violation of positive law' (278). It is possible that this legal practice was applied in Paul's case, too.

61. For general information about government, Roman administrative

and financial offices, personal archives and regular statistical inquiries, see W.E.H.Cockle, 'State Archives in Graeco-Roman Egypt from 30 BC to the Reign of Septimius Severus', *JEA* 70, 1984, 106-22. For registration of the birth of a new Roman citizen in Alexandria see 118; the registration was also passed on to Rome and put in the archives there. Cf. F.Schulz, 'Roman Registers of Birth and Birth Certificates', *JRS* 32, 1942, 78-91 and 33, 1943, 55-64; Sherwin-White, *Roman Citizenship* (n.58), 314-16, 'The Registration of Citizenship', and J.F.Gardiner, 'Proofs of Status in the Roman World', *JCS* 33, 1986, 1-14, which discusses these questions using the example of the status of a freedman, taking Schulz's work as a starting point. He describes the process as follows: the parents reported the child to be entered in the register (*professio liberorum*), giving name, origin, sex and date of birth, and also place of birth. 'Lastly, the *professio* contained the declaration that the child was a legitimate child and a Roman citizen. Such a declaration was indispensable, as only legitimate children in possession of the Roman citizenship could be registered' (87). This registration had to take place within thirty days of birth and be made before a magistrate in a *tabularium*, in Rome before the Aerarium Saturni, in the provinces before that of the governor. The *professio* was entered twice in a register (cf. Suetonius, *Vita Caliguli* 8.2): *in actis Anti* [Antium is the birthplace of Caligula] *editum*, see also 8.5: *publici instrumenti auctoritas*); first provisionally in the *album professionum* (or on tablets displayed in public) and then finally in a codex or papyrus scroll; it is unclear whether this itself or the building in which it was kept was called the *tabellarium*. The purpose of this registration 'was to facilitate the proof of a child's birth and status' (63). Possession of proof of birth and status was not obligatory, but very useful, especially when the person concerned did not permanently live in one place, or in the case of children of freedmen, who only in this way could demonstrate their status. These certificates were also used as proof of age (important for marriage, admission to particular offices, legal competence), cf. the instructive account in Apuleius, *Apologia* 89.1f., where he rejects the false accusations about the age of his wife with a reference to the paternal *professio* and the document produced on this occasion which he can show to the court: 'Her father acknowledged her as his daughter in the usual way. His notices are preserved partly in the public tabularium, partly at his house.' Copies from these albums are known (Schulz, 78f.: a list of the texts known to that point), so-called *testationes* which served as birth certificates: 'It was the Roman custom, practised already in Republican times, to make such *testationes* and to submit them to the court.' However, the judge was not forced to believe this evidence, though the reference to Roman citizenship contained in it 'furnished a *prima facie* evidence of the Roman citizenship of the bearer, being in so far a substitute for a passport' (63). Evidently forgeries of legal texts were by no means rare at that time, cf. Suetonius, *Vita Neronis*; Apuleius, *Apologia* 89.3ff., who stresses the intactness of the artificial seal which is to protect against forgery. Moreover appropriation of Roman citizenship evidently did not happen very often, because of the Draconian punishment to which it laid people open, cf. Suetonius, *Vita Claudii* 15,25: trial and execution in the case of false information concerning Roman citizenship, and at the same time a prohibition against the bearing of Roman family names by foreigners (if Pau[l]lus was the family name of the apostle, this would be an indication of his citizenship). Cicero's defence speech for the poet A.Licinius Archias is illuminating here, as the latter was accused of having wrongly claimed his citizenship (*pro Arch*. 1-11, see also the introduction to this speech by M.Fuhrmann, *Marcus Tullius Cicero. Sämtliche Reden* V, Zurich and Munich 1978, 61-5). For giving false personal information and the consequences see Pliny the Younger, *Ep.*X, 29 + 30 and on this Gardiner, 11. The event among the Christians of Lyons narrated in Eusebius, *HE* 5,1,47, also shows that it was possible to examine citizenship from the official side, since 'those who appeared to have Roman citizenship had their heads cut off': they were executed immediately in Lyons. By contrast, Pliny the Younger, *Ep.* X, 96,4, sent citizens to Rome.

On Paul's case Schulz writes: 'When St Paul alleged his Roman citizenship before the Roman authorities... he must have produced his birth certificate for corroboration. As he was Roman born he was in possession of such a document, which he doubtless carried with him wherever he travelled' (63f.). This more technical information may be helpful in understanding Paul's punishments: Paul certainly did not carry his birth certificate in his coat pocket; it was probably among his scrolls and tools, i.e. at the place where he was a guest or where he lived. Some time could elapse before he got this document. Moreover, the official concerned could challenge its validity.

62. The evidence can be found in M.Hengel, *Crucifixion*, London and Philadelphia 1982, 39-45: 'Crucifixion and Roman Citizens'. Cf. A.H.M.Jones, 'I appeal unto Caesar', in id., *Studies in Roman Government and Law*, Oxford 1968, 51-65, who in 56f. mentions cases where Roman citizens were executed in the provinces.

63. Josephus, *BJ* 2,308.

64. Dio Cassius 60.24.4, cf. Hengel, *Crucifixion* (n.62), 80. Rhodes was therefore threatened by the emperor Claudius with a restriction of its *libertas*, cf. also Sherwin-White, *Roman Citizenship* (n.58), 273.

65. See n.57 above.

66. For Jonathes see Josephus, *BJ* 7.437-50; for Eleazar, see Josephus, *Antt.* 20.161, and M.Hengel, *The Zealots*, Edinburgh 1989, 359ff.

67. W.Schmithals, ZBK 3.2, 1982. He sees the Roman citizenship simply as 'a motif crudely emphasized by the author Luke' and 'the reference to Paul's having this citizenship belongs in the framework of the apologetic tendency of Luke the author, who in this way makes emphatically clear the political innocence of the missionaries' (153), cf. 205: 'And from all that we know, it is hardly conceivable that already at the time of Augustus, when Roman citizenship was still very restricted, a Jew could be born in Tarsus a Roman citizen.' For the journey to Rome see 219ff. According to Schmithals, to find the historical facts we have to 'depart from Luke's description' and come to the conclusion that 'Paul travelled to Rome as a free man and was only arrested – sooner or later – or suffered martyrdom there' (219).

68. Cf. also Lampe, *Stadtrömische Christen* (n.27), 124-53; Meeks, *Urban Christians* (n.12), 55ff.; see below n.73.

69. Tertullian's full name was Quintus Septimius Florens Tertullianus, and Cyprian's Thascius Caecilius Cyprianus. It should also be noted that not even the complete tripartite name of the historian Titus Livius is known. Cf. P.R.C.Weaver, *Familia Caesaris. A Social Study of the Emperor's Freedmen and Slaves*, Cambridge 1972, 37ff., who has investigated over 4000 inscriptions of freedmen; he states 'that over one in three of the Imperial freedmen of whom we have record do not in fact use their *nomen* or have it recorded on their inscriptions as part of their name' (37). See also G.Fuks, 'Where have all the Freedmen gone? On an Anomaly in the Jewish Grave-Inscriptions from Rome', *JJS* 36, 1985, 25-32: among more than 500 Roman tomb inscriptions of Jews, at least 10% of which had Roman citizenship, there is not one which mentions the full Roman name. This shows how much this alien name was inwardly repudiated.

70. Cf. Phil.3.20f.; Gal.3.28; Col.3.11.

71. Josephus mentions a Paulus Apuntius (*Antt.* 19.102) and two Romans by the name of Paulinus (*BJ* 3.44; 7.434) and a Roman woman called Paulina (*Antt.* 18.66, 69, 72, 75, 77).

72. In the ruined door of the family tomb which consists of two rooms, there is ΠΑΥΛΙΝΟΥ ΜΥΡΕΥ(ΟΥ), and within the rooms there is the inscription ΠΑΥΛΙΝΟΥ on three coffins, see N.Avigad, *Beth She'arim* 3, Jerusalem 1971, 29f. and plate XII (in Hebrew).

73. Unfortunately it cannot be decided with any certainty whether Paulus was the *praenomen* or *cognomen*. As freedmen normally took over the *nomen* and *praenomen* of their patron, this could explain the background to the acquisition of citizenship by Paul's family, cf. Tajra, *Trial* (n.37), 83, who regards Paulus as the *cognomen*; thus also Welles, 'Hellenistic Tarsus'

(n.11), 62, who conjectures a completely speculative name, C.Iulius Paulus. The classic article on this theme is H.Dessau, 'Der Name des Apostels Paulus', *Hermes* 45, 1910, 347-68, though he also puts forward the disputed theory that the cognomen was changed because of Sergius Paulus. Also important for understanding the Σαῦλος ὁ καὶ Παῦλος in Acts 13.9 is A.Deissmann, *Bibelstudien*, Marburg 1895, reprinted Hildesheim 1977, 181ff.; id., *Die Urgeschichte des Christentums im Lichte der Sprachforschung*, Tübingen 1910, 16f. n.4; id., *Paul* (n.5), 91f. (especially n.6 against Dessau), who has demonstrated that Paul already had the names Saul and Paul before his visit to Cyprus, and that the Greek expression cited above corresponds to the Latin *qui et*, so that the ancient reader could only understand it as 'Saul who is also called Paul' (see also above 9f.). Building on that, G.A.Harrer, 'Saul who is also called Paul', *HTR* 33, 1940, 19-33, conjectured that Saul was the *signum* or *supernomen* of Paul (21), i.e. the name by which he was called, whereas in his view the Sau*lus* of Acts is only a later name formed in analogy to Paulus in the third or fourth century (25), as P⁴⁵ mentions only Σαούλ. In that case Paulus would be the *cognomen* (26) and could refer to the *gens Aemilia*, in which Paul(l)us occurred frequently. The tripartite name could then have run something like *L.Aemilius Paullus qui et Saul* (33); Bornkamm, *Paul* (n.2), 6, also argues for Saul as a *signum* or *supernomen*; cf. Riesner, *Frühzeit* (n.12), 125. But too much stress should not be put on the terminology of P⁴⁵, since it could also be a bigoted whim of the copyist, who preferred for the Jewish name of Paul the version which had as it were divine approbation and therefore kept throughout to the form of the name used by the Damascus voice (moreover P⁴⁵ does not have the complete text of Acts, so that it is not possible to examine all the Saul passages). See also G.H.R.Horsley, 'The Use of a Double Name', *NewDocs* I, 1981, 89-96, who gives an impressive demonstration of the wide distribution of double names; also E.A.Judge, 'Greek Names of Latin Origin', in *NewDocs* II, 1982, 106-8, who refers to correspondence which is to be evaluated as an indication of the social structure of the early communities in the Pauline mission sphere: 'NT social history must therefore face the possibility that the churches drew heavily upon those classes of lower-level Greeks whom Roman patronage was systematically advancing to citizenship during an era when eminent members of the ruling classes in the Greek cities were still by no means regularly granted Roman citizenship' (107); C.J.Hemer, 'The Name of Paul', *TynB* 36, 1985, 179-83; id., *Acts* (n.9), 128 n.77.

74. Cf. e.g. Harrer, 'Saul' (n.73), 30f. For Sergius Paulus and his family see now Riesner, *Frühzeit* (n.12), 119-24, and appendix 2, 'Stemma der Sergier', taken from D.Halfmann, *Die Senatoren aus dem östlichen Teil des Imperium Romanum*, Göttingen 1979, 106. See below 108 n.83.

75. A.N.Sherwin-White, *Roman Society and Roman Law in the New Testament*, Oxford 1963, 153f. Moreover it is uncertain whether Paul was thought to correspond at all to Saul; cf. Lüdemann, *Earliest Christianity* (n.6), 241.

76. *CIJ* II, no.803 (55f.); the inscription comes from 391 CE.

77. Acts 9.4.; 22.7; 26.14; cf. Ananias, 9.17; 22.13. Σαῦλον appears in 9.17 because of the declension; see also 13.21 Σαοὺλ υἱὸν Κ[ε]ίς.

78. The inscription from Phthiotis is published in B.Lifshitz, Prolegomenon to the reprint of *CIJ* by Ktav Publishing House, New York 1975, no.696a (p.79). The text reads: Μνῆμα Σαοὺλ καὶ τῆς αὐτοῦ γαμητῆς Ἄννας. Lifshitz regards this passage as the earliest evidence for Saul on an inscription, but the symbols represented (menorah, lulab and dove) seem to point to the fourth/fifth century. Moreover, both names indicate Palestinian influence. For Palestine see *CIJ* II, no.953 (p.146) from Jaffa, *CIJ* II, no.1208 (p.243) from Touba, south of the Dead Sea (433 CE, *š'wl*, line 2); a further ossuary inscription from Kiriat Tiv'on mentions ΜΑΡΙΑ/ΣΑΟΥΛΟΣ (see *RB* 79, 1972, 575; the other objects in the grave point to the first century CE). In addition are the inscriptions on ostraca and jars collected from Masada (*Masada, The Y.Yadin Excavations 1963-65, Final Reports*: Vol.1, Y.Yadin and J.Naveh, *The Aramaic and Hebrew Ostraca and Jar Inscriptions*, Y.Meshorer, *The Coins of Masada*; Vol.II, H.M.Cotton and J.Geiger, *The Latin and Greek Documents*, Jerusalem 1989), in which the name *š'wl* still appears three times: once (I.22, no.410) on an ostracon which was probably used for the distribution of food in Masada (I.18), twice as the name of an owner on sherds from jars (I.43, nos.508-9). In Josephus, apart from king Saul (*BJ* 5.51, and 191 times in the *Antiquities*, we always find Σαοῦλος; Saul's place of origin is called Γαβαθὰ Σαούλ or Σαούλη) we find a relative of Agrippa II with this name (*BJ* 2.418,556,558; *Antt.* 20.214, Σαοῦλος or Σαῦλος) and a Jew from Scythopolis (*BJ* 2.469, Σαοῦλος). From the rabbinic literature we know Abba Sha'ul b.Batnith (second generation of the Tannaim, see H.L.Strack and G.Stemberger, *Einleitung in Talmud und Midrasch*, Munich ⁷1982, 78); Abba Sha'ul (third generation of Tannaim, see Strack and Stemberger, 84) and Abba Sha'ul b.Nannos (Tannaite, ARN A 29). The Rabbi Sha'ul mentioned in Sifre Deut.185 is possibly identical with the latter, see the note in Finkelstein, *Sifre Debarim*, ad loc. (226). There is also mention in bKet 876a of an Abba Sha'ul b.Imma Miriam; in bPes 34a of an Abba Sha'ul as a dough kneader in the house of the rabbi. Sha'ul appears as a paternal name in the Palestinian Chalaphta (Billerbeck I, 457), for Johanan (Bill.I,466) and Jose (a Tannaite around 220, see Strack/Stemberger, 88). Finally, from the fourth century, there is the Palestinian Sha'ul from Nave (Bill. II,589). The form of the name *šyl'*

seems to be a parallel form to Saul, and in Rabbinic literature there are similarly some bearers of this name, see Bill.V/VI, 227f., 222. Finally, a R.Johanan ben Sha'ula (*š'wlh*) is mentioned in BerR 94.3 (on Gen.45.27), see the edition by Albeck, 1173. The relatively rare occurrence of the name is certainly connected with the tragic fate of the biblical Saul; the most popular names at this time were the famous names of the Maccabaean period, as is also attested by the names found in Masada (see *Masada*, II,10).

79. Phil.3.6; Rom.11.1.

80. Acts 13.9, see above n.73 and Haenchen, *The Acts of the Apostles*, Oxford and Philadelphia 1971, 399 n.1.

81. Cf. W.M.Ramsay, *Traveller* (n.45), 81ff., who connects the accord in the change of the Jewish name Saul to the Roman name Paul in Luke with the Pauline principle expressed in I Cor.9.20f.

82. Cf. Riesner, *Frühzeit* (n.12), 124 (see n.74 above).

83. Thus e.g. E.Groag, 'Sergius' (no.34), *PW* 2.R., II A 2, 1923, 1714ff.

84. Cf. also W.M.Ramsay, 'The Statesmanship of Paul', in id., *Pauline and Other Studies*, New York 1906 (reprinted 1970), 47-100.

85. Eloquent testimony to the virulent, anti-Roman and at the same time anti-Jewish national pride of the Greek upper classes is provided by the *Acta Alexandrinorum* (text, translation and commentary, H.Musurillo, *The Acts of the Pagan Martyrs, Acta Alexandrinorum*, Oxford 1954; id. [ed.], *Acta Alexandrinorum. De mortibus Alexandriae nobilium fragmenta papyracea graeca*, Leipzig 1961). Cf. M.Hengel, 'Messianische Hoffnung und politischer "Radikalismus" in der "jüdisch-hellenistischen Diaspora"', in *Apocalypticism in the Mediterranean World and the Near East, Proceedings of the International Colloquium on Apocalypticism, Uppsala August 12-17, 1979*, ed. D.Hellholm, Tübingen 1983, ²1989, 655-86; id., 'Hadrians Politik gegenüber Juden und Christen', in *Ancient Studies in Memory of Elias Bickerman*, JANES 16-17 (1984-5), 1987, 153-82.

86. See above 1 with the literature mentioned in n.12. For Lüdemann, *Earliest Christianity* (n.6), 241, too, the apostle's travel plans which emerge from his letters are also an indication that he was a Roman citizen; similarly also Becker, *Paulus* (n.2), 37, who at the same time regards the Pauline geography as an indication of the 'Hellenistic city air' that the young Paul breathed in Tarsus, a 'microcosm of the Hellenistic Mediterranean area'.

87. See now also R.Feldmeier, *Fremde in einer entfremdeten Welt. Die Erschliessung christlichen Selbstverständnisses und Weltverhältnisses durch die Kategorie der Fremde im 1.Petrusbrief*, Tübingen Habilitationsschrift 1991, to appear in WUNT. For Phil.3.20 cf. 68ff.

88. For a survey of the status of the Jews within the Roman empire cf.

Tajra, *Trial* (n.37), 14-21: 'The Juridical Situation of Judaism during the Early Principate'; A.M.Rabello, 'The Legal Condition of the Jews in the Roman Empire', *ANRW* II. 13, Berlin and New York 1980, 662-70, who estimates the number of the Jewish population in the Diaspora at 4 million (691) and writes this about the privileges granted them by the Roman rulers: 'the privileges were intended to enable the Jews to live "in accordance with their own laws"' (632); T.Rajak, 'Was there a Roman Charter for the Jews?', *JRS* 74, 1984, 107-23, on Caesar, 110ff., 117; id., 'Jews and Christians as Groups in a Pagan World', in *To See Ourselves as Others See Us: Christians, Jews, 'Others' in Late Antiquity*, ed. J.Neusner and E.S.Frerichs, Chico 1985, 247-62. The standard work here is Smallwood, *Jews under Roman Rule* (n.50). For the relationship of Augustus to the Jews see Kienast, *Augustus* (n.47), 208 n.155, 254-7.

89. Cf. Josephus, *Antt.* 14. 127ff., 140ff., 190ff. In the course of the civil wars which accompanied Caesar's rise to power the bestowing of privileges, which of course also included citizenship, was a favourite way of guaranteeing oneself the sympathies of those thus favoured, cf. Kienast, *Augustus* (n.47), 11f., and for Caesar's policy of colonization, ibid., 388f.; the most vigorous critics of this policy of colonization and citizenship were Cicero and his conservative colleagues, cf. ibid., 386f. n.10. For an illustration see Suetonius, *Vita Caesaris* 8.28,42, and for the complaint of the Jews about Caesar, ibid., 84.5, where he reports on funerals: 'In all this public mourning, a great crowd of foreign peoples were weeping all around, each according to their own custom, and in particular the Jews, who even came to visit his funeral pyre night after night', see M.Stern, *GLAJJ* II, Jerusalem 1980, 109f. (= no.302).

90. Josephus, *Antt.* 14. 228-240, cf. Schürer, *History* (n.27), III.1, 22-4, and as a supplement H.Bloedhorn, *JSS* 35, 1990, 67; A.L.Connolly, 'Jews at Ephesos', *NewDocs* 4, 1987, 231f.

91. Josephus, *Antt.* 14.235, cf. Schürer, *History* (n.27), III.1, 20-2, and similarly Bloedhorn, *JSS* (n.90), 66f. For the late (fourth century) grand synagogue see now H.Botermann, 'Die Synagoge von Sardes: Eine Synagoge aus dem 4.Jahrhundert?', *ZNW* 81, 1990, 103-21.

92. Cf. M.Kaser, *Das römische Privatrecht*, HAW X.3.3.1, Munich ²1971, 115-19, 293-301; Weaver, *Familia Caesaris* (n.69); H.Chantraine, 'Zur Entstehung der Freilassung mit Bürgerrechtserwerb in Rom', *ANRW* I. 2, Berlin and New York 1972, 59-67; Lampe, *Stadtrömische Christen* (n.27), 68, who in n.196 quotes G.Alföldy with the words: 'On the basis of juristic and epigraphic sources "it might be asserted that the freeing of a slave, at the latest when he reached the age of 30-40, was presumably almost the norm".'

93. Cf. the inscriptions of Jewish freedmen from Pantikapaion and

Georgippia (see M.Hengel, 'Proseuche and Synagoge', in *FS K.G.Kuhn*, ed. G.Jeremias, H.-W.Kuhn and H.Stegemann, Göttingen 1971, 173f.; Schürer, *History*[n.27], II.1, 36-8), and P.Ox 1205 from Egypt (*CPJ* III, no.473, pp.33-6), where there is a report of the ransom of a Jewish girl by Palestinian Jews (291 CE); Josephus, *Vita* 418-21: after the capture of Jerusalem Josephus exerts his influence on Vespasian to ask for the release of relatives and friends; see also bJeb 45 and bQid 29a/b: the father is obliged to have his son circumcised, to release him to learn the Torah, to take a wife for him and make him learn a trade...; cf. S.Krauss, *Synagogale Altertümer*, Berlin 1922 (reprinted 1966), 197, 305; M.Hengel, *Judaism and Hellenism*, London and Philadelphia 1974, I, 41f.; Bill.4.1, 572f.; W.Haubeck, *Loskauf durch Christus*, Giessen and Basle 1985, 114-21. See also n.112 below.

94. Philo, *Leg ad Cai*. 155,157: 'He was not unaware that the great section of Rome across the river Tiber was inhabited and occupied by Jews. Most of them were Roman freedmen; for prisoners of war were brought to Italy by their owners and then freed, and were not forced to compromise any of their traditional customs... Nonetheless, he did not expel them from Rome, nor deprive them of Roman citizen rights because they were concerned to keep their Roman citizenship, nor interfere with their synagogues, nor forbid them to gather together for the teaching of the laws, nor prevent them from offering sacrifices.'

95. Stegemann, 'Römischer Bürger' (n.58), 225.

96. See the relevant instances in Stern, *GLAJJ* I (n.89), 321-7 (Horace); 429-34 (Seneca); II, 94-107 (Juvenal); M.Whittaker, *Jews and Christians: Graeco-Roman Views*, Cambridge Commentaries on Writings of the Jewish and Christian World 200 BC to AD 200, 6, Cambridge 1984, 85-91. People like the Jewish playwright Aliturus, who was a member of Poppaea's court (Josephus, *Vita* 16) are the exception. On the other hand, she, too, seems to have been interested in the Jewish faith, see Josephus, *Antt*. 20.195 and Tacitus, *Ann*.6.5.

97. Cf. e.g. Suetonius, *Vita Caesaris* 42: 80,000 Roman citizens were compelled to migrate to the East (see also 8 and 28, the bestowing of citizenship on colonists and its later revocation); *Vita Tiberii* 36: Tiberius posted young Jews who were Roman citizens on military service to regions with an unhealthy climate, and expelled the rest of the Jews from Rome, as later also did Claudius (*Vita Claudii* 25), cf. Lampe, *Stadtrömische Christen* (n.27), 67; Riesner, *Frühzeit* (n.12), 136-69.

98. Not 'perhaps'; thus Stegemann, *Apostel Paulus* (n.58), 216f.

99. Thus also, along with many others, G.Schille, ThHK 5, 175, see also Bill.II, 661ff., and Deissmann, *Paul* (n.5), 87ff.; on Paul, 89: 'This synagogue of the Cilicians and those from Asia Minor in Jerusalem is

probably the one to which the young Cilician Jew, Saul who is surnamed Paul, whose family probably originally came from Galilee, was attached while for a considerable time in his youthful years he stayed in Jerusalem.'

100. Hengel, 'Between Jesus and Paul', in *Between Jesus and Paul* (n.9), 17f.; id., *'Hellenization'* (n.37), 11,13. The inscription is also in *CIJ* II, no.1404.

101. Acts 16.37. Haenchen thinks that it was probably also attributed to Silas for simplicity (*Acts* [n.80], 498). This solution seems too facile. Perhaps there were also quite practical considerations in the choice of travelling companions, and Roman citizenship guaranteed those who had it a certain freedom of movement and legal protection. As a Greek-speaking Jew from Jerusalem and a Roman citizen Silas could have been a particularly appropriate companion on a journey which was to lead to Greece and indeed possibly to Rome. This strategic thought would also correspond to Paul's missionary methods in other respects, cf. M.Hengel, 'Der Jakobusbrief als antipaulinische Polemik', in *Tradition and Interpretation in the New Testament. FS E.Ellis*, ed. G.F.Hawthorne and O.Betz, Grand Rapids and Tübingen 1987, 248-78, above all 255ff.

102. Cf. R.Hachlili, 'The Goliath Family in Jericho: Funerary Inscriptions from a First-Century AD Jewish Monumental tomb', *BASOR* 235, 1979, 31-65; on Theodotus see 33.45-47.

103. See above 8f. and n.69.

104. Jerome, *Comm. in Ep. ad Philemonem*, on v.23 (*PL* 26, 653): 'We know a story like this: They say that the parents of the apostle Paul were from the region of Gischala in Judaea. When the whole province was destroyed by the Romans, and the Jews were scattered across the world, they were carried off to Tarsus, a city in Cilicia; the young Paul followed the fortunes of his parents'; in *De viris ill.*5 (*PL* 23,645f.): 'Paul the apostle... was from the tribe of Benjamin and the town of Gischala in Judaea; when it was captured by the Romans he moved with his parents to Tarsus in Cilicia, and they sent him to Jerusalem to study the law. He was taught by Gamaliel, a very learned man, whom Luke mentions.'

105. But cf. A von Harnack, *Der kirchengeschichtliche Ertrag der exegetischen Arbeiten des Origenes* (2.Teil), TU 42/4, Leipzig 1919, 145f., who assumes that Jerome derived his information from Origen's commentary on Philemon which he used. According to Harnack, Photius' information (see n.106 above) similarly goes back to Origen himself.

106. *Quaest.Amphil.*116, *PG* 101, 687-90: 'Paul... by both his ancestry and his conception, would have had as his *patris* Gischala (now a village in the region of Judaea, but formally a wealthy small town). When his parents, along with many others of his race, were taken captive by the Roman forces, their removal to Tarsus, where his mother went into labour

and gave birth to him, gave him that place as his *patris*... Now the greatness
of the Romans' love of honour exceeds in magnitude their military might,
and outranks the love of honour even of foreigners themselves; this
greatness happily brought to many people the noble status of Roman
citizenship and a Roman name, the one as a gift, the other at a price. As
a result of this, by means of a few syllables for his parents, and by the
laws of men, Rome and the Roman people became the *patris* of St Paul.
Thus, not only can two *patrides*... be found for the teacher of truth, but a
third can be added to them. Of these, he refers to Gischala, in the region
and jurisdiction of the tribe of Benjamin; the people of Tarsus were given
to him through his captivity; his letter to the Romans describes him as
Roman through his parents, and his ancestry as an honour that came to
him by lot.'

On his origin from Gischala, Zahn, 'Lebensgeschichte' (n.1), 29, writes:
'But the latter tradition is intrinsically all the more credible since
Gischala... is not mentioned in the Bible, and so had no renown for early
Christianity, which could mislead people into associating the history of
the apostle with this city'; thus also Deissmann, *Paul* (n.5), 90 n.5. Zahn
also attempted to investigate the historical content of the patristic evidence
(ibid., 24-34), and it seemed to him probable that Paul's parents were
enslaved by Varus in 4 BCE. But an earlier date is also quite possible, cf.
Fuks, 'Freedmen' (n.69), 26ff., who cites all the known enslavements of
Palestinian Jews from 63 BCE. Zahn's argument was taken over by
Harnack (*Mission* [n.27], 63f. n.1), but is mostly rejected by more recent
scholars – perhaps wrongly, see e.g. Burchard, *Zeuge* (n.14), 34 n.2.

107. Ramsay, *Paul the Traveller* (n.45), 34.

108. Lietzmann, *Paulus*, in WdF 24 (n.1), 318 (originally vol.5 of *Der
Weg der Kirche*, Berlin 1934).

109. Meyer, *Ursprung* (n.7), III, 308. Steinmann, *Werdegang* (n.1), 17,
also guesses that Paul's father was a 'manufacturer' of Cilician textiles or
a merchant.

110. T.Mommsen, 'Die Rechtsverhältnisse des Apostles Paulus', *ZNW*
2, 1901, 81-96: 82. But this conclusion is erroneous if, as I have attempted
to demonstrate, the citizenship was not acquired for special services but
in connection with the emancipation.

111. Cf. Stegemann, 'Apostel Paulus' (n.58), 226-8; A.J.Saldarini,
Pharisees, Scribes and Sadducees in Palestinian Society, Edinburgh 1989, 139:
'As an artisan Paul was in principle a member of the lower classes.
Artisans were not an independent middle class, but a subservient class
who were limited by their ability to produce only a small amount of
work by hand.' Fundamental here are the works by R.F.Hock, 'Paul's
Tentmaking and the Problem of his Social Class', *JBL* 97, 1978, 555-

64; id., *The Social Context of Paul's Ministry. Tentmaking and Apostleship*, Philadelphia 1980, but he evaluates the work of the apostle more as snobbish spleen, comparable to that of the Cynic itinerant missionaries. By origin Paul is one of the socially privileged class. For criticism of Hock see Tajra, *Trial* (n.37), 48; Hemer, *Acts* (n.9), 119 n.46; G.Clark, 'The Social Status of Paul', *ExpT* 96, 1985, 110f.; see also the remarks by Deissmann (n.31). For the social status of Aquila, Paul's colleague in the profession, cf. Lampe, *Stadtrömische Christen* (n.27), 156-64.

112. For this extensive complex on the social position of freedmen in the Roman empire cf. A.M.Duff, *Freedman in the Early Roman Empire*, Cambridge ²1958; L.R.Taylor, 'Freedman and Freeborn in the Epitaphs of Imperial Rome', *AJP* 82, 1961, 113-32; H.Chantraine, *Freigelassene und Sklaven im Dienst der römischen Kaiser*, Wiesbaden 1967; id., 'Entstehung der Freilassung' (n.92); S.Treggoari, *Roman Freedmen during the Late Republic*, Oxford 1969; Weaver, *Familia Caesaris* (n.69); id., 'Social Mobility in the Early Roman Empire. The Evidence of the Imperial Freedmen and Slaves', in *Studies in Ancient Society*, ed. M.I.Finley, London and Boston 1974, 121-40; G.Fabre, *Libertus. Recherches sur les rapports Patron-Affranchi à la fin de la république romaine*, Rome 1981.

113. Ramsay, *Paul the Traveller* (n.45), 35f.

114. Acts 18.3. The meaning is uncertain. For the different traditions of the early church see Hock, *Social Context* (n.111), 20f. In addition to the traditional 'tentmaker', a trade which is usually seen in connection with the linen-weaving industry in Tarsus (cf. e.g. G.Dalman, *Arbeit und Sitte in Palästina*, Gütersloh 1937, reprinted Hildesheim 1987, 18, 116f.) nowadays it is usually interpreted as 'leather worker', beginning from the fact that tents were often made of leather, cf. Haenchen, *Acts* (n.80), 534 n.3; recently Lampe in particular has again argued for tentmaker, seeing Paul's linen tents as being made of expensive materials; see his 'Paulus – Zeltmacher', *BZ* 31, 1987, 256-61; id., *Stadtrömische Christen* (n.27), 157f. The degree to which intensive preoccupation with the secular side of Paul's life also gives wing to fantastic associations which then frees the material for a Paul romance is clear from Lampe's pretty suggestion that even before he became a missionary Paul had business links with Lydia, the textile merchant in Philippi. Returning to serious business, see also M.Hengel, 'Die Arbeit im frühen Christentum', *ThBeitr* 17, 1986, 196 and nn.78f.

115. Hengel, 'Arbeit' (n.114), 174-212 (cf. the bibliography, 174); R.Meyer, 'Das Arbeitsethos in Palästina zur Zeit der werdenden Kirche' (originally in *Neues Sächsisches Kirchenblatt* 42, 1935, 465-76), in id., *Zur Geschichte und Theologie des Judentums in hellenistisch-römischer Zeit*, Neukirchen

1989, 11-20, and on Paul, 17f.; J.Jeremias, *Jerusalem in the time of Jesus*, London and Philadelphia 1969, 31-57.

116. On this see Meyer, 'Arbeitsethos'(n.115), 16f.: too much work keeps a person from study of the law; on the other hand a certain income is needed to pay for the religious and ritual duties of a pious Pharisee. The journeys to Jerusalem for the annual pilgrimages presuppose that the pilgrims concerned could afford one (or more) 'family holidays' of around two weeks, see Steinmann, *Werdegang* (n.1), 17.

117. Sir.38.24-39.11; see Hengel, 'Proseuche und Synagoge' (n.93), 146-50, 243ff.; H.Stadelmann, *Ben Sira als Schriftgelehrter*, WUNT II.16, Tübingen 1980, 284ff., see also 28.38f.

118. Cf. G.Schrenk, 'Rabbinische Charakterköpfe im urchristlichen Zeitalter', in id., *Studien zu Paulus*, ATANT 26, Zurich 1954, 17ff. (originally in *Jud.* 1, 1945, 117-56); Jeremias, *Jerusalem* (n.115), 112f., 115ff.

119. mAbot, 1.10b, against Hock, *Context* (n.111), 22ff., who wrongly tends to dismiss these traditions about the Pharisees before 70 as 'late and legendary'. The foundations for the relatively rapid formation of the rabbinate and the spiritual revival of Palestinian Judaism after the fearful catastrophe of 70 were already laid by the Pharisees Hillel and Shammai, see also below, 19, 28, 45.

120. See Hock, *Context* (n.111), 23f. and 75 nn.36-38 (literature on articles on papyri).

121. T.Mommsen, 'Cilicium', *PW* 3.2, 1899, col. 2545.

122. So Hock, *Context* (n.111), 24; F.F.Bruce, *Paul: Apostle of the Free Spirit*, Exeter 1977, 37. For the leather tents of the army see G.Webster, *The Roman Imperial Army*, ²1979, 167: 'They... were made of best-quality leather', see also 334 (index s.v.tents).

123. Saldarini, *Pharisees* (n.111), 143. The whole section on Paul is on 134-43.

124. Becker, *Paulus* (n.2), asks whether it is worth writing a separate section on the Jew Paul at all as 'the few biographical details as such hardly justify this'. But the decisive thing is not their amount but the importance that they have in particular letters: often, when Paul is addressing the themes which are central for him both personally and theologically, he emphatically speaks of the Jewish origin or past that in a particular way still also influences his future. Paul's testimonies about himself in Luke confirm this picture, for Luke, too, always makes Paul speak of his Jewish past when he is bearing witness before Jews to his decisive theological and biographical experience. Luke has been accused of making Paul more 'Jewish' and 'Pharisaic' than he really was. However, this is correct only up to a point and in the case of his pre-Christian past

does not even apply to his study under Gamaliel, whereas the origin from Tarsus tends rather to contradict the 'Lukan concept'. It is true that Luke puts particular stress on the Jewish features in the Christian Paul, but here one should not overlook I Cor.9.20 and Rom.9.1ff.!

125. For Hillel see the works of J.Neusner: 'Die Suche nach dem historischen Hillel', in id., *Das pharisäische und talmudische Judentum*, TSAJ 4, Tübingen 1984, 52-73; 'Die Gestalt des Hillel – Ein Gegenstück zur Frage nach dem historischen Jesus', in *Judentum in frühchristlicher Zeit*, Stuttgart 1988, 69-98; also of course, as on all the other Pharisees from the period before 70, the three-volume standard work *The Rabbinic Traditions about the Pharisees before 70*, Leiden 1970. For all the justified criticism of the older, more naive, and unhistorical accounts of Hillel, Neusner's attitude again seems to me to be too 'naively critical'; that is, he sweeps away the historical problem too easily. For Johanan b.Zakkai compare J.Neusner, *A Life of Johanan ben Zakkai*, StPB 6, Leiden [2]1970; id., *Development of a Legend. Studies on the Traditions concerning Yohanan ben Zakkai*, StPB 16, Leiden 1970. We have strikingly few primary sources from this period. The Psalms of Solomon were written between the middle and the end of the last century BCE and in all probability come from a Pharisaic milieu. The Fast Scroll may come from the time immediately before the outbreak of the war (66-70); the lists of thirty-five times of joy on which fasting is forbidden give at least some indication of the political dates which are important for the Pharisaic interpretation of history (see H.Mantel, 'Fastenrolle', *TRE* 11, 1983, 59-61; the text is in K.Beyer, *Die Aramäischen Texte vom Toten Meer*, Göttingen 1984, 354-8). In Josephus, only those Pharisees are significant for this period who are in contact with the Zealot movement (*Antt*. 18.4.9-17, 23-25; also in the so-called 'eagle pericope' [*Antt*. 17.149-167, 206-16; *BJ* 1.648-655; 2.5-13] Pharisaic and Zealot motives stand in the background, see Hengel, *Zealots* [n.66], 86ff.) or that peace party which wants to avoid an escalation of the rebellion (*BJ* 2.411; 4.158-161; *Vita* 17-23). Cf. the work by J.Wellhausen, *Die Pharisäer und die Sadducäer. Eine Untersuchung zur inneren jüdischen Geschichte*, Greifswald 1874 (reprinted Hanover 1924 and Göttingen 1967), 109ff., which is still valid for this period; G.Alon, 'The Attitude of the Pharisees to Roman Rule and the House of Herod', in id., *Jews, Judaism and the Classical World*, Jerusalem 1977, 18-47 (originally written in Hebrew in 1935); R.Meyer, *Tradition und Neuschöpfung im antiken Judentum. Dargestellt an der Geschichte des Pharisäismus*, SSAW.PH 110.2, Berlin 1965 (reprinted in *Geschichte und Theologie*, n.115, 130-87; below it is cited from this edition), 145ff.; id and H.F.Weiss, Φαρισαῖος, *TDNT* 9, 1974, 26ff. See also the summary in Schürer, *History* (n.27), II, 381-403, and Saldarini, *Pharisees* (n.111). Further literature below 128f. n.213. Josephus (37/38-after 100

CE) wrote the Aramaic version of his *Jewish War* between 73 and 79, the *Antiquities* in 93/94 and the *Life* a little later, i.e. parallel in time to the writings of the NT: Paul from 50, Mark around 70, Luke around 75-80 CE; the most remote here are Matthew, c.85-90, and John, 95-100. Over and above that we have hardly any contemporary sources. The statements are similarly sparse and can hardly conceal the fact that we know less about this period, which is most important for New Testament study, than about any phase of Phariseeism; unfortunately even Josephus reports only individual episodes and is almost silent about the period between 6 and 27 CE which leads up to Christianity. He limits himself almost completely to the political history of the rulers. See also P.Schäfer, 'Der vorrabbinische Pharisäismus', in M.Hengel and U. Heckel (eds.), *Paulus, Missionar und Theologe und das antike Judentum*, WUNT, Tübingen 1991.

126. Acts 22.3.

127. Acts 26.4f.

128. Acts 23.8.

129. Phil.3.4-6.

130. However, we know of no serious persecutions for the time between 75 and 85. Accordingly Luke still believes in a tolerant attitude of Roman authorities towards Christians, which for him means fair treatment. A real tightening up only came in the late period of Domitian, sometime after 90, and therefore too late for Luke-Acts, which was written before Matthew. Saldarini's verdict (*Pharisees* [n.111], 142, following A.J.Hultgren, 'Paul's Pre-Christian Persecutions of the Church. Their Purpose, Locale and Nature', *JBL* 95, 1976, 97-111) is: 'In Acts Luke depicts Paul as engaged in violent persecution, but this type of persecution is a late first-century experience for the Jewish community.' This completely misses the point because he does not distinguish between Jewish persecution, which already began early (cf. I Thess.2.14f.; Acts 4.3ff.; 5.17ff.; 12.1ff., etc.; Josephus, *Antt.* 20.200), and that by the Roman state, see also Hengel, *Acts and the History* (n.9), 73f.

131. II Cor 11.21b-22.

132. Rom.11.1.

133. Rom.9.3b-5a.

134. For both quotations see van Unnik, *Tarsus or Jerusalem* (n.11), 301.

135. Ibid., 304, see also 325, 'the apostle's mental language'. See also id., 'Aramaisms in Paul' (1943), *Sparsa Collecta* II, NT.S. 29, Leiden 1973, 129-143.

136. H.Conzelmann, *Acts*, Hermeneia, Philadelphia 1987, 209f.; cf. van Unnik, *Tarsus or Jerusalem* (n.11), 296f.

137. Mommsen, 'Rechtsverhältnisse' (n.110), 85f.

138. Thus G.Strecker, 'Befreiung und Rechtfertigung', in *Rechtfertigung*.

FS E.Käsemann, ed. J.Friedrich, W.Pöhlmann and P.Stuhlmacher, Tübingen 1976, 482 n.10 (also in *Eschaton und Historie. Aufsätze*, Göttingen 1979, 232).

139. Ibid. Cf. also Becker, *Paulus* (n.2), 40f., whose starting point is similarly that 'in view of the small scale of the society of Jerusalem' Paul as a persecutor of the group around Stephen must also have become known to the group around Peter. So in his view we must 'keep to the clear words of Gal.1.22-24: at the time of the persecution of Stephen, Paul was not in Jerusalem'. At the same time, however, he wants to salvage the tradition that Paul was brought up with Gamaliel, and therefore transfers this to the time before Jesus emerged and there was a Christian community. To this it must be objected that at that point the Galilean Cephas-Peter and his friends were in Jerusalem for a relatively short period, and probably were engaged in missionary work in the country for most of the time (cf.Gal.1.19); moreover Jerusalem was not such a restricted society as the above quotation seeks to suggest. Dealing with Lukan traditions in this way can hardly escape the charge of being a very subjective, if not arbitrary use of the sources. Here we have the impression that only what can be fitted into a scholar's own picture of Paul is taken over from Luke, and all the rest is dismissed as Lukan fiction, cf. e.g. the list on p.15.

140. Cf. J.Wilkinson, 'Ancient Jerusalem; Its Water Supply and Population', *PEQ* 106, 1974, 33-51; M.Broshi, 'La Population de l'ancienne Jérusalem', *RB* 82, 1975, 5-14.

141. P.Stuhlmacher, 'Die Stellung Jesu und des Paulus zu Jerusalem', *ZTK* 86, 1989, 140-56, on Paul, 148ff.; J.Jeremias, *Der Schlüssel zur Theologie des Paulus*, CH 115, Stuttgart 1971.

142. Acts 23.16-22; cf. Burchard, *Zeuge* (n.14), 32 nn.33, 34f.

143. For the translation see W.Bauer, *Lexicon of New Testament Greek*, ed. W.F.Arndt, F.W.Gingrich, F.W.Danker, Chicago ²1979, s.v. κύκλῳ (456f.). For this verse see already 25 above and n.86; for a possible connection between Rom.15.16-28 and Isa.66.18-21, see Riesner, *Frühzeit* (n.12), 205-14.

144. EKK VI.3, 1982, 120.

145. O.Michel, KEK IV, ¹⁴1978, 460 n.23, rightly stresses that for Paul Jerusalem has a central position both biographically and theologically. His statement in Rom.15.19b therefore indicates 'how far he has carried the gospel'.

146. Cf. Sirach, Prol.22, the oldest evidence for ἑβραϊστί in the sense of 'Hebrew language'; IV Macc.12.7; 16.15: the mother admonishes 'in the Hebrew language' her sons who are being tortured to death to stand fast in martyrdom 'for the ancestral law'. A very late legend about Paul

also relates that in the hour of his death he prayed in Hebrew (*Passio Sancti Pauli Apostoli* XVI, in *Acta Apostolorum Apocrypha*, ed. R.A.Lipsius and M.Bonnet, Leipzig 1891 [reprinted Hildesheim 1972] I, 40: the Greek text runs: καὶ καταπαύσα[ς τὴν προσευχὴν κοινολογησάμεν]ος ἑβραιστεὶ πρὸς τοὺς πατέρας, cf. C.Schmidt [ed.], ΠΡΑΞΕΙΣ ΠΑΥΛΟΥ. *Acta Pauli. Nach dem Papyrus der Hamburger Staats- und Universitäts-Bibliothek*, Glückstadt and Hamburg 1936, 38). Further see Philo, *Vita Mosis* II.31, whereʹΕβραῖοι from Judaea are those who can translate the Old Testament into Greek (cf. also *ConfLing* 68,129) and Gutbrod, *TDNT* 3, 1966, 372-5. On Acts 6.1; II Cor.11.22; Phil.3.5 see 392-4, though there the aspect related to language is somewhat undervalued. Cf. also Hengel, 'Between Jesus and Paul' (n.9), 1-15.

147. J.B.Lightfoot, *St Paul's Epistle to the Philippians*, London and Cambridge 1868, 144. Similarly also E.Lohmeyer, KEK IX [12]1961, 129f.

148. Cf. Luke 1.59; 2.21; John 7.22 and Bill. 4.1, 23-27, with mShab 19.5. Circumcision was not without dangers for the small child, see tShab 15.8 (line 88).

149. Cf. Hengel, 'Hellenization' (n.37), 7, 113f. (nn.19-22). For the history of exegesis see H.-W.Neudorfer, *Der Stephanuskreis in der Forschungsgeschichte seit F.C.Baur*, Giessen and Basle 1983, 19-85, 219-34, 309f., 329-31.

150. Jeremias, *Jerusalem* (n.118), 287f., 278f.

151. Ibid., 227, 287.

152. Bill.3.622, cf. Gen.35.16f.

153. The attempts of Böhlig, *Geisteskultur* (n.11), and Barnikol, *Vorchristliche Zeit* (n.1), 31-46, to refer these remarks to the Jews of Tarsus fully fail to understand the significance of Judaea and Jerusalem for Pharisaic theology, cf. also Gal.4.25f. and on it Bill.3.573f. Oepke, 'Probleme' (n.1), 444, already commented rightly: 'So if to all appearances Paul had had a rabbinic high school education, where else was this to be found than in Jerusalem? Can one think of a Pharisee of strict observance (Phil.3.5) with no connection with the mother country?' See also Jeremias, *Jerusalem* (n.115), 247.

154. Acts 22.3; cf.26.5.

155. The traditions attributed to him have been collected in Neusner, *Rabbinic Traditions* I (n.120), 341-76.

156. *BJ* 4,159; *Vita* 190f., 194-6, 216, 309. John of Gischala, the archenemy of Josephus, attempted with Simon's help to relieve him of his Galilean comand.

157. J.Jeremias in particular has argued that Paul was a Hillelite: 'Paulus als Hillelit', in *Neotestamentica et Semitica, FS M.Black*, ed. E.E.Ellis and M.Black, Edinburgh 1969, 88-94; M.Enslin, 'Paul and Gamaliel',

JR 7, 1927, 360-75, judged otherwise. Paul is also understood as a Shammaite by K.Haacker, 'Die Berufung des Verfolgers und die Rechtfertigung des Gottlosen', *TheolBeitr* 6, 1975, 1-19, and H.Hübner, 'Gal.3,10 und die Herkunft des Paulus', *KuD* 19, 1973, 215-31: 228f.; id., *Das Gesetz bei Paulus*, FRLANT 119, Göttingen ³1982, 142f. n.16, who here rightly limits his position by regarding the division into two schools of Hillelites and Shammaites as a tendency which conceals a great multiplicity.

158. Strack/Stemberger, *Einleitung* (n.78), 26-30.

159. Oepke, 'Probleme', (n.1), 412-21, already objected to this, but with other arguments. The rabbinic material on ordination appears in Bill.2.648-61; the excessively early date for rabbinic ordination still appears in E.Lohse's monograph *Die Ordination im Spätjudentum und im Neuen Testament*, Göttingen 1951. For criticism see M.Hengel, *Nachfolge und Charisma* BZNW 34, Berlin 1968, 48 n.22; cf. also Riesner, *Frühzeit* (n.25), 266-74; Burchard, *Zeuge* (n.14), 33 n.36.

160. jMeg 3.73d, 23ff. is certainly an exaggeration, but probably contains a historical reminiscence: 'There were 480 synagogues in Jerusalem and each had a school and a house of learning, a school for teaching the Bible and a house of learning for teaching the Mishnah, and Vespasian attacked all of them.' The quotation goes on to single out the house of learning of Johanan ben Zakkai, cf. Bill.2.150, 662 (parallel passages which sometimes give a different number); there is a report of a house of learning on the Temple mount in which the Sanhedrin met and from which the Torah extended over all Israel (jSanh 1,17, 19c.11ff.; tSanh 7.1 [line 425]); the legendary great house of learning in Jerusalem (*byt hmdrš [h]gdwl yrwšlym*) is mentioned often in SER, p.10 (F 49 and 51); 16 (F 80); 21 (F.122). ARN also often presupposes that Johanan ben Zakkai was active in Jerusalem as a teacher in the temple, cf. ARN 6 (and bPes 26a), where the story of Nakdimon ben Gorion is also told. In it the temple as a place of prayer and *byt hmdrš* is identical. Cf. Hengel, 'Proseuche und Synagoge' (n.93), 150f., 243; S.Safrai, *Die Wallfahrt im Zeitalter des Zweiten Tempels*, Neukirchen-Vluyn 1981, 261f. For the Sirach passage cf. also Stadelmann, *Ben Sira als Schriftgelehrter* (n.117), 305ff.

161. Cf. Strack/Stemberger, *Einleitung* (n.78), 19-21.

162. Strecker, 'Befreiung' (n.138), 482 n.10.

163. Schoeps, *Paul* (n.5), 24ff.

164. Cf. D.E.Garland, *The Intention of Matthew 23*, NT.S, Leiden 1979, 129f.: 'The term proselyte denotes one who has fully accepted circumcision and the requisite submission to the Torah in its entirety. This was especially true in Palestinian circles. Hellenistic Judaism in the Diaspora showed signs of conciliation toward the Gentiles in its missionary activity. These Diaspora missionaries seem to have been less concerned that

Gentile adherents keep the cultic commandments, including circumcision, than that they should believe in the one God of Israel and live
according to basic ethical requirements. The Palestinian Jews were much
more stringent in their requirements, as were those Jewish Christians,
identified in Acts 15:5 as Pharisees, who demanded circumcision of new
converts to Christianity.'

165. On this see M.Hengel, 'Hadrians Politik gegenüber Juden und
Christen', *JANES* 16/17, 1984/85, 155f.; cf. P.Schäfer, *Der Bar-Kokhba-
Aufstand*, TSAJ 1, Tübingen 1981, 24ff. (= TanB mishpatim 3; ExR 30,2,
CantR 1,1, §1).

166. *Antt.* 20.71; cf.*BJ* 2.520; 6.356f.

167. *Antt.* 20.34-48: like his mother Helena, Izates too had moved
towards Jewish religion but at first without being circumcised. Strecker
(482 n.10) mentions the Josephus passage along with Matt.23.15, without
going into it more closely.

168. *Antt.* 20.43. For ἀκρίβεια as a characteristic of the Pharisees in
Josephus see A.I.Baumgarten, 'The Name of the Pharisees', *JBL* 102,
1983, 411-28: 413-17; S.N.Mason, 'Priesthood in Josephus and the
"Pharisaic Revolution"', *JBL* 107, 1988, 661; G.Theissen, *Lokalkolorit und
Zeitgeschichte in den Evangelien*, NTOA 8, Fribourg CH and Göttingen 1989,
241f.

169. G.Bornkamm, 'Paulus', *RGG*[3] 5, 1961, col.168.

170. J.Neusner, 'Die pharisäischen rechtlichen Überlieferungen', in
id., *Judentum* (n.120), 43, see also 51: the regulations for priestly purity for
the whole people called for by the Pharisees was to 'sanctify all Israel and
transform everyone into a priest and the whole people into a holy people'.
However, it is important to guard against certain exaggerations here:
certainly questions about purity of food were very important, but they
are only one part of the lifestyle orientated on the law that was represented
by the Pharisees. Cf. E.P.Sanders' legitimate criticism of J.Neusner, 'Did
the Pharisees Eat Ordinary Food in Purity?', in id., *Jewish Law from Jesus
to the Mishnah*, London and Philadelphia 1990, 131-254, 212 (from his
summary): 'This many pages on purity may seem to imply that the
Pharisees were interested in it above all else and that they were, if not a
"pure food club", at least a "purity club". A full and evenhanded
treatment of Neusner's passages – that is, the rabbinic legal passages
which are attributed to Pharisees or to the Houses – would result in many
pages about Work, a large number under the heading "Non-purity
aspects of tithes, sacrifices and offerings", a good number on "Festivals"
and "Private Worship", several on "Agriculture", "Charity" "Civil law"
and "Family law" (especially if vows are included), and a few on "Food"
(food itself, not its purity). Purity has generally been taken as defining

the Pharisees, and I think that their purity practices have been misde-
scribed and misinterpreted. On the other hand, purity really was important to them.' The Pharisaic ideal was a total one, cf. also K.W.Niebuhr,
*Gesetz und Paränese. Katechismusartige Weisungsreihen in der frühjüdischen
Literatur*, WUNT II.28, Tübingen 1987, who in the first part investigates
the summaries of the law by Pseudo-Phocylides, Philo, *Hyp.* 7.1-9, and
Josephus, *c.Apionem* 2.190-219, which he then compares with further
catechetical sets of paraenesis from early Jewish literature. Here in terms
of content – for all the profound differences – he comes to a similarly
complex result to that of Sanders in the above quotation, in which the
texts that he investigates are more directed against the behaviour of the
pagan environment and are also conditioned by the situation of Diaspora
Judaism: 'The wealth of texts discussed in the course of the investigation
allows us to make representative statements about focal points of content
in early Jewish paraenesis. First in the concrete admonitions comes the
sphere of sexual ethics... A second important theme of admonition is the
call for mercy towards the weak and disadvantaged within the social
community... Further concrete admonitions can be collected under the
heading of truthfulness (lies, calumny, perjury, deceit). Finally we have
various modes of conduct connected with the neighbour (anger, envy,
hatred, pride, disputes)... The modes of behaviour listed all come from
everyday life. In the face of the wealth of such moral admonitions,
instructions from the cultic sphere clearly fade into the background,
though they are not completely absent or even replaced by statements
which are critical of the cult. Cultic and oral admonitions do not form an
alternative, nor is there any evidence of a tendency to spiritualize the cult'
(234f.). This agreement is all the more striking since Niebuhr himself in
his investigation completely ignored the rabbinic sources and the texts
which he investigated are only to the slightest degree attributable directly
to Judaism with a hasidic, Pharisaic stamp (Ps.Sol.); otherwise they relate
to this Judaism only in a wider sense (Josephus, *c.Apionem*; TestXII;
Tobit; ApcAbr). I.e., the ethics it contains corresponds to that of the
Pharisees and a broad trend of popular piety within the Jewish people. For
Josephus, *c.Apionem*, cf. also H.F.Weiss, 'Pharisäismus und Hellenismus.
Zur Darstellung des Judentums in Geschichtswerk des jüdischen Histori-
kers Flavius Josephus', *OLZ* 74, 1979, 421-33, who shows that precisely
in his apologia for Judaism Josephus adopts a Pharisaic standpoint and
understands this to be representative. For the parallels in content between
c.Ap.2.190-219 and rabbinic texts see now also G.P.Carras, *Paul, Josephus
and Judaism: The Shared Judaism of Paul and Josephus*, Oxford dissertation
1989 (typescript), 79f. The work shows further the degree to which Paul
also remained bound to Judaism as a Christian. That starting from the

temple the ritual ideal of purity played a very important role among the Pharisees (Mark 7; Luke 11; Matt.23) must not therefore be doubted. Outside Eretz Israel strict ritual purity was possible only to a limited degree, and large parts of the Torah could not be observed there. See n.171 below.

171. The priestly conception was the ideal; the efforts of the Pharisees are '*a minor symbolic gesture* towards "living like a priest"' (thus Sanders, *Jesus, Paul and Judaism* [n.170], 192, his italics; he here contradicts the current picture of Pharisees and so restores the Pharisees to everyday life, see also 233-5, 248, etc., see index s.v. Pharisees, 'Ritual' or 'priestly' purity, Did not live like priests). Here, however, I ask myself whether Sanders does not start too much from the situation after the destruction of the Second Temple, as it is presupposed in the Tannaitic sources. That at the time of the late Second Temple ritual questions were dynamite is now shown by 4Q MMT: the priestly ideal lived out in real life had even stronger weight at that time.

172. Gal.2.12f.; but cf. also I Cor.5.11.

173. Cf. Bill. 2,759f.; Sanders, *Jesus, Paul and Judaism* (n.170), 191: 'The idea of concentric circles of purity is basically biblical, but it was elaborated during the period of the second temple. Palestine is purer than Gentile lands, Jerusalem purer than the rest of Palestine, and the temple purer yet.' On the other hand, of course, ways had to be found of being able to live as a Pharisee abroad, for even Paul's parents were in a position to raise their son in Gentile Tarsus as a 'Pharisee of the Pharisees', even if they sent him to Jerusalem relatively soon. It is interesting to see how in their foreign policy the Hasmonaeans worked towards enabling Jews to observe their home customs (πάτρια ἔθη) even in foreign lands; these measures included exemption from military service because of the sabbath and provision with 'home foods' (τροφαὶ πάτριαι), see Josephus, *Antt.* 14.223-7, see also *Antt.* 14.245, where in addition to the sabbath the Jews are also allowed to 'perform their native rites or manage their produce in accordance with their custom'. In Sardes the aedile (ἀγορανόμος) was required to see that they could buy 'suitable food' (τροφὴ ἐπιτήδεια). Nevertheless the most probable starting point is that Jews in the Greek Diaspora could not observe 'those same stringent standards of purity' (Rajak, 'Jews and Christians' [n.88], 253) as in Israel itself (and were not obliged to by the mother country). For these questions see now the excellent article by E.P.Sanders, 'Purity, Food and Offerings in the Greek-Speaking Diaspora', in *Jewish Law* (n.170), 255-308.

174. *Vita* 14. They need not have been Pharisees, but wanted rigorously to live up to their priestly ideal of purity – which was a model for the Pharisees on their side. However, as the Pharisee Josephus calls them

ἱερεῖς τινας συνήθεις ἐμοί ('certain priests of my acquaintance'), they could have been close to the Pharisees. Cf. also the numerous didactic narratives in which model pious people do not make themselves unclean with pagan food: Dan.1.8ff.; Tobit 1.10f.; II Macc.7; III Macc.3.4-7; IV Macc.5.1-6.30; Esther 4.17x (Rahlfs LXX), on this see Sanders, *Jewish Law* (n.170), 274-6.

175. G.Stemberger, 'Die Bedeutung des "Landes Israel" in der rabbinischen Tradition', *Kairos* 25, 1983, 176-99.

176. Ibid., 178f.

177. Ibid., 180f.

178. pSheq 3,4,47c par. pShab 1,5,3c. For this significant and influential pupil of Aqiba see W.Bacher, *Die Agada der Tannaiten* II, Strasbourg 1890, 1-69; Strack/Stemberger, *Einleitung* (n.78), 82. He was possibly the child of proselytes and had to escape from Palestine during the Bar Kokhba rebellion, but then returned. He again spent the evening of his life abroad, among other places in Asia Minor, but before his death he ordained that his body should be buried in Israel (jKil 9,4,32c), see Bacher, 24 and nn.2, 28.

179. In the life of Jonah in the *Vitae Prophetarum* there is the interesting information that the prophet repented of his false prophecy against Nineveh by going abroad to Tyre, because in this way he hoped to expurgate his guilt. There Elijah found him and stayed with Jonah and his mother because he could not live with uncircumcised people. When Jonah died he was raised from the dead again by Elijah. Here Jonah is identified with the son of the widow of Sareptah (I Kings 17.17ff.). The miracle is meant to show the prophet Jonah that he cannot escape God. The stay in the pagan surroundings in which Jonah dies is here interpreted as a flight from God (*Vitae Prophetarum* 10,2-6; *Old Testament Pseudepigrapha* [n. 25] II, 392, Greek text: *Prophetarum vitae fabulosae...*, ed. T.Schermann, Leipzig 1907, 82-5: I owe this reference to A.M.Schwemer).

180. Cf. *BJ* 1.98: 8,000 refugees under Alexander Jannaeus = *Antt.* 13.383; both times Josephus stresses that their exile came to an end with the death of the king, and so they returned as quickly as possible to the mother country. That Jannaeus's opponents were Pharisees emerges clearly from the advice to his wife Salome Alexandra at the end of his life, *Antt.* 13, 399-404, cf. *BJ* 1,110f. par. *Antt.* 13, 408-10; cf. further the saga of Jehuda b.Tabbai and his pupils (jHag 2,2 77d; bSanh 107b par. b.Sota 47a), a legend which was later, *inter alia*, associated with the polemic against Jesus. Text and translation in H.L.Strack, *Jesus, die Häretiker und die Christen*, SIJB 37, Berlin 1910, §8 (pp.9ff., 30*ff.); cf. also J.Maier, *Jesus von Nazareth in der talmudischen Überlieferung*, EdF 82, Darmstadt 1978, 114ff.

181. The figure of 6000 Pharisees who refused to give an oath to Herod, mentioned in Josephus, *Antt.* 17.42, is the only information about the number of Pharises before 70. These are the supporters and followers of Sammeas and Pollio (cf. *Antt.* 15. 269f.), and therefore possibly the group around Hillel and Shammai (for the identification of Hillel and Shammai with the Sameas and Pollio who appear only in Josephus see Schalit, *König Herodes* [n.47], 316ff., 768ff.).

182. For him see J.Neusner, *A History of the Jews in Babylonia* I, StPB 9, Leiden 1965, 43-9, 121-4: 'Judah b.Bathyra represents the first known important tannaitic authority resident outside of Palestine' (48).

183. For the situation in Rome see Bill.3.23f.; for the inscriptions see Schürer, *History* (n.27), III.1, 95-101; W.Wiefel, 'Die jüdische Gemeinschaft im antiken Rom und die Anfänge des römischen Christentums', *Jud.* 26, 1970, 65-88; H.J.Leon, *The Jews of Ancient Rome*, Philadelphia 1960; Lampe, *Stadtrömische Christen* (n.27), 61 n.174. Todos/Theodotos is certainly not identical with the man of the same name in the famous synagogue inscription in Jerusalem, but see *CIJ* I, no.358.

184. The rabbinic information on houses of learning in the Greek-speaking Diaspora is extremely sparse. For Rome see above n.183, cf. also mAZ 4.7: the discussion between the Gentiles and the elders (*hzqnym*) in Rome (tAZ 6.7 [line 469] and bAZ 54b read *[h]plwswpyn*, the philosophers) on the question why God did not destroy the idolatry has nothing to do with a house of learning there but deals with a typical Jewish apologetic problem. For Nisibis see n.182; for Antioch see S.Krauss, *JE* 1, 1901, 632; bKet 88a; GenR 10.4: Ephes preaches in Antioch; 19.4: R.Tanchuma is asked about Gen.5 in Antioch (by heretics?). These are not clear indications of a school; bErub 21a: there are no pillars of wells outside the land (i.e. Eretz Israel) because there are no houses of learning there (*mty bt'*: I owe this reference to Dr F.Hüttenmeister).

185. Acts 21.37,40; 22.2.

186. Acts 21.39-22.3.

187. Kuss, *Paulus* (n.2), 19 n.1; Becker, *Paulus* (n.2) also gives a similar date. For Philemon 9 see M.Dibelius, HNT 12, ³1953, 104 (new ed. by H.Greeven), where the authors discuss the ancient division of times of life. According to this, πρεσβύτης denotes the period between forty-nine and fifty-six years of age (in this scheme the νεανίσκος is between twenty-two and twenty-eight). For the alternative 'messenger' or 'ambassador' see P.Stuhlmacher, EKK 18, ²1981, 37f. From the context, however, the πρεσβύτης which alone has been handed down in the text seems more meaningful than Bentley's conjecture πρεσβευτής.

188. See 3 above with n.31. Cf. also Becker, *Paulus* (n.2), 35,37,55f., who mentions, in addition to the good style, further references to Greek

as a mother tongue; thus the Pauline distinction between 'Jews and Greeks' (Rom.1.16; 2.9, etc.), which *also* (of course not 'just'!) indicates that for Paul the non-Jewish world is characterized by its language, though he himself writes his letters in Greek. Becker also mentions the Pauline letter formulary, which similarly, despite the arbitrary prescript, is of Greek origin, as also are the patterns of argument which Paul uses. Greek rhetoric and letter forms were, however, also well established among the Jewish upper classes in Palestine.

189. Becker, *Paul* (n.2), 55: 'He also cites holy Scripture – usually by heart – from the Septuagint, which he evidently read from his youth and from which he learned; otherwise he could hardly quote it so extensively. So for Paul Greek is not just a marginal assimilation to his readers and hearers but an aspect of his own education. For this reason it makes sense here to presuppose schooling from his youth.' For the use of a partly revised Septuagint see D.A.Koch, *Die Schrift als Zeuge des Evangeliums*, BHTh 69, Tübingen 1986, 48ff.: 'A number of Isaiah quotations and both of Paul's Job quotations are not taken from the LXX: they are essentially nearer to the MT and in part show clear agreements with the (later!) translations of Aquila, Symmachus and Theodotion. At the same time this indicates that here Paul is not referring back independently to the Hebrew wording of scripture but in these passages is using a model assimilated to the Hebrew text' (57). I myself think it quite possible that Paul worked out a text of his own on the basis of his knowledge of revised versions.

190. For the scroll of the Twelve Prophets see now E.Tov, *The Greek Minor Prophets Scroll from Naḥal Ḥever (8ḤevXIIgr)*, DJD VIII, Oxford 1990.

191. Against Koch, *Schrift als Zeuge* (n.189), 81. But cf. already O.Michel, *Paulus und seine Bibel*, BFCT II.18, Gütersloh 1929 (reprinted with an appendix, Darmstadt 1972), 57ff., though he rejects the use of a LXX recension corrected by Paul himself (63ff.). Compare also E.E.Ellis, *Paul's Use of the Old Testament*, Edinburgh 1957, 15, 19f., 139-41, who similarly goes for an independent treatment of the Hebrew Bible by Paul. This reference back to the sacred language is quite understandable in a 'zealot' who has 'made progress in Judaism'. Particularly if he had grown up with the Greek Bible, he must have been concerned to examine the familiar text and if need be correct it (just as even now theology students compare the translation with which they have grown up and often even mention this process in sermons). Deissmann, *Paul* (n.5), 99-101, somewhat neglected this twofold character of Paul's treatment of holy scripture in calling him a 'Septuagint Jew'; but he too observes that at some points Paul uses a revised verson of the LXX, though without going into the question how he came by it.

192. Koch, *Schrift als Zeuge* (n.189), 92. He seeks to distinguish 'between a general familiarity with the most important content of the tradition of scripture and an assured knowledge of the text'. Koch will allow Paul the former, but the latter only to a very limited degree. On this see the quotation above from Becker, who begins from the assumption that Paul learned Aramaic as well as Greek at home (37) and 'because of his Pharisaic education' he also regards Hebrew as probable, 'as he could probably have read and understood the text of the Hebrew Bible'. Koch then continues: 'However, as a Christian Paul nowhere certainly translates directly from the Hebrew Bible into Greek' (38). Here, however, we should remember that Paul was principally missionizing in pure Greek-speaking communities which as a rule knew only the LXX, and further that on his journeys he had no access to a Hebrew text. He *had to* work with the Greek text.

193. Cf. Acts 17.2,17; 18.4,19; 20.7ff.; 24.25; cf. also Apollos, Acts 18.28.

194. C.D.Stanley, 'Paul and Homer: Greco-Roman Citation Practice in the First Century CE', *NovT* 32, 1990, 48-78, compares Paul's technique of quotation with that customary in ancient literature, and in discussion of Koch's work, which despite all the criticism is masterly, comes to the conclusion: 'Despite Koch's own summary dismissal of the possibility of Greco-Roman parallels, a careful consideration of the evidence reveals a near identity of conceptions between Paul and his Greco-Roman contemporaries regarding the acceptable parameters for citing literary texts' (77). That with his deviations from the text before him Paul is at the upper limit (comparable, significantly, with Qumran, see 78 n.91) makes the hypothesis of his own critical recension of the text at least probable.

195. Cf. Luke 11.45f., 52 (par. Matt.23.4,13); see also Luke 10.25 (par. Matt.22.34; Mark 12.28). Luke 7.30; 14.3 have no parallels.

196. H.G.Liddell, R.Scott and H.S.Jones, *A Greek-English Lexicon*, Oxford [9]1940 (reprinted 1985) give as a translation s.v.: '*secretary, registrar*, title of officials at Athens and elsewhere;... also of subordinate officials, *clerk*'. Only one instance points to 'scholar' (358f.). In Acts 19.35 the word is similarly used for an official; for Josephus cf. *BJ* 1.479, 529; 5.532; *Antt.* 11.26, 248; 20.208f. etc. (the Josephus-Concordance edited by K.H.Rengstorf [four vols., Leiden 1973-83] similarly translates γραμμα-τεύς as 'scribe, secretary') and A.Schlatter, *Die Theologie des Judentums nach dem Bericht des Josephus*, BFCT II.26, Gütersloh 1932, 200ff. For Matthew see M.Hengel, 'Zur matthäischen Bergpredigt und ihrem jüdischen Hintergrund', *TR* 52, 1987, 374f.

197. Cf. Riesner, *Jesus* (n.25), 115f., etc., who stresses 'that most Jews in their environment stood out for the particularly intensive way in which

they learned the precepts of their law off by heart', cf. Josephus, *c.Ap.*
2.178, 257; Juvenal, *Sat.* XIV 100f. (= *GLAJJ* [n.89], no.301, p.102).

198. E.Norden, *Die antike Kunstprosa vom VI. Jahrhundert v.Chr. bis in die
Zeit der Renaissance*, II, Leipzig and Berlin ²1909, 496f. An example of what
from a historical point of view are 'useless' allusions is the drawing of a
parallel between Paul's talk about speaking as a fool in II Cor.11f. and
the drunken Alcibiades' praise of Socrates in Plato's *Symposium*, 221ff., in
H.Windisch, H.D.Betz and C.Wolff (see n.27 above) and H.-J.Klauck,
NEB 8, Würzburg 1986, 86.

199. Ibid., II, 506f.

200. Ibid., II, 502, cf. 509, 'language of the heart'.

201. Zahn, 'Lebensgeschichte', 283.

202. Zahn, KNT V.2, ³⁺⁴1927, 751.

203. Around 100? see Bacher, *Tannaiten* (n.178), 1,372; 2,556f.

204. CantR 1,3,1 (= *Midrasch rabba*, ed. Shimson Dunsqi, Jerusalem
1980: 1.20; p.22); cf. Bill. 2.763f. and Luke 2.46, where the twelve-year-
old Jesus is depicted sitting in the temple among the scholars. Elsewhere
Jesus also teaches seated, cf. Luke 4.20; 5.3; Matt.5.1; 13.1f.; 15.29; 24.3;
Mark 4.1, 9,35; 13.43; 26.55; John 6.3; 8.2. Here it is presupposed that
the pupils sit round the teacher in a circle. The Pharisees, too, sat like
this at his feet, see Luke 5.17 (cf. Mark 2.6). Matthew 23.2 mentions the
special teacher's chair. For more detail about the order of seating among
the Babylonian rabbis see D.M.Goodblatt, *Rabbinic Instruction in Sasanian
Babylonia*, SJLA 9, Leiden 1975, 252-9 (I owe this reference to F.Ave-
marie).

205. *Vita* 191, see above 30 n.168 and F.Mussner, HTK 9, ⁴1981, 80.

206. Isa.2.3; Sir 24.8,11,23, cf. H.Gese, *Zur biblischen Theologie*, Tübingen
²1983, 69ff.; on the concept of the messianic Torah from Zion, which he
coined, see 83f. For Zion as the place from which the Torah goes forth
see above n.160.

207. Gal.1.13f.

208. Mommsen, 'Rechtsverhältnisse' (n.110), 85; thus also Barnikol,
'Vorchristliche Zeit' (n.1), 35ff. For criticism cf. A.Oepke, ThHK 9,
⁵1984, 59.

209. Cf. Gal.4.17: even Paul's opponents in Galatia are described as
being 'zealous', and from the rest of the information about them it can
be concluded with some probability that they were probably Jewish
Christians from Jerusalem who attempted to convince the young Christians in the province of Galatia to adopt a Judaizing lifestyle, analogous
to the Galilean Eleazar with King Izates of Adiabene, Josephus, *Antt.*
20.43 (see above n.167); on this see the good survey in Mussner, HTK
(n.205), 11-29. R.Jewett, 'The Agitators and the Galatian Congregation',

NTS 17, 1970/71, 198-212 (Mussner, 21f.) sees a direct connection between the opponents and the Zealots; Acts 21.20f.; 22.3. For details see Hengel, *Zealots* (n.66), 149-228. See also below 70f. and nn.305-7.

210. Cf. J.W.Doeve, 'Paulus der Pharisäer und Galater i 13-15', *NovT* 6, 1963, 170-81, esp. 179f. For 'progress' in education see also 1QSa I, 8b. If the novice makes good progress (*ybw' btb*), he can go into the next higher class. Cf. Josephus, *Vita* 191, on the Pharisees: 'who seem to be most scrupulous in observing ancestral customs'.

211. Cf. V.C.Pfitzner, *Paul and the Agon Motif. Traditional Athletic Imagery in the Pauline Literature*, NT.S, Leiden 1967, 21f. (The Greek Gymnasium and its Ideals): 'The entire curriculum of the gymnasium, including the studies in grammar and the musical arts, became saturated with the spirit of competition, so that examinations in all spheres were regarded as contests, offering the possibility of showing personal superiority over the next person. Victory lists of the succesful competitors were issued. Life in the gymnasium was a continual winning or being defeated, a continuing measuring of one's own powers over against those of the other, whereby superiority was an aim in itself without necessarily being directed towards any practical use of the strength and skill developed.' See also 38-72, 'Hellenistic Judaism and the Agon Tradition', where Philo, LXX, IV Macc. and Josephus are cited as examples; for rabbinic Judaism cf. jBerakh 4,7d par.; bBerakh 28b; for the motif of competition among Jews and Greeks in the Hellenistic period see also Hengel, 'Proseuche und Synagoge' (n.93), 124, 145ff., 402; id., 'Qumran und der Hellenismus', in *Qumrân. Sa piété, sa théologie et son milieu*, ed. M.Delcor, BETL 46, Paris and Louvain 1978, 333-72: 351f.; H.I.Marrou, *Histoire de l'Education dans l'antiquité*, Paris 1948, index s.v. 'concours', 590.

212. Thus the English title of the work by E.P.Sanders which provoked wide and controversial discussion. See also his subsequent work *Paul, The Law and the Jewish People*, London and Philadelphia 1985.

213. See E. Rivkin, 'Defining the Pharisees: The Tannaitic Sources', *HUCA* 40/41, 1969/70, 205-49, esp. 234f.. Rivkin's starting point is that *prwšym* only refers certainly to the Pharisees where it is used in opposition to *sdwqym*. In isolation it therefore stands for heretics, ascetics and sectarians. See also id., *A Hidden Revolution. The Pharisees' Search for the Kingdom Within*, Nashville 1978, 129ff., 162-6, 321-4, where he also postulates the meaning 'fanatics' for Josephus, *Antt.* 17.41-45. But this last seems improbable to me; for this episode connected with the wife of Herod's brother Pheroras see below 45 and n.227. Rivkin was vigorously criticized by J.Lightstone, who on the basis of a radical historical scepticism virtually rules out the possibility of inferring anything from this controversy between Pharisees and Sadducees for the period before

70: 'Sadducees versus Pharisees. The Tannaitic Sources', in *Christianity, Judaism and other Greco-Roman Cults. FS M.Smith*, ed. J.Neusner, SJLA XII.3, Leiden 1975, 206-17. Against this is now 4Q MMT, the controversies of which partly emerge in the discussions between *prwšyn* and *ṣdwqyn* in mJad 4.6-8, where the *ṣdwqyn* probably refers more to the Essenes. But Sadducees are no longer attested after 70, so there is much to be said for Rivkin's assumption that where the texts refer to controversies between Pharisees and Sadducees, we have traditions from before 70.

For the designation Pharisee see basically R.Meyer, 'Tradition und Neuschöpfung im antiken Judentum', in *Arbeitsethos* (n.115), 130-87 (originally Berlin 1965), here 132-4; id., Φαρισαῖος, *TDNT* 9, 1974, 12f.; Baumgarten, 'Name of the Pharisees' (n.168), who attempts to understand *pᵉrūšīm* as a positive self-designation by the Pharisees, which like the Greek ἀκρίβεια means 'those who specify'; he then interprets it as a participle in the active: 'That is, the Pharisees claimed to be the party of accurate and specific observance of the law by understanding their name as *parōšīm* and maintaining that it meant "the specifiers". I propose that we consider the circle complete and conclude that *parōšīm* was the Semitic original behind the use of *akribeia* in Josephus, Acts and Nicolaus' (420). But he then leaves open the question whether this is a subsequent euphemistic interpretation of a designation originally given polemically by outsiders or is from the beginning an expression of Pharisaic self-understanding. If the last assumption were correct, it is hard to see why it should have been abandoned in the second century.

214. Here the changed political and social situation is important: the Pharisees, who hitherto were fighting for their influence in the people, and who canvassed for their ideals among the people, now became the leading group, without any real competition.

215. See above p.29 and n.161; below, pp.51ff.

216. For him see Josephus, *Vita*, 190ff., 216, 309; *BJ* 4,159; Schürer, *History* (n.27), II, 368f.; III.2, 994 (Index). For Gamaliel I see pp.28f. above.

217. W.Bacher, *Die Agada der Tannaiten I: Von Hillel bis Akiba*, Leipzig and Berlin ²1903, is indispensable as a collection of material; for a survey see Schürer, *History* (n.27), II, 1979, 356-9; Strack/Stemberger, *Einleitung* (n.78), 71-6; cf. also the summary with which Neusner concludes his three-volume investigation of the rabbinic traditions about the Pharisees (n.120), II, 301-19: 'We have this account, so far as it is early, primarily through the medium of forms and mnemonic patterns used at Yavneh and later on at Usha. What we know is what the rabbis of Yavneh and Usha regarded as the important and desirable account of the Pharisaic traditions: almost entirely the internal record of the life of the party and

its laws, the party being no more than the two factions that predominated after 70, the laws being mainly rules of how and what people might eat with one another' (319). However, I do not believe that the school of Shammai still gained *substantial* influence after 70. The controversies between the two schools point back to the time before 70. After that the more liberal school of Hillel gradually established itself.

218. Cf. the relevant sections in the general accounts of the New Testament period (e.g. W.Grundmann, 'Gruppen und Kräfte, Einsichten und Gestalten', in J.Leipoldt and W.Grundmann, *Umwelt des Urchristentums* I, Berlin ⁷1985, 217-91), though as a rule they only mention the movements known from the NT, and the Essenes; we should not forget that in addition there is still a series of further, often much smaller and largely unknown conventicles and groups. See what to us is the enigmatic list of Jewish sects in Justin, *Dial.*90.4; Hegesippus (in Eusebius, *HE* 4.22.6) and Epiphanius (*Ancoratus* 13.3-15; *Panarion* 16.1ff.; 19.1-6; 53.1-9). Cf. also the Jewish accounts in Josephus, *Vita* 11; mJad 4.6ff., and the rabbinic accounts of the *minim* collected in Strack, *Jesus* (n.180), 19-40, 47*-80. These Jewish 'heretics' partly go back to marginal groups which already existed before 70.

219. Jeremias, *Jerusalem* (n.118), 147-245: the upper classes; R.Meyer, Σαδδουκαῖος, *TDNT* 7, 1971, 35-54; also the monumental work by J.LeMoyne, *Les Sadduciens*, EtB, Paris 1972; M.Stern, 'Aspects of Jewish Society: The Priesthood and Other Classes', in *The Jewish People in the First Century*, CRINT I 2, Assen and Amsterdam 1976, 561-630; Schürer, *History* (n.27), II, 238-56, 'The Priesthood as a Class'; 404-14, 'The Sadducees', Saldarini, *Pharisees* (n.111), 298-308: 'The Sadducees and Jewish Leadership'. For the Boethuseans see Josephus, *Antt.* 15.320f.; 17.78, 164, 339; 18.3,26 (*BJ* 2.55); *Antt.* 19.297f.; *BJ* 5.527 and on this Hengel, 'Proseuche und Synagoge' (n.93), 142 n.151; id., *'Hellenization'* (n.37), 14, 70 n.62; Jeremias, *Jerusalem*, 97; Meyer, Σαδδουκαῖος, 42f., 45f.; Stern, *Aspects*, 603-6. There is an account in terms of social history in M.Goodman, *The Ruling Class of Judaea*, Oxford 1987.

220. Josephus, *Antt.* 15.320ff.; 17.78, 339; 18.3,109, 136; also Schürer, *History* (n.27), II, 229, 334.

221. R.Riesner, 'Das Jerusalemer Essenerviertel und die Urgemeinde', *ANRW* II.26,3 (in preparation); id., 'Essener und Urkirche in Jerusalem', *BiKi* 40, 1985, 64-76; B.Pixner, D.Chen, S.Margalit, 'Mount Zion: The "Gate of the Essenes" Re-excavated', *ZDPV* 105, 1989, 84-95; R.Riesner, 'Josephus' "Gate of the Essenes" in Modern Discussion', ibid., 105-9.

222. These include the Zealots, Sicarii and the followers of eschatological prophets like Theudas the Egyptian, see Hengel, *Zealots* (n.66).

223. H.Lichtenberger, 'Täufergemeinden und frühchristliche Täufer-

polemik im letzten Drittel des 1. Jahrhunderts', *ZTK* 84, 1987, 36-57. See also the lists of Christian sects in n.215 below and in detail J.Thomas, *Le mouvement baptiste en Palestine et Syrie (150 av.J.-C. – 300 ap.J-C.)*, DGMFT 2.ser, Louvain 1935.

224. We know of them on the basis of the literature that they have left behind, but detailed features of the different groupings are not recognizable behind these texts; however, cf. as an example the group standing behind the *Assumptio Mosis*, whose profile A.Schalit attempted to work out in his commentary on this work, of which there are only fragments (*Untersuchungen zur Assumptio Mosis*, ALGHJ 17, Leiden 1989). In his view this is an emphatically nationalistic group which stresses the election of Israel in a mystical-eschatological way; the text arose in the period shortly before the outbreak of the great war (66-70) in a circle which seems to have broken away from Pharisaism.

225. Deissmann, *Paul* (n.5), 89; Jeremias, *Jerusalem* (n.118), 58-77, on trade with Jerusalem; because of the religious significance of the city the result was that many people settled in this city 'so that they might die in the Holy Place and be buried in the place of the Resurrection and the Last Judgment' (75), see also 120ff.; Hengel, *'Hellenization'* (n.37); id., 'Between Jesus and Paul' (n.9), 14.

226. M.Smith, 'Palestinian Judaism in the First Century', in M.David (ed.), *Israel: Its Role in Civilization*, New York 1956, 67-81, disputes the influence of the Pharisees on large parts of the Jewish people for the period before 70 CE. In his view, at the time we can recognize only an 'orthodox', i.e. normative, Judaism, if there was any at all; it may not be identified with Pharisaism. For him the Pharisees are only one of the many sects and special groups of the time, without any social or political influence. The accounts in Josephus' *Antiquities* which attribute determinative influence to the Pharisees are constructs with the aim of portraying this group to the Roman occupying forces as loyal and influential. This thesis would abandon a long-lasting consensus according to which, while as a firmly organized party the Pharisees were a relatively small nucleus, in their views and their scriptural exegesis they were nevertheless representative of the majority of Palestinian Judaism of the time; see the classic account in E.Schürer, *Geschichte des jüdischen Volkes im Zeitalter Jesu Christi* II, Leipzig ⁴1907, 447-75. The following description is characteristic: the Pharisees are 'therefore those who also sought to accomplish earnestly and consistently in practice the ideal of a life according to the law put forward by the scribes. That means that they are the classical representatives of that trend which set the inner development of Israel in the post-exilic period generally. What applies to them in general applies specifically to the Pharisaic party. This is the real nucleus of the people,

which is distinct from the rest of the mass only by its greater strictness and consistency' (456, cf. 472). See also the new version of this section in *History* (n.27), II, 388-403, esp. 402.

The work of Morton Smith was continued by J.Neusner, 'Josephus's Pharisees', in *Ex Orbe Religionum. FS G.Widengren*, SHR 22, Leiden 1972, 224-44, and S.D.Cohen, *Josephus in Galilee and Rome. His Vita and Development as a Historian*, CSCT 8, Leiden 1979. There is a critical discussion of this by, among others, D.R.Schwartz, 'Josephus and Nicolaus on the Pharisees', *JSJ* 14, 1983, 157-71, and S.N.Mason, 'Josephus on the Pharisees Reconsidered: A Critique of Smith/Neusner', *SR* 17, 1988, 455-69, cf. also his dissertation announced for 1991, *Flavius Josephus on the Pharisees*, to be published by Brill, Leiden. D.Goodblatt, 'The Place of the Pharisees in First-Century Judaism: The State of the Debate', *JSJ* 20, 1989, 12-30, is a survey of scholarship with clear sympathy for the Smith/Neusner theory; on 12 n.1 he also cites the present advocates of the traditional view. For the problem see also the contribution by P.Schäfer, *Pharisäismus* (n.125).

227. Josephus, *Antt.* 17.41-49; unfortunately it is no longer possible to illuminate the details of this process. It seems certain that the Pharisees had an influential position among the wives of Herod's 'harem' (17.41); among these in turn the consort of Herod's brother Pheroras had an exalted position (cf.17. 33f., 46). She paid the certainly not inconsiderable sum which Herod imposed on the 6000 Pharisees as a penalty for their refusal to take a loyal oath. In return, Pharisaic teachers prophesied the kingship for her and her consort and their descendants. Evidently Herod's courtiers were also influenced by this, including the eunuch Bagoas, who had been promised that the messianic king Pheroras would restore his procreative powers. Pharisaic messianology seems to have interpreted texts like Isa.56.3f in this direction. Unfortunately we have this account only from the tendentious report of the court historian Nicolaus of Damascus, whom Josephus is following here. For this episode see Wellhausen, *Pharisäer* (n.125), 24-6; Schalit, *Herodes* (n.47), 630f. Ps.Sol. 17 and 18 which appeared at this time are also evidence of the Pharisaic messianic expectation of the time.

228. Hengel, *Zealots* (n.66), 330-7, 369-79.

229. Cf. the various traditions which formed around the so-called eighteen Halakhot (mShab 1.4 9), the content of which represents a radical separation from all that is not Jewish, and their imposition by the Shammaites on pain of death against the Hillelites, cf. jShab 3c, 34ff.; bShab 17a, and Hengel, *Zealots* (n.66), 199-207; cf. also Shir haShirim Zuta on Song of Songs 8.14 and Alon, 'Attitude' (n.125), 43f.; S.Lieberman, *Greek in Jewish Palestine*, New York 1965, 179-84.

230. tSota 14.9 (Zuckermandel, p.320); Bill. 3, 106, see P.Schäfer, *Studien zur Geschichte und Theologie des rabbinischen Judentums*, AGAJU 15, Leiden 1978, 196: 'The primary concern of the school of Yavneh was to stop *this* development (the separation of the two Torot) and preserve or impose a unitary teaching', cf.also 203. That Johanan ben Zakkai was also a member of the party that was ready for compromise becomes clear from his flight from Jerusalem, cf. id., 'Die Flucht Johanan b.Zakkais aus Jerusalem und die Gründung des "Lehrhauses" in Jabne', *ANRW* II 19.2, Berlin and New York 1979, 42-101.

231. Cf. E.E.Urbach, *The Sages – Their Concepts and Beliefs*, Jerusalem 1975, I, 42-101.

232. For this question, which can only be sketched out here, see the works by Michel (n.91), 91-102; J.Bonsirven, *Exégèse Rabbinique et Exégèse Paulinienne*, Paris 1939; id., *Textes Rabbiniques des deux premiers siècles chrétiens pour servir à l'intelligence du Nouveau Testament*, Rome 1955 (797-800, index of Pauline passages); Davies, *Paul and Rabbinic Judaism* (n.5); id., *Jewish and Pauline Studies*, Philadelphia 1984, 89-224; D.Daube, *The New Testament and Rabbinic Judaism*, London 1956, 336ff. (see also the index, 452f.); Schoeps, *Paul* (n.5), 37-40; A.T.Hanson, *Studies in Paul's Technique and Theology*, London 1974, 126ff.; O.Hofius, *Paulusstudien*, WUNT I.51, Tübingen 1989. Special mention should also be made here of the commentaries by Adolf Schlatter on I and II Corinthians and Romans, which, drawing on a wealth of knowledge, he wrote at the end of a long and industrious life.

233. G.Strecker, *Die Johannesbriefe*, KEK 14, 1989, 21 n.4. His criticism is directed against my comment in *Nachfolge und Charisma* (n.159), 89, where I observed on the relationship of Jesus to his disciples that 'the pressing nearness of the kingdom of God itself left no time for a teacher-pupil relationship and for learned studies in rabbinic fashion'.

234. Cf. the completely different verdict of an English scholar, who writes on Billerbeck's commentary: '... it would be worth learning the German language just to be able to use that book' (R.Beckwith, *Themelios* 15, 1990, 81).

235. Cf. e.g. Josephus, *c.Apionem* 1.225, 254; 2.80ff. with Rom.1.23 (Bill. 3, 60f.); *c.Apionem* 2.217f. with Rom.2.15 (Bill. 3, 92); *c.Apionem* 2.293f. with Rom.2.19f. (Bill. 3, 98f.); *BJ* 5.419 with Rom.9 (Bill. 3, 261); *Antt.* 4.233 with I Cor.9.9 (Bill. 3, 384); *Antt.* 15.136 with Gal.3.19 (Bill. 3, 556). The sequence could be continued indefinitely.

236. On this cf. E.Grafe, 'Das Verhältnis der paulinischen Schriften zur Sapientia Salmonis', in *Theologische Abhandlungen, FS C.von Weizsäcker*, Freiburg 1892, 251-86; A.Fridrichsen, 'Zur Auslegung von Röm.1.19f.', *ZNW* 17, 1916, 154-68 (this shows by means of the Romans passage the

proximity of the Pauline statements to Wisdom and similar Hellenistic material); O.Eissfeldt, *The Old Testament: An Introduction*, Oxford 1965, 602; H.Hübner, 'Zur Ethik der Sapientia Salomonis', in *Studien zum Text und zur Ethik des Neuen Testaments. FS H.Greeven*, ed. W.Schrage, Berlin and New York 1986, 166-87. For the subject see also J.M.Reese, *Hellenistic Influence on the Book of Wisdom and its Consequences*, AnBib 41, Rome 1970.

237. See Michel, KEK (n.145), 63-5.

238. Cf. A.Fridrichsen, *Der wahre Jude und sein Lob. Röm.2,28f.*, SO 1, 1922, 39-49. The whole chapter Romans 2 corresponds to a synagogue preaching in diatribe style, see also Sanders, *Paul and Palestinian Judaism* (n.212), 123, 'homiletical material from Diaspora Judaism'; Michel, KEK (n.145), 96f.; W.Schmithals, *Der Römerbrief. Ein Kommentar*, Gütersloh 1988, 72ff.

239. See now A.M.Schwemer, 'Gott als "König" und seine "Königsherrschaft" in den Sabbatliedern aus Qumran', in *Königsherrschaft Gottes und himmlischer Kult*, ed. M.Hengel and A.M.Schwemer, WUNT I.55, Tübingen 1991, 75–118.

240. See Riesner, *Frühzeit* (n.12), and above n.221.

241. For the sources see esp. W.Bauer, 'Essener', *PW Suppl* 4, 1924, 386-430 (also in id., *Aufsätze und Kleine Schriften*, Tübingen 1967, 1-59); A.Adam, *Antike Berichte über die Essener*, new ed. by C.Burchard, KlT 182, Berlin ²1972.

242. *Vita*, 10f.

243. Hengel, *Judaism and Hellenism* I (n.93), 175ff.

244. Cf. H.Braun, *Qumran und das Neue Testament* I, Tübingen 1966, 169-240; J.Murphy O'Connor and J.H.Charlesworth (ed.), *Paul and the Dead Sea Scrolls*, New York ²1990 (originally London 1958). The preface to the new edition by J.H.Charlesworth describes how since the first publication 'the Jewishness of Paul and his indebtedness to early Jewish thought' has gradually become (re-)established in the scholarly world (XI).

245. For the question of free will see G.Maier, *Mensch und freier Wille*, WUNT I.12, Tübingen 1971; Hengel, *Judaism and Hellenism* II (n.93), 333 (index s.v. Will, Freedom of); id., 'Qumran' (n.211), 353f., 364f.

246. 1QS 11.9 *bāśār 'āwel*; Braun, *Qumran* (n.244), 178.

247. 1QS 11.14; cf. I Cor.6.11; Braun, *Qumran* (n.244), 191.

248. 1QpHab 5.7f.; CD 15.7; Braun, *Qumran* (n.244), 205.

249. 1 QH 13.11f.; Braun, *Qumran* (n.244), 200.

250. Cf. Rom.2.7; 7.12f.; 12.2; II Cor.9.8. The translation derives from the photograph in E.Qimron and J.Strugnell, 'An Unpublished Halakhic Letter from Qumran', *Biblical Archaeology Today*, Israel Exploration Society, Jerusalem 1985, 400-7. See also below n.306 on 'reckoning for righteousness'.

251. J.Gnilka, '2.Kor 6,14-7,1 im Lichte der Qumranschriften und der Zwölf-Patriarchen-Testamente', in *Neutestamentliche Aufsätze. FS J.Schmid*, ed. J.Blinzler et al., Regensburg 1963, 86-99 (English version in *Paul and the Dead Sea Scrolls* [n.244], 48-68); J.A.Fitzmyer, 'Qumran and the Interpolated Paragraph 2 Cor.6.14-7.1', *CBQ* 23, 1961, 271-80 (also in *Qumran*, WdF 410, ed. K.E.Grözinger et al., Darmstadt 1981), 'a non-Pauline interpolation'. But how could this fragment have strayed into a letter of Paul in Corinth? Are the letters of Paul full of such interpolations? Might it even come from an unknown letter of Paul? Cf. also H.D.Betz, '2 Cor.6.14-7.1: An Anti-Pauline Fragment?', *JBL* 92, 1973, 88-108. By contrast, the authenticity of the 'fragment' has been argued for in recent times by G.D.Fee, 'II Corinthians VI, 14 – VII,1 and Food offered to Idols', *NTS* 23, 1977, 140-61; M.E.Thrall, 'The Problem of II Cor.VI,14 – VII, 1 in some Recent Discussion', *NTS* 24, 1978, 132-48; G.K.Beale, 'The O.T. Background of Reconciliation in 2 Cor 5-7 and its Bearing on the Literary Problem of 2 Cor 6,15-7,1', *NTS* 35, 1989, 550-81. Cf. also N.A.Dahl, *Studies in Paul*, Minneapolis 1977, 69: 'The possibility that the apostle himself incorporated the fragment may after all have to be reconsidered.'

252. Hengel, *Zealots* (n.66), 190-7; see also R.Meyer, 'Die Figurendarstellung in der Kunst des späthellenistischen Judentums', in id., *Arbeitsethos* (n.115), originally *Jud* 5, 1949, 1-40, 40-62, esp. 42ff. on Zealot iconoclasm; V.Sussman, 'Early Jewish Iconoclasm on Pottery Lamps', *IEJ* 23, 1973, 46-9. There was more leeway here before the Maccabaean revolt. One might compare the late-Persian early Hellenistic YHWD coins with those of the Hasmonaeans, Herodians, procurators and the two rebellions. For the earliest period see L.Mildenberg in H.Weippert, *Palästina in vorhellenistischer Zeit*, Handbuch der Archäologie II/1, Munich 1988, 721-8; also Y.Meshorer, *Jewish Coins of the Second Temple Period*, Tel Aviv 1967.

253. Cf. also the polemical answer of R.Johanan (died 279) to R.Abdimi, who thought that after the destruction of the temple prophecy had been taken from the prophets and given to the wise: 'Since the day the temple was destroyed, prophecy was taken from the prophets and given to fools and small children' (bBB 12a/b).

254. tPes 4.2; jPes 6,1,33a line 40; bPes 66a: see P.Schäfer, *Die Vorstellung vom Heiligen Geist in der Rabbinischen Literatur*, StANT 23, Munich 1972, 124f. For Hillel and his school as bearers of the Spirit see ibid., 94f., 147.

255. I Cor.5.6-8; Acts 20.6.16; cf. 2.1; John 2.13,23; 4.45; 5.1; 7.2-14,37.

256. Cf. also Jeremias, *Jerusalem* (n.115), 66ff.; Safrai, *Wallfahrt* (n.160), 65-93 on the pilgrimage from the Diaspora; Hengel, *'Hellenization'* (n.37), 12ff.

257. Ibid. The picture that I have drawn of linguistic and cultural conditions in Judaea in the first century CE is now amazingly confirmed by writing, ostraca, graffiti and papyri discovered from Masada; see the concluding report (n.78) and below, n.259. For Qumran see now E.Ulrich, 'A Greek Paraphrase of Exodus on Papyrus from Qumran Cave 4', in *Studien zur Septuaginta Robert Hanhart in Ehren*, ed. D.Fraenkel et al., AAWG.PH. F 190 = MSU 20, 1990, 287-298: 289f.

258. There are exact figures in the catalogue of Jewish ossuaries prepared by L.Y.Rahmani: 228 inscriptions, 178 Hebrew or Aramaic; 71 Greek, 15 or 16 bilingual; 2 Latin, 1 Palmyrene, see *'Hellenization'* (n.37), 10.

259. See Goodman, *Ruling Class* (n.219), 51-75. Cf. now also the Greek ostraca found in Masada which go back to its Jewish inhabitants and defenders; while they are quantitatively much scarcer than the Aramaic and Hebrew ostraca, they are nevertheless significant for 'the Jewish habit of employing Aramaic and Hebrew on the one hand and Greek on the other for informal writing... It seems that Greek was used for writing names, for writing abecedaria and rarely for longer instructions or letters' (*Masada* [n.78] II, 113). Bilingual *tituli picti* were also found at Masada (nos.878-90, 924-7; II, 188-90, 202f. and plate 41). Cf. the resumé by H.M.Cotton and J.Geiger (Vol.II, 9f.) on the use of Greek by the inhabitants of Masada: 'The evidence presented here... may provide at least a part of the long sought-for missing link in the discussion of the Jews of Palestine' (9). 'The most remarkable fact is the apparent absence of barbarisms and solecisms... Nor does the Greek script attest anywhere a lack of familiarity with it' (10). Further on the Greek names found in Masada: 'Many of these, such as Simon, Judas, Eleazar, Salome and Mariam, are among the most widely current Jewish names of the Second Temple period; other names are Greek but can often with good reason be assigned to Jews. Zenon, Abaskantos and Kosmas are elsewhere only rarely attested as Jewish names, while others, such as Aminias, Lykias and Kypselos, make their first appearance here as Jewish names. The higher degree of Hellenization of people bearing Greek names is suggested by the fact that Greek names are written more often in Greek than in Jewish script. Hebrew names, on the other hand, appear frequently both in Jewish and in Greek characters' (10).

260. See Hengel, 'Jakobusbrief' (n.101), 251, 270 nn.31,33.

261. Safrai, *Wallfahrt* (n.160), 89f. with good reason identifies this Tarsian synagogue with that of the Cilicians in Acts 6.9, cf. Hengel, *Jesus and Paul* (n.9), 16f.

262. See the extended collection in Hengel, *'Hellenization'* (n.37), 81ff.

Cf. also in Masada (*Masada* [n.78] I,26, no.424) an ostracon which with *hqrny* perhaps denotes a Jew from Cyrenaica.

263. Cf. *CIJ* no.1265, the similarly written *tdywn*.

264. On this see A.F.Zimmermann, *Die urchristlichen Lehrer*, WUNT II.12, Tübingen²1988, 69-91. The teachers' graves seem to have belonged to a family. According to pottery finds in these tombs they come from the time of Herod the Great (70 n.3). Here it seems likely that this family is identical with that of Theodotus, who founded the synagogue, which can similarly be traced back into the Herodian period, see Hengel, 'Between Jesus and Paul' (n.9), 17. In his investigation of the ossuary inscriptions Zimmermann comes to the conclusion that these must be 'Jewish religious teachers from the period before 70, and most likely Pharisaic scribes' (85f.).

265. See above 13 and n.102; cf. also Safrai, *Wallfahrt* (n.160), 69f., 82ff.; F.Hüttenmeister and G.Reeg, *Die antiken Synagogen in Israel*, TAVO.B 12.1, Tübingen 1977, 192-5, 525.

266. The Pharisees are the only group known to us to have been interested in a broad and intensive education of the people in the law. Therefore they also had the greatest influence on the people.

267. Cf. E.Rivkin, 'Prolegomenon', in *Judaism and Christianity*, reprint in one volume of the work which appeared under this title in 1937-1938, New York 1969, LV, LVV, cf. also XXVI; by contrast L.L.Grabbe, 'Synagogues in Pre-70 Palestine: a Reassessment', *JTS* 39, 1988, 401-10, disputes any connection between Pharisaism and the synagogue. Unfortunately Grabbe gives no answer to the basic question why the expansion of the synagogue in Jewish Palestine is only attested so late, coincides chronologically with the heyday of Pharisaism in Eretz Israel, and is taken over not only without any problems in Talmudic literature but also in close connection with the school is dated back to the time of Moses and Joshua.

268. Hengel, 'Proseuche und Synagoge' (n.93), 143-52.

269. Norden, *Kunstprosa* (n.198), 506f.

270. T.Schmeller, *Paulus und die "Diatribe"*, NTA NF 19, Münster 1987. E.A.Judge, 'St Paul and Classical Society', *JAC* 15, 1972, 19-36: 33, is critical of a derivation of Pauline rhetoric from the praxis of the diatribe.

271. See above n.25. Siegert describes the sermons as 'free omissions by a theologically trained orator... on a biblical story, ...using all the means of the *genus epidicticum*... Playful practices are interspersed with the *genus judiciale* and the *genus deliberativum*... clear recollections of the orator to his school' (6, for the style of the diatribe, 7).

272. *De oratore* I, 146, cf. Norden, *Kunstprosa* (n.198), I, 81. In direct connection with Paul, Augustine, *Doct. Christ*.IV.7.11 (ed. I.Martin,

CCSL 32, 123.26ff.), asserts: 'So just as I do not say that the apostle followed the precepts of eloquence, I do not deny that eloquence followed his wisdom' (I owe this reference to U.Heckel). C.F.G.Heinrici, KEK 6, Göttingen [8]1900, who notes 'contacts with Hellenistic culture' and 'analogies of thought construction' with Paul (441), regards the apostle 'not as a studied orator in a legal, ceremonial or teaching context', since 'the real features of the school, like indications of parts, technical transitional formulae and summaries, are lacking in Paul'. However, 'his way of arguing and fighting is closely related to the achievements of classical eloquence... But if in Paul's letters one can recognize an original use of means of persuasion which are discussed theoretically in ancient rhetoric, this shows how congenial he found the Hellenistic education of his time, his capacity to be an apostle to the Gentiles' (39-41). Schmeller, *'Diatribe'* (n.270), 91f., wants to assume for Paul 'most of all, alongside an indubitable Jewish education a moderate influence of elements of Hellenistic education, since this was just as possible with a Diaspora Jew as with a Graeco-Palestinian'.

273. See Hengel, *'Hellenization'* (n.37), 35ff.

274. See above, n.219.

275. Josephus, *Vita* 16: see Hengel, *'Hellenization'* (n.37), 23f.

276. Acts 24.1-9 (2-4). For the teachers of rhetoric in antiquity see Marrou, *Education* (n.21), 268ff., 283ff., 380ff.; for its dissemination in the Latin West of the empire, 405-12. Presumably Roman state power had a certain interest in teaching grammar and rhetoric in Jewish Palestine, as there it disseminated the predominant culture of the empire, see Hengel, *'Hellenization'* (n.37), 32-44.

277. See E.A.Judge, *St Paul and Classical Society* (n.270), 32: 'When Paul withdrew from the synagogue in one city after another he must have carried on his activities under the umbrella of some accepted social convention or institution which made such meetings easy. It does little to help answer this question to examine Paul's enterprise in the light of subsequent ecclesiastical practice, or that of the mystery cults. In these cases we are dealing with religious procedures, in which order and ceremony, decorum and restraint were of the essence of the matter. But Paul belongs to a society of vigorous talk and argument about behaviour and ideas, carried on through privately organized meetings.' 'Vigorous talk and argument' was what he had learned in Jerusalem.,

278. On this see Hengel, 'Proseuche und Synagoge' (n.93), 183-90; id., *'Hellenization'* (n.37,) 23-9; Safrai, *Wallfahrt* (n.160), 261f.

279. R.Jewett, *A Chronology of Paul's Life*, Philadelphia 1979 (English edition *Dating Paul's Life*, London 1980), largely keeps to the existing consensus. On the other hand for Lüdemann, *Paul* (n.6), it was 'suspect'

(1), so he attempted a completely new approach, seeking to rely only on the information in the letters of Paul. Here he took up earlier approaches by J.Knox and D.W.Riddle (1, 29 nn.2f.). Now cf. Riesner, *Frühzeit* (n.12), who has defended the traditional view with new and better arguments.

280. Irenaeus, *Adv.haer.* I.3.2; I.30.14, cf. W.Schneemelcher, *Neutestamentliche Apokryphen* I, Tübingen ⁵1987, 237, 239; II, ⁵1989, 558.

281. A.v.Harnack, *Geschichte der altchristlichen Literatur bis Eusebius* II.1, Leipzig 1897, 236f.; id., 'Chronologische Berechnung des "Tags von Damaskus"', SPAW.PH 1912, Berlin 1912, 673-82 (= *Kleine Schriften zur Alten Kirche*, Leipzig 1908, 2, 190-9); id., *Mission* (n.27), 60f. n.5. Harnack's arguments were taken up by Riesner, *Frühzeit* (n.12), 57-64, who moreover refers in this connection to neglected traditions of the church's calendar of feasts, which celebrates the conversion of Paul on 25 January; it is said to have taken place in the second year after the ascension of Jesus. Riesner then arrives at the possible date of 31/32 CE (64). Cf. Jewett, *Chronology [Dating]* (n.279), 29f.

282. Cf. P.R.Jones, 'I Corinthians 15:8: Paul the Last Apostle', *TynB* 36, 1985, 3-34.

283. Cf. M.Hengel, 'Christology and New Testament Chronology', in *Between Jesus and Paul* (n.9), 30-47.

284. On this see A.Strobel, *Die Stunde der Wahrheit*, WUNT I.21, Tübingen 1980, 61-94; O.Betz, 'Probleme des Prozesses Jesu', *ANRW* II. 25.1, Berlin and New York 1982, 546-647, esp. 625-39: 'Therefore the arrested Jesus must have been regarded as a false prophet and deceiver of the people who according to the Torah deserved no mercy' (639), cf. Deut.13.9.

285. Cf. above all the old confession Rom.1.3f. and on it M.Hengel, *The Son of God*, London and Philadelphia 1976, 59ff.; U.Wilckens, EKK VI.1, ²1987, 57-61, 64-7. For Ps.110.1 and christology see my forthcoming article in the Festschrift to celebrate the 65th birthday of Ferdinand Hahn, *Anfänge der Christologie*, Göttingen 1991, 43–73.

286. Josephus, *Antt.* 20, 200-2. The sentence 'Those of the inhabitants of the city who were considered the most fair-minded and who were strict in observance of the law were offended at this' can only mean Pharisees, see M.Hengel, 'Jakobus der Herrenbruder – der erste "Papst"?', *Glaube und Eschatologie, FS W.G.Kümmel*, Tübingen 1985, 71-104: 73ff.

287. For the literature (see also nn.1,2 above): Burchard, *Zeuge* (n.14), 40-51; Haacker, 'Berufung' (n.157); A.J.Hultgren, 'Persecutions' (n.130); S.Kim, *The Origin of Paul's Gospel*, WUNT II.4, Tübingen ²1984, 32-50: 'Paul the Persecutor'; C.Dietzfelbinger, *Die Berufung des Paulus als Ursprung*

seiner Theologie, WMANT 58, Neukirchen-Vluyn 1985, 4-42: 'Paulus als Verfolger'; Riesner, *Frühzeit* (n.12), 53-6.

288. For the translation see below, 41.

289. His designation of himself as ἔκτρωμα in I Cor.15.8 is certainly also to be understood in this connection; on this see A.Fridrichsen, 'Paulus Abortivus. Zu I Kor.15.8', in *FS O.A.Danielsson*, Uppsala 1932, 78-85, who rightly stresses that with this vivid expression Paul is describing his pre-Christian period as a persecutor; cf. also C.Wolff, ThHK VII.2, 1982, 169f.

290. Cf. I Cor.15.8ff.; 9.1; Phil.3.6: all these texts presuppose earlier information if they are to be understood by the reader.

291. Acts 7.58; 22.20; cf. mSanh 6.4.

292. Acts 8.3; 9.1f.; 22.4f,19, cf. 71f. below on πορθεῖν.

293. Cf. Burchard, *Zeuge* (n.14), 50f.

294. Ibid., 51. G.Klein, *Die Zwölf Apostel*, FRLANT 77, Göttingen 1961, 115-28, argues that Luke deliberately drew a terrifying picture of Paul as persecutor: 'All these features serve to give the formal profile of a picture of "Saul" the content of which is clearly concerned to bring the individual to the level of his environment, but also to cause horror at his action' (127, cf. 122: for him Paul is a typical Jew, nothing else).

295. See above, 28.

296. According to Bauer, *Lexicon* (n.143), 'youth, young man, from about the 24th to the 40th year', 534.

297. Acts 8.1. See Hengel, 'Between Jesus and Paul', in *Between Jesus and Paul* (n.9).

298. For the history of research into Acts 6-7 generally see H.W.Neudörfer, *Stephanuskreis* (n.149).

299. Even in Tübingen there is an English-language church service for students and guests from the Anglo-Saxon world.

300. Acts 6.9; see Bill.2.662-5; Hengel, 'Between Jesus and Paul' (n.9), 16f.

301. It is remarkable that these Jews (Jewish Christians) from Cyrenaica and Cyprus who are often stressed in the earliest tradition play no further role later on. They come from what was formerly the Ptolemaic sphere of rule, which had a particularly large Jewish Diaspora and therefore also many inhabitants who returned to Jerusalem (Cyrenaica: Mark 15.21 par.; Acts 6.9; 11.20; 13.1, Lucius of Cyrene; Cyprus: Acts 4.36, Barnabas; 11.19f.; 13.4; 15.39; 21.16). Presumably predominantly Jewish Christian missionaries were active there, as also in Egypt; the Christians in this area were almost completely wiped out along with the Jews by the fearful rebellion of 115-17 CE. On this see Schürer, *History* (n.27), III.1, 60ff., 94f.: Cyrenaica; 68f.: Cyprus; G.Lüderitz, 'Zeugnisse'

(n.27); Hengel, 'Between Jesus and Paul' (n.9), 17f., on inscriptions in Jerusalem.

302. Acts 6.11,13; on this see Stephen's speech in 7.48-53 and the accusation against Paul in 21.28. See also below 81ff.

303. Stephen's speech does not really fit the charge, nor is it sufficient reason for the tumultuous reaction of the distinguished court. It is difficult to connect it directly with Stephen, of whom in fact we know hardly anything. The language is Lukan, but Luke has incorporated presumably earlier tradition coming from the circle of the Hellenists, cf. G.Stemberger, 'Die Stephanusrede (Apg 7) und die jüdische Tradition', in *Jesus in der Verkündigung der Kirche*, SNTU Ser.A 1, Vienna and Munich 1976, 154-74; J.Kilgallen, *The Stephen Speech*, AnBib 67, Rome 1976. Cf above, 83.

304. On this see Burchard, *Zeuge* (n.14), 26ff., with what to my mind are the best reflections on the matter. That Luke does not describe the stoning in accordance with mSanh 6.1-4 need not rest on ignorance, as Schneider, *Die Apostelgeschichte* I, HTK V.1, assumes. This is not a legal execution, and the tractate Sanhedrin depicts more ideal than real legal conditions.

305. See Hengel, *Zealots* (n.66), 177f.,180f.

306. For the exemplary zeal of Phinehas cf. Hengel, *Zealots* (n.66), 150-77. The formula in Gen.15.6, ἐλογίσθη αὐτῷ εἰς δικαιοσυνήν, which is so significant for Paul in Rom.4.3; Gal.3.6 (cf. John 7.23), now appears in the letter from Qumran to the godless high priest, at the end of the final warning: *wnḥšbh lk lṣdqh* (4Q MMT c33). See also above 51 and n.250.

307. See Hengel, 'Luke the Historian' (n.9), 119-21.

308. F.Passow, *Handwörterbuch der griechischen Sprache* s.v. (Vol.2.1, Lepizig ⁵1852 [reprinted 1970], 1032); see also Bauer, *Lexicon* (n.143), s.v.: 'pillage, make havoc of, destroy, annihilate' (693). In the LXX it appears, significantly, only in IV Macc.4.23; 11.4; in Symmachus still in Deut.2.34; Jer.34 (41).22; 37(44).8 as a translation of *lqd*. It is applied to the destruction of Jerusalem in Josephus, *Antt.* 10.135; Greek Apocalypse of Baruch 1.1, and often in the Jewish Sibyls, cf. C.Spicq, *Notes de Lexicographie Néotestamentaire II*, OBO 22.2, Fribourg CH and Göttingen 1978, 723f.

309. Spicq, *Notes* (n.308), 723.

310. 'Le sens du verbe πορθεῖν (Gal.1.13,23; Acts 9.21)', in APOPHO-RETA, *FS E.Haenchen*, BZNW 30, Berlin 1964, 178-86.

311. Hengel, *Zealots* (n.66), 163-70, 174-7.

312. On this see Bill. 3, 527-30. Attempts were made to avoid death by limiting the punishment, but cf. mMakk 3.13, 'And the striker strikes with one hand and with all his force' and further (3.14), 'If he dies under

his hand, he is free'. Cf. also Hengel, 'Between Jesus and Paul' (n.9), 21ff. and 158 nn.133f. For the possibility of lynch justice see mSanh and id., *Zealots* (n.66), 480, index s.v. lynch law, but especially 186f., 395f.; also J.Juster, *Les Juîfs dans l'Empire Romain*, Paris 1914, II, 158f.; A.N.Sherwin White, *Roman Society and Roman Law in the New Testament*, Oxford 1963, 39-43.

313. Burchard, *Zeuge* (n.14), 50 n.37, also produces good arguments in favour of Jerusalem as the place of Paul's persecuting activity.

314. On this see Riesner, *Frühzeit* (n.12). Paul could have received the five synagogue punishments (II Cor.11.24) above all during the fourteen years 'in the region of Syria and Cilicia' (Gal.1.12; 2.1). The emphatic early position of 'in Damascus' in II Cor.11.32 suggests that the details of place are also important for Paul; the point here is that Paul is now speaking to the Corinthians not of the vision at his call, but of his experience of weakness and persecution in Damascus (I owe this comment to U.Heckel [see n. 27]).

315. O.Betz, 'Judäa', *EWNT* II, 470; Hengel, 'Luke the Historian' (n.9), 99.

316. Josephus, *BJ* 2.559-61; 7.368; cf. *Vita* 27; see also Schürer, *History* (n.27), III.1, 13f.; R.Riesner, 'Damaskus II. Im Neuen Testament', *GBL* I.3, Wuppertal and Giessen [2]1990, 249f.; M.Görg, 'Damaskus', *Neues Bibellexikon*, fasc.3, Zürich 1990, 379ff.; for the history of the city in the Hellenistic-Roman period see Benzinger, 'Damascus', *PW* IV.2, 1901, cols.2042-8, for its economic significance, T.Weber, 'ΔΑΜΑΣΚΙΝΑ', *ZDPV* 105, 1989, 151-65.

317. Cf.CD 6.19; 8.21; 19.33f.; 20.12.

318. According to the Tannaitic list of the boundary of the land of Israel which was important for halachic practice (tShevi IV.11, Lieberman 181; Sifre Dtn §51, Finkelstein 117f.; jShevi VI, 1, 36c; Jalqut Dtn 874; TgNum 34; on this see Stemberger, 'Landes Israel' [n.175], 182; further Neubauer, *La géographie du Talmud*, Paris 1868 [reprinted Hildesheim 1967], 10-24); S.Klein, 'Das tannaitische Grenzverzeichnis Palästinas', *HUCA* 5, 1928, 197-59), Damascus belongs at least to the frontier area of the Eretz Israel. This text may be relatively old (Klein, 240, dates it to the time of Herod, around 20 BCE; Stemberger, 'Landes Israel', by contrast is sceptical), and at any rate belong to the earliest texts of the Tosephta (thus P.Freimark, *Die Tosefta* I.2, Stuttgart 1971, 197ff.) and orientates itself on what is in fact the Jewish population within the biblical land of Israel in its time (thus Stemberger). In halachic terms the Syrian sphere has an 'intermediary status between Israel and abroad' (Stemberger, 'Landes Israel', 198 n.224; cf. Orl III,3; AZ I,8; tTer II, 9; Lieberman, 113f.). This status was the subject of intensive discussion

which Stemberger reports: 'The question is discussed by the rabbis in Jabneh, but also in Usha. R.Aqiba declares in respect of the sabbath year: "All that is allowed to the like in the land is done in Syria" (Shebi VI.2; cf.TShebi IV.12, Lieberman 181). It is not clear from the text whether this parallel between the land of Israel and Syria also applies to the prohibitions of the sabbath year. R.Simeon puts forward a halachic identification of Syria with Israel in Shebi VI.5-6: he refers to the tradition that products of the sabbath year may not be sent abroad, but may go to Syria. Hallah IV.7 is about fields which a Jew in Syria has leased from a non-Jew. According to R.Eliezer its produce was subject to the tithe and the law of the sabbath year, but not according to Rabban Gamaliel II. Evidently Eliezer regarded Syria as part of the land of Israel and Gamaliel did not' (183). Stemberger (184f.) assumes here that the halachic boundaries of the country were first extended and then later reduced again in order to stem the incipient migration of Jews from Palestine for economic reasons. Accordingly the wider halachic boundary line which includes Syria will have to be regarded as the earlier (more nationalistic?) tradition.

In addition there were also certain messianic expectations in connection with Damascus. On the basis of the promise to Abraham in Gen.15.18-21, in rabbinic tradition of the messianic time an extension of the frontiers of the land of Israel was expected (thus e.g. GenR 44.23; jQid I,9,61d; jShevi VI.1.36b; bBB 56a, 13; cf. in Bill.4, 899, and Stemberger, 'Landes Israel', also Bill.2, 689) which in that case should also embrace Arabia and Damascus – which is mentioned several times and indeed according to II Sam.8.6 was part of the kingdom of David. Behind this is a broader exegetical tradition, cf. Stemberger, 193: 'One biblical example is Zech. 9.1: "Saying. The word of the Lord rests on the Land of Hadrach, Damascus is its resting place." That attests "that Jerusalem will reach to Damascus"; for it says, "and Damascus is its resting place", and "its resting place" is one other than Jerusalem; for it says, "That is my resting place for ever" (Ps.132.14). The continuation is concerned with the exegesis of Ezek.41.7: "And it will extend and turn above, for the house will be surrounded above, around the house; therefore the house will be broad above." This description of the future temple is interpreted in such a way "that the land of Israel will extend and rise from all sides like this fig tree, which is narrow below and broad above. And the gates of Jerusalem will reach to Damascus." And so it says: "Your nose is like the tower of Lebanon that looks towards Damascus" (Song of Songs 7.5). And the exiles will come and camp in it; for it is said, "And Damascus is his resting place" (Zech. 9.1)...' (Sifre Deut. 1, Finkelstein 7f.). Cf.

further A.Levanon, 'Damascus', *JE* V, 1239; A.Neubauer, *La géographie du Talmud*, Paris 1868 (= Hildesheim 1967), 293, 296.

319. It is nevertheless striking that in Stephen's speech Amos 5.26 is quoted with a remarkable deviation from the Massoretic and LXX text; the 'to Damascus' is replaced by 'Babylon' (7.43). Is the reason for this simply the historical fact of the exile in Babylon or is Damascus omitted here as a place of judgment for theological reasons? On this question cf. N.Wieder, 'The "Land of Damascus" and Messianic Redemption', *JJS* 30, 1969, 86-8; S.Sabugal, 'La conversión de S.Pablo en Damasco: ciudad de Siria o región de Qumrân?', *Augustinianum* 15, 1975, 213-24, esp. 219f. (but his conclusion that the conversion of Paul took place near Qumran is to be rejected); Riesner, *Frühzeit* (n.12), 197-201.

320. This is stressed by Burchard, *Zeuge* (n.154), 50 n.37. This would also correspond to Paul's later action, which is usually very self-willed.

321. A.Fridrichsen, 'Zur Stephanusrede AG.7', *Le Monde Oriental* 25, 1931, 44-52, esp.50f. Stephen and Paul probably met for the first time at the stoning.

322. On this see the argument between J.D.G.Dunn, 'The Relationship between Paul and Jerusalem according to Galatians 1 and 2', *NTS* 28, 1982, 461-78, and O.Hofius,'Gal.1.18: ἱστορῆσαι Κηφᾶν', *ZNW* 75, 1984, 73-85, and now in id., *Paulusstudien* (n.232), 255-67; J.D.G.Dunn, 'Once More – Gal. 1.18....', *ZNW* 76, 1985, 138f.

323. For the psychological interpretation as one example among many see Deissmann, *Paul* (n.5), 66, 79, 91, who reads out of Rom.7.9-11: 'Paul, who had experienced this fall, cannot have had a sunny, cheerful youth. Law, Sin and Death already in early life cast their gloomy shadows in the soul of the gifted boy.' The merit of having deprived these theories of foundation is that of W.G.Kümmel, whose 1929 dissertation, *Römer 7 und die Bekehrung des Paulus*, Leipzig 1929, is reprinted in expanded form as *Römer 7 und das Bild des Menschen im Neuen Testament*, ThB 53, Munich 1974.

324. Luke 18.10-12 is the narrative transposition of this self-understanding.

325. II Cor.4.6; cf. Rom.4.17b; I Cor 1.28.

326. Phil.3.7; cf. II Cor.5.17.

327. Thus the impressive formulation of A.Schweitzer, *The Mysticism of the Apostle Paul*, London 1931, 225: 'The doctrine of righteousness by faith is therefore a subsidiary crater, which has formed within the rim of the main crater – the mystical doctrine of redemption through the being-in-Christ.' Schweitzer is taken up again and defended by Sanders, *Paul* (n.212), 434-42; F.Watson, *Paul, Judaism and the Gentiles*, SNTS.MS 56, Cambridge 1986, 179, also comes to the conclusion, 'It is therefore completely wrong to regard the phrase *sola gratia* as the key to Paul's

theology.' Here in my view Paul is basically misunderstood because this approach does not really take seriously his origin as a Pharisee and his activity as a persecutor, or his shaping as a theological teacher. Romans is no chance product, but a fundamental theological account by the apostle. Paul, the persecutor and enemy of Christ, has experienced in himself the significance of radical grace.

328. Cf. Kim, 'Origin' (n.287), 269-329 and 355-8, where he argues with H.Räisänen, *Paul and the Law*, WUNT I.29, Tübingen ²1987. Räisänen denies the fundamental significance of the Damascus experience for Pauline theology (cf.255f.). It is significant that in chapter 8 of his work, 'The Origins of Paul's Conception of the Law' (229-63), among the seven possibilities he cites he does not mention the Damascus event at all. Räisänen defended his position in 'Paul's Call Experience and his Later View of the Law', in id., *The Torah and Christ*, PFES 45, Helsinki 1986, 55-92, and in 'Paul's Conversion and the Development of his View of the Law', *NTS* 33, 1987, 404-19. For the fundamental significance of the conversion before Damascus for Pauline theology cf. also M.Goguel, 'ΚΑΤΑ ΔΙΚΑΙΟΣΥΝΗΝ ΤΗΝ ΕΝ ΝΟΜΩ (Phil.3.6). Remarques sur un Aspect de la Conversion de Paul', *JBL* 53, 1934, 257-67; Dietzfelbinger, *Berufung* (n.287), Part III, 'Konsequenzen der Berufung' (90-147); U.Luck, 'Die Bekehrung des Paulus und das Paulinische Evangelium. Zur Frage der Evidenz in Botschaft und Theologie des Apostels', *ZNW* 76, 1985, 187-208. See also O.Hofius, 'Das Gesetz des Mose und das Gesetz Christi', in *Paulusstudien* (n.232), 75-102, esp.75ff. and 'Wort Gottes und Glaube bei Paulus', ibid., 148-74: 162.

329. See M.Hengel, *The Johannine Question*, London and Philadelphia 1989, 40ff., 51ff.

330. See Hengel, *Between Jesus and Paul* (n.9), 18ff., nn.257-9.

331. Cf. Acts 11.20ff.; see also 15.1; Gal.2.1ff., 11ff.

332. See Hengel, 'Between Jesus and Paul' (n.9), 23ff.; id., 'Jesus und die Tora', *ThBeitr* 9, 1978, 152-72. See also A.Weiser, 'Zur Gesetzes- und Tempelkritik der "Hellenisten"', in *Das Gesetz im Neuen Testament*, ed. K.Kertelge, QD 108, Freiburg, Basle and Vienna 1986, 146-68. Cf. also above, n. 69ff.

333. M.Hengel, *The Atonement*, London 1981, 47-55.

334. On this see 11 QT 64,7-12, where this curse is transferred to the person executed by crucifixion. For the disputed question whether crucifixion or hanging is in question here cf. D.J.Halperin, 'Crucifixion, the Nahum Pesher and the Rabbinic Penalty of Strangulation', *JJS* 32, 1981, 32-46; with further literature A.S.van der Woude, *ThR* 54,1989, 242f. On this see Hengel, *Crucifixion* (n.62), 84f. and id., 'Rabbinische

Legende und frühpharisäische Geschichte. Simon b.Shetach und die achtzig Hexen von Askalon', *AHAW.PH* 1982, second section, 27-35.

335. On this see Hofius, 'Gesetz des Mose' (n.328), 63f., 73. The Christian Paul then finds the positive understanding of the death of the messiah Jesus on the cross as representative dying for all in Isa.53, which in all probability had already been applied to the death of Jesus by the Hellenists (I Cor.15.3; cf. Acts 8.32ff.) or even by himself, Mark 10.45; 14.24; I Cor.11.23ff.

336. In quotations and allusions Ps.110.1 is by far the most cited Old Testament messianic text in the NT, cf. already the kerygmatic formula Rom.8.34 and D.M.Hay, *Glory at the Right Hand*, SBL.MS 18, Nashville 1973; M.Gourgues, *A la droite de Dieu*, Paris 1978; Hengel, 'Ps.110' (n.285).

Abbreviations

AAWG.PH	Abhandlungen der Akademie der Wissenschaften in Göttingen. Philologisch-historische Klasse
AHAW.PH	Abhandlungen der Heidelberger Akademie der Wissenschaften. Philosophisch-historische Klasse
AGAJU	Arbeiten zur Geschichte des antiken Judentums und des Urchristentums
AJBI	*Annual of the Japanese Biblical Institute*
AJP	*American Journal of Philology*
ALGHJ	Arbeiten zur Literatur und Geschichte des hellenistischen Judentum
AnBib	Analecta Biblica
ANRW	*Aufstieg und Niedergang der römischen Welt*
ATANT	Abhandlungen zur Theologie des Alten und Neuen Testaments
BASOR	Bulletin of the American Schools of Oriental Research
BCH	*Bulletin de Correspondance Hellénique*
BETL	Bibliotheca Ephemeridum Theologicarum Lovaniensium
BFCT	Beiträge zur Förderung christlicher Theologie
BGBE	Beiträge zur Geschichte der biblischen Exegese
BiKi	*Bibel und Kirche*
BHTh	Beiträge zur historischen Theologie
BS	*Biblische Studien*
BSGRT	Bibliotheca Scriotorum Graecorum et Romanorum Terbneriana
BZ	*Biblische Zeitschrift*
BZNW	Beiträge zur Zeitschrift für die neutestamentliche Wissenschaft
CBQ	*Catholic Biblical Quarterly*
CCSL	Corpus Christianorum Scriptorum Latinorum

CIJ	*Corpus Inscriptionum Judaicarum*
CPJ	*Corpus Papyrorum Judaicorum*
CRINT	Compendia Rerum Iudaicarum ad Novum Testamentum
CSCT	Columbia Studies in the Classical Tradition
DGMFT	Dissertationes ad gradum magistri in facultate theologica
DJD	Discoveries in the Judaean Desert
EcHR	*Economic History Review*
EdF	Erträge der Furschung
EtB	*Études bibliques*
ExpT	*Expository Times*
EKK	Evangelisch-katholischer Kommentar zum Neuen Testament
EWNT	*Exegetisches Wörterbuch zum Neuen Testament*
FEUC	Forschungen zur Entstehung des Urchristentums, des Neuen Testaments und der Kirche
FRLANT	Forschungen zur Religion des Alten und Neuen Testaments
FS	Festschrift
GBL	*Das Grosse Bibellexikon*, ed. H. Burkhardt et al.
GLAJJ	*Greek and Latin Authors on Jews and Judaism*, ed. M.Stern
HespSuppl	Supplements to *Hesperia*
HTK	Herders theologischer Kommentar zum Neuen Testament
HTR	*Harvard Theological Review*
HUCA	*Hebrew Union College Annual*
IEJ	*Israel Exploration Journal*
ISBE	*International Standard Bible Encyclopedia*
JAC	*Jahrbuch für Antike und Christentum*
JANES	*Journal of the Ancient Near Eastern Society*, Columbia University
JAOS	*Journal of the American Oriental Society*
JBL	*Journal of Biblical Literature*
JCS	*Journal of Classical Studies*, Kyoto
JE	*Jewish Encyclopedia*
JEA	*Journal of Egyptian Archaeology*
JHS	*Journal of Hellenic Studies*
JJS	*Journal of Jewish Studies*
JR	*Journal of Religion*

JRS	*Journal of Roman Studies*
JSHRZ	Jüdische Schriften aus hellenistisch-römischer Zeit
JSJ	*Journal for the Study of Judaism*
JSS	*Journal of Semitic Studies*
JTS	*Journal of Theological Studies*
Jud	*Judaica*
KEK	Kritisch-exegetisches Kommentar über das Neue Testament
KIG	Kirche in ihrer Geschichte
KlT	Kleine Texte
KP	*Der Kleine Pauly*
KNT	Kommentar zum Neuen Testament
KuD	*Kerygma und Dogma*
LCL	Loeb Classical Library
LD	Lectio Divina
MSU	Mitteilungen des Septuaginta-Unternehmens der Gesellschaft/Akademie der Wissenschaften in Göttingen
MUSJ	*Melanges de l'université Saint-Joseph*
NEB	Die Neue Echter Bibel
NES	Nordelbingische Studien
NewDocs	*New Documents Illustrating Early Christianity*, ed. G.H.R. Horsley
NF (NS)	Neue Folge (New Series)
NKZ	*Neue kirchliche Zeitschrift*
NovT	*Novum Testamentum*
NTA	Neutestamentliche Abhandlungen
NTOA	Novum Testamentum et Orbis Antiquus
NTS	*New Testament Studies*
NT.S	*Novum Testamentum*, Supplements
OBO	Orbis Biblicus et Orientalis
OLZ	*Orientalische Literaturzeitung*
PEQ	*Palestine Exploration Quarterly*
PFES	Publications of the Finnish Exegetical Society, Helsinki
PL	Patrologia Latina, ed. J.P.Migne
PVTG	Pseudepigrapha Veteris Testamenti Graeca
PW	*Paulys Real-Encyclopädie der classischen Altertumswissenschaft*
QD	Quaestiones Disputatae

RAC	*Reallexikon für Antike und Christentum*
RB	*Revue Biblique*
RÉG	*Revue des Études Grecques*
RevPhil	*Revue de Philosophie*
RGG	*Die Religion in Geschichte und Gegenwart*
RHPR	*Revue d'historie et de philosophie religieuses*
RSJB	*Receuils de la société Jean Bodin*
SAWW.PH	Sitzungsberichte der Akademie der Wissenschaften in Wien – Philosophisch-historische Klasse
SBL.MS	Society of Biblical Literature, Monograph Series
SHR	Studies in the History of Religions
SIJB	Schriften des Institutum Judaicum in Berlin
SJLA	Studies of Jewish Life in Antiquity
SNTS.MS	Societas Novi Testamenti Studiorum, Monograph Series
SNTU	Studien zum Neuen Testament und seiner Umwelt
SO	Symbolae Osloensis
SPAW.PH	Sitzungsberichte der preussischen Akademie der Wissenschaften – Philosophisch-historische Klasse
SR	Studies in Religion
SSAW.PH	Sitzungsberichte der sächsischen Akademie der Wissenschaften zu Leipzig – Philosophisch-historische Klasse
StANT	Studien zum Alten und Neuen Testament
StPB	Studia post-biblica
StUNT	Studien zur Umwelt des Neuen Testaments
TAVO.B	Tübinger Atlas des Vorderen Orients, Beihefte, Reihe B
TDNT	*Theological Dictionary of the New Testament*, ed. G.Kittel
ThB	Theologische Bücherei
ThBeitr	*Theologische Beiträge*
ThHK	Theologischer Handkommentar zum Neuen Testament
ThR	*Theologische Revue*
ThStKr	*Theologische Studien und Kritiken*
TRE	*Theologische Realenzyklopädie*
TRG	*Tijdschrift voor rechtsgeschiedenis*
TSAJ	Texte und Studien zum Antiken Judentum
TU	Texte und Untersuchungen
TynB	*Tyndale Bulletin*

VigChrSuppl	Supplements to *Vigiliae Christianae*
WdF	Wege der Forschung
WMANT	Wissenschaftliche Monographien zum Alten und Neuen Testament
WUNT	Wissenschaftliche Untersuchungen zum Neuen Testament
ZBK	Zürcher Bibelkommentar
ZDPV	*Zeitschrift des deutschen Palästina-Vereins*
ZNW	*Zeitschrift für die neutestamentliche Wissenschaft*
ZTK	*Zeitschrift für Theologie und Kirche*

Index of Biblical References

NEW TESTAMENT

Index of Modern Scholars

claims to be a Christian or not, is more or less guided by Judeo-Christian standards. Brought up in the average home, attending the average school, he is bound to come under the influence of Christian teaching in spite of himself. With the result that even the raw pagan (in the biblical sense) living in America will order his life along Christian lines. Consequently we have a familiar phenomenon: the good man whose conduct is Christian but whose heart is not. Outwardly he acts like a Christian, yet he has no interest in Christ's church, much less any loyalty or personal attachment for Jesus Christ Himself.

As a matter of fact there is a distinct, basic difference between a Christian and a merely good man. It is an inner difference! The truly Christian man has a completely different outlook on life. He has a strong sense of obligation to God. The non-Christian does not feel this but rather feels self-made. The Christian believes himself to be a sinner saved by grace. The non-Christian does not feel he is a sinner, or if he does, he figures he can work his own way out of it. Hence the Christian sees Christ as Savior and Lord while the non-Christian sees Him merely as a good man or a great teacher. The Christian worships Christ. The non-Christian at best admires Christ, may even patronize Him. The Christian gives priority to the kingdom of God and its righteousness. The non-Christian never thinks of this. He is motivated by self-interest! Even the philanthropy of the non-Christian has a self reference. He wants credit for it. The Christian handles his resources as a steward of God. The non-Christian has the attitude of a squatter. The Christian gives God first place in financial considerations. The non-Christian figures he owns what he has: he's made it! Nobody, not even God, dictates how he'll use it! Self is at the center of the non-Christian's life, no matter how thoroughly he embraces Christian ethics. Jesus Christ is the center of the Christian's life. The Christian and non-Christian are at opposite poles when the secrets of their hearts are exposed!

> *Now this is eternal life: that men may know you, the only true God, and Jesus Christ, whom you have sent.*
> —John 17:3

Tuesday

There could be a hundred million new Christians in the world today—one hundred million new converts to Jesus Christ—if just one in every nine professing Christians was really interested in winning a friend to Christ. One hundred million persons might be born into the Christian family through the power of God today, translated by the heart-changing dynamic of the Gospel from darkness to light, out of death into life—if one-ninth of us who claim to be Christian were really faithful followers of the One who said, "Follow me and I will make you fishers of men."

Of course you don't regiment the Spirit of God, and it is He who gives birth to the children of God. You don't dictate to God, setting quotas or schedules for the harvest of souls. Nevertheless, the statistics dramatize the thrilling possibilities of one day, any day, if we Christians were really serious about the mission to which our Lord has called us. Who can measure what the Spirit of God might do today if we who make profession of faith in Jesus Christ were obedient to the mandate which He left His church? What an absolutely exciting prospect if today each of us decided it was his duty, his vocation, his holy calling, to be a witness—by the Spirit—among his colleagues, friends, and associates.

Certainly the failure is not God's! It is "not His will that any should perish." He who loved the world so much that "He gave His one and only Son" is certainly not indifferent to the lostness, the waywardness, the disorientation of men. He who loved the world so much that He laid down His life on the cross, submitting to the ignominious treatment and shame of ruthless and profane men, letting His own blood pour out as a sacrifice for the sin of the very men guilty of the atrocity—surely He is not without care and concern for men everywhere. Surely He would speak to the hearts of men, woo them to Himself, if He had a faithful servant through whom to speak and love.

Jesus Christ has His people everywhere! But many are indifferent. They are cold and heartless and preoccupied with their own achievements and acquisitions. You aren't responsible for the nine hundred million who call themselves Christian, but you are responsible for you—and those around you.

> *But you will receive power when the Holy Spirit comes on you; and you will be my witnesses in Jerusalem, and all Judea and Samaria, and to the ends of the earth.* —Acts 1:8

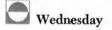 **Wednesday**

In a very real sense Christian witness is a secret service. The Christian who takes seriously his duty to God and man, who desires to exert a positive and constructive influence for Christ where he lives, has no infallible criteria whereby he may know how he is doing. In fact, those most deeply influenced by him may not be aware of that influence in the process. As the sun can tan a body without the conscious awareness of the one being tanned, so the godly influence of a thoughtful Christian may sink in and affect other lives without their knowledge. And the serious Christian is not aware of the transmission of his influence. He is just being himself, committed to Christ, dependent upon the Holy Spirit.

Today, in a hundred million places around the world, Christ-possessed Christ-filled persons will go quietly to their tasks and places in society, and throughout the day they will be permeating that society like a "benevolent infection" with Christian influence. They will not advertise, will not sound a trumpet before them, may not even talk a lot about it. They will not preach, will not "evangelize" in the conventional sense; but they will be a sermon. Their lives will "witness" to the reality and relevance of Christ. Today, parliaments, offices, schools and campuses, labor unions, military installations, clubs, markets, and homes all over the world will be silently infiltrated by faithful Christians whose lives, managed by the Holy Spirit, will bless and sweeten and challenge and preserve the little world in which they move. This is the heart and soul of the impact of the church in the world. This is the cutting edge, the point of thrust, the central impact of authentic Christian witness and influence as it penetrates the secular system.

Jesus said, "You are the salt of the earth." Salt is useless as long as it retains its identity in the salt shaker; only as it is spread on the food, losing its identity as it disappears, does it enhance and make palatable and preserve. So faithful Christians, "rubbed" by Christ into the society around them, disappear as they dissolve into that secular structure. And there, daily, they enhance and make palatable and preserve and make men thirsty for God and righteousness. Bless you, salt of the earth!

> *You are the salt of the earth. But if the salt loses its saltiness, how can it be made salty again? It is no longer good for anything, except to be thrown out and trampled by men.* —Matthew 5:13

Thursday

The fruit of the teaching is the test of the teacher. It is one thing to take an academic interest in religion, any religion, far from the culture it produces; it is another to live in the environment the religion creates and perpetuates. It is easy enough to patronize a religion when one is an observer rather than an authentic participant; easy enough while one enjoys the bountiful benefits of a Judeo-Christian culture to be a proponent of a religion about which one has only theoretical knowledge. It is easy to forget our heritage, take its priceless benefits for granted, and ignore the source from which they come.

But spend some time in a non-Christian environment where even simple cleanliness is a rare treasure and one begins to realize things are as they are, not in spite of the non-Christian religion, but because of it. Complacency, indifference to dirt and misery and suffering, filth, total absence of incentive, cheapness of life, unimportance of the individual, exploitation, corruption, superstition, etc. These are the status quo in a world without the influence of the Bible.

Whereas the great humanitarian benefits—hospitals, schools, hygiene, individual dignity, social welfare, orphanages, leprosariums—derive directly or indirectly from the Judeo-Christian tradition. Either they are the result of Christian nationals or foreign missions, or they are borrowed by imitation from the Christian world. Lean, hungry, sore-infested dogs, spit and vermin and dung; children with running noses, matted hair, open sores and scabs and scars, watery eyes; people bathing, washing dishes and clothes, brushing their teeth, swimming and excreting in the same river from which they get their drinking water; pathetic, abandoned old people; broken distorted bodies; and some will say, "They have their religion. Why should we send missionaries?" What terrible parasites are we who enjoy all the benefits of a Christ-generated civilization, yet reject

Him whose redemptive love produced the climate in which those benefits thrive and ignore the need and want of others!

> *Beware lest you say in your heart, "My power and the might of my hand have gotten me this wealth." You shall remember the Lord your God, for it is he who gives you power to get wealth.*
> —Deuteronomy 8:17-18

Friday

"A pill to make sex safe."

That statement, from a contemporary best seller, expresses the ultimate in human selfishness, license, and irresponsibility. Followed to its logical conclusion, it would mean the end of the human family. It is to take the profoundest, most intimate, most deeply selfless, most meaningful, most personal human relationship and pervert it for utterly selfish, totally physical purposes. It is idolatry in its most subtle, most devastating form!

Sex is God's idea; created to give man his greatest pleasure, thereby guaranteeing the perpetuation of humanity; so constituted to give maximum satisfaction only when it is an exclusive relationship between one man and one woman committed to each other for life. It was intended to be the ultimate in self-surrender of a lover to his beloved and she to him.

Sex on any other basis is a will-o'-the-wisp, promising ecstasy and never really fulfilling, substituting animal pleasure for human commitment and surrender. The pay-off is sex purely as a technique: fail to get satisfaction, read another book, experiment with a new technique, use the sex partner like a guinea pig. That's exploitation of personality at its ugliest worst! That's sex without love!

How wonderfully, joyfully, gloriously different is God's plan. "Then the Lord God said, 'It is not good that the man should be alone. I will make him a helper.' ... (he) brought her to the man. Then the man said, "This at last is bone of my bones and flesh of my flesh" (Gen. 2:18, 22-23).

> *Therefore a man leaves his father and his mother and cleaves to his wife, and they become one flesh.* —Genesis 2:24

 Monday

The incredible fact of the Jew! Have you ever thought it through? The Jew is one of the strongest evidences for a personal God persevering in history to bring to pass His own eternal purpose. History is His-story! Begun with Abraham, two thousand years before Christ, the Jews have been dispersed and enslaved time after time in history, yet never obliterated. Disappearing from history as a nation six hundred years before Christ, persecuted generation after generation by some of the most fiendish and contemptibly cruel pogroms (consider the destiny of those nations which persecuted Jews); reappearing as a nation twenty-five centuries later, prospering and rising to international significance in twenty years!

Centuries before Christ, in the midst of rawest paganism, the Jew preserved the purest form of monotheistic religion with the highest ethical standards. From the Jew came the Ten Commandments, the most precise and comprehensive statement of moral law ever formulated. Think of the art and science and music the Jew has given to mankind. Think of the financial genius the Jew has given the world. The three great revolutions with which our modern world is wrestling were born of three Jews: Karl Marx precipitated the politico-economic revolution which is the focus of the present world crisis; Albert Einstein triggered the scientific revolution which may decide the progress of civilization, or its incineration; and Jesus Christ brought the spiritual and moral revolution upon which hangs the eternal destiny of humanity.

From Abraham to modern Israel; from Jerusalem under King David to Jerusalem under Golda Meir; the continuity of the Jew argues for the trustworthiness of the Bible, the validity of the Judeo-Christian tradition, the relevance of Christian faith. Let any man who would ignore the Bible or reject the faith of our Lord and Savior Jesus Christ give some intelligent thought to the incredible phenomenon of the Jew!

Salvation is from the Jews! —John 4:22

Tuesday

Corporate guilt is an illusion! The only relief is to the one who is imposing it, for the prophet seems to exclude himself from the indictment. By blaming everyone else he's home and free; his blanket accusation salves his own conscience. He may even feel he's a hero, daring to take such a bold stand against society in general.

Actually corporate responsibility is meaningless. People feel responsible individually or not at all. To be sure, responsible persons identify with other responsible persons and thus assume responsibility corporately; but as soon as individuals within such a collective lose their sense of responsibility, the whole structure weakens. The only ones who take corporate guilt seriously are those who suffer personal guilt; those not bothered by personal guilt couldn't care less. Corporate guilt gives them a perfect opportunity to cop out!

For the thoughtful person there's no way out of corporate guilt. He may regret his failure, his prejudice, his sin, and attempt to do something about it, but he finds no relief, for the prophet of doom, painting everybody with the same brush, includes him in his relentless blanket condemnation. God promises to forgive and bless a repentant nation, but repentance itself is a one-by-one proposition. Apart from individual repentance there is no corporate forgiveness and renewal. Persisting in the accusation of corporate guilt finally immobilizes a society because there is no way for the individual to respond and there is no other way society can respond to any challenge except individually. Perpetrating social guilt is futile!

> *If my people who are called by my name humble themselves, and pray and seek my face, and turn from their wicked ways, then I will hear from heaven, and will forgive their sin and heal their land.*
> —2 Chronicles 7:14

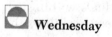 **Wednesday**

Three ways (at least) men use Scripture: some

use it as a collection of proof texts to support what they believe. They develop their theology, usually out of personal experience, then find Scripture to support their views. They suffer the false security that their belief is biblical whereas it may be unscriptural or even contradictory to the Bible. Experience, not the Bible, is their final authority. They learn little from the Scriptures, but search for texts to prove what they already hold to be true.

Others use Scripture as the starting point of their faith, from which they soon depart on their spiritual journey. The farther they go in their quest for spirituality, the farther they remove from their biblical beginning. Often they boast of a biblical faith when, as a matter of fact, their faith is biblical only in its genesis.

To others, Scripture is the foundation and the superstructure upon which and with which they build faith, "line upon line, precept upon precept."

The first group, using Scripture to their own subjective ends, develop an experience-centered faith which is tragically vulnerable because it is so helplessly dependent upon a sustained experience. The second group move horizontally from the Bible, generally boast of their orthodoxy, while the reality of biblical faith dims and dies. The third group move vertically and more deeply into Scripture, depend upon it for their sustenance, faith, and knowledge. Their confidence is based upon the Bible itself. The Bible becomes their meat and drink, their direction and goal, their teacher and motivator.

> *And he said to them, "You have a fine way of setting aside the commands of God in order to observe your own traditions."*
> —Mark 7:9

Thursday

You've got one life. What are you doing with it? One life to live, one life to give. What are you living for? To what are you giving your life? Either you give your life to something, or you give it to nothing. In any case, you give it!

What consummate tragedy—good men who give their lives for nothing. Waste their lives on that which is temporary and transient when they could be investing their lives in that which is eternal. Good men they are too, but good for what? What a pity that there are men who are good, but good for nothing!

This is the greatest option in life: the privilege of giving your life to the highest and best or settling for the lowest and cheapest. Think of the men you know who have invested the best life has given them in that which has no significance in the light of eternity. They put all their eggs into the basket of life this side of the grave, and the payoff is disillusionment, frustration, boredom, and emptiness. They achieve everything they fight for and get nothing they really want. Everything turns to ashes in the sunset of life. They have everything they want and want little that they get.

> *My people have committed two evils; they have forsaken me, the fountain of living waters, and hewed out cisterns for themselves, broken cisterns, that can hold no water.* —Jeremiah 2:13

 Friday

The Christian hope is retroactive! Unlike all man-made utopias, its promise is relevant to those who have lived in past generations. Communism, for example, holds out no hope for Abraham, progenitor of Israel, who lived two thousand years before Christ. But Christianity does! In fact, Christianity, rightly understood, is the fulfillment of Abraham's hope.

The promise God made to Abraham (Gen. 12), two thousand years before Christ, is coming to its consummation and fulfillment in Jesus Christ. Every man who had faith in the God of Israel, from Abraham to Christ, is included in that promise and that hope! And the Apostle Paul declared (Rom. 8:18-23) that the whole created universe stands to benefit.

It is not uncommon for men to lay down their lives for one human dream or another, but apart from the heroism which is admirable, the dream will never pay off for the man who laid down his life. The most that he could hope for was that his posterity would enjoy the legacy left by his sacrifice. Every man who has sacrificed his life for the Christian "dream" is going to "collect" on the benefits, though he may have been dead a thousand years.

God began something with Adam, the first man (Gen. 2), which He is still working out in history. That plan, relevant not only to Adam but to the entire cosmos, will be consummated the day Jesus Christ makes His Second Advent on earth. He came once as a "suffering servant" to lay down His life on the cross for the sins of mankind. He is coming a second time as a conquering King to bring to fruition all the glorious prospects promised in the plan God began with Adam. All the legitimate dreams and aspirations of mankind from its beginning will find their perfection and fulfillment in Christ's return.

> *Creation itself will be liberated from its bondage to decay and brought into the glorious freedom of the children of God.*
> —Romans 8:21

Peace wears different costumes: it may be real or an illusion! The peace of ignorance, for instance: one may have peace simply because he is uninformed; not knowing the facts, he remains undisturbed. "Ignorance is bliss." Or the peace of mental gymnastics: one pretends things are not as they are or actually convinces himself contrary to the truth like an ostrich with head in sand. There is the peace of fatalism: "What will be will be." Neither God (if there be a God) nor man can change inexorable, inflexible destiny. Such peace dooms a man to helplessness, feeds apathy, makes man a vegetable. It is also a beautiful defense for laziness. Then there is the peace of anesthesia, making one insensitive to reality. It may be induced by dope, liquor, or a mad whirl of pleasure; or one may just get very busy. This is the peace of escape. In one way or another some do whatever is necessary to remain numb to reality. All such peace is not only illusion, but it can be very dangerous! Like a "high threshold of pain" is dangerous. If a man doesn't feel pain, he will be indifferent to its cause. And he may be destroyed by it!

The peace of God is the only authentic peace! It works with things as they are! Apart from Jesus Christ, a man has two alternatives when faced with cold, hard facts: anxiety or false security.

Either he lets himself be distracted by trouble or he takes refuge in unreality. False peace disarms, puts one at the mercy of the facts. The peace of God mobilizes, enables one to keep his equilibrium in the face of the facts; makes him poised, efficient, capable. He is the master, never the victim, of circumstances. He is aware of the facts, but He is more than a match for them in the strength of Christ. He enjoys the genuine "undisturbedness" of the Lord Jesus. Such peace the world cannot give, and it cannot take it away either!

> *Do not let your hearts be troubled. Trust in God; trust also in me.* —John 14:1
> (See Philippians 4:6-7.)

Christmas Week, Tuesday

Christmas has a carry-over, a follow-through. In fact that is the most important thing about it! If you have really kept Christmas, the joy of it has only begun. It is not meant to be a once-a-year spree or spasm; God meant it quite differently. Christmas is the beginning of God's program, just the beginning. And if you have really kept Christmas, then things have just begun for you. Do you keep Christmas or just observe the day? There is a vast difference!

Observing Christmas day is a cursory thing—momentary frills, tinsel, a flash-in-the-pan sort of thing. It's shallow, unreal, and exhausting. When it's over it's over. And frankly, people who just celebrate the day are relieved that it is over. They can return to normal; by which they mean that they can get back into the same old rut! But if you know the real meaning of Christmas, it is infinitely more than a mere celebration; it is a realization. It is not exhausting; it is transforming. It is a new birth! That's what it meant in the first place. Literally! It meant a new birth: the advent of God, in human form, in the Person of Jesus Christ into the world, into human affairs, human problems.

The birth of Jesus Christ into this world was only the beginning. The fundamental meaning of Christmas is that God demonstrated His interest, His concern for us, His love—a love that led to action. Love that led God to do something about man's need. It means that God desires to be born in the hearts of men everywhere: "God so loved the world that he gave his one and only Son."

God loved and gave, but we don't receive. That's the crux of our need! There's simply not a problem which touches our life in which God is not interested. He is a Father. His love is personal, practical, down-to-earth, realistic, available, continual, dependable.

Santa Claus is a usurper and the celebration an evil if it has no lasting effect in one's life—if we haven't Christmas in our heart. "Christ in you is the hope of glory." Not until Christ is in you can He help you. God had to enter the world to help it; He has to get into your heart to help you. Until you let Christ in, Christmas is a travesty, a fairy tale, a mockery, quiet blasphemy!

> *To all who received him . . . he gave the right to become children of God.*
> —John 1:12

Christmas Week, Wednesday

"Peace on earth—among men of good will." That's the promise of Christmas! And what peace! It surpasses the ability of words to express or imagination to conceive. Paul describes it as "The peace which transcends all understanding." It is the legacy of those who take the promise of Christmas seriously.

There are many kinds of peace: the peace of ignorance, for example. As the saying goes, "Ignorance is bliss." Some people are at peace simply because they don't know any better; they are uninformed. No news is good news for them, and they would prefer to remain in their ignorance rather than have their peace disturbed. Then there is the peace of the sepulchre, the peace of apathy and inertia and indifference. "Couldn't care less" is its slogan, irresponsibility its hallmark.

But the peace of Christmas is the antithesis. It means peace whatever the news, however deeply one is involved, no matter how contrary the circumstances. It is a peace which helps a person fulfill responsibility efficiently and effectively. "An island of tranquillity at the center of my soul," is the way one young person described it recently. Circumstances were difficult, but a force within kept her steady and cool, like a giant gyroscope in the bowels of a great ship keeps it sailing smoothly however rough the seas.

The peace of Christmas at the center of one's life maintains the equilibrium despite swirling, turbulent, stormy circumstances. It is the antidote for fear, panic, and hysteria! It is the gift of God. Receive it this Christmas! You'll find it offered in Jesus Christ.

> *He himself is our peace.*
> —Ephesians 2:14

Christmas Week, Thursday

Christmas is over. Its impact on the world staggers one. It is really amazing when you stop to think about it—the fuss the world makes over a baby born in a barn nineteen centuries ago. Christmas Eve, most of that day—in fact for several days preceding it—hour after hour over radio and television, as well as in newspapers and magazines, we are reminded of the strange fascination the birth of that babe holds for the whole world. The finest talent of art and music and literature, of the stage and screen, seem almost to vie with one another to portray this disarmingly simple event of history. No human power could perpetuate that kind of reverence and respect for such a humble event. No gimmick that Madison Avenue could think up today could promote such perennial excitement and adoration world-wide. (To be sure they do their best to capitalize on it.)

Why this universal focus on such an unpretentious fact of history occurring as it did in relative obscurity? Have you ever asked yourself that question? Ever wondered? What is there about the birth of a Jewish baby in a little suburb of Jerusalem, half a dozen miles from the civic center? Rome hardly noticed. Still today, nineteen hundred years later, its celebration is felt universally, even inspires a truce between warring nations. The answer to that question is that the birth of Jesus was tied into two thousand years of Hebrew history. God's promise to Abraham, progenitor of Israel, made 2000 B.C., was about to enter its most significant phase. The Messiah promised so long ago was about to enter history in supreme redemptive strategy. Two thousand years of history were about to see fulfillment! Two thousand years of anticipation, hope, aspiration, were to be satisfied. That is why Dr. Charles Malik, eminent Lebanese statesman, refers to Jesus Christ as "the hinge of history."

> *Do not be afraid. I bring you good news*
> *of great joy that will be for all people.*
> *Today in the town of David a Savior has*
> *been born to you; he is Christ the Lord.*
> —Luke 2:10-11

Christmas Week, Friday

Indignation rose within me as I returned home from our Christmas day service. The golf course across the street was busy, and I wondered how many golfers were merchants or suppliers who had realized a neat profit from the Christmas trade. Impatient for Thanksgiving to be over (many could not wait), they had gone all out on their Christmas drives. The crowds came and the money poured in—all because "God so loved the world that he gave his one and only Son."

Many who prospered couldn't care less. They had exploited a Christian festival, gotten all they could out of it; now it was over, they had made their pile, and they hadn't the slightest thought for the One who made it possible. Not a moment's notice to God's gift! In total indifference to the Son of God whose birthday generated the sales, they ignored His church on Christmas day.

> *Take care lest you forget the Lord your God when you have eaten your fill, and have built fine houses to live in, and your silver and gold have increased, and everything you own has prospered, beware lest your heart grow haughty and you forget the Lord your God, and you say to yourselves, "My own power and might of my own hand have won this wealth for me." Remember that it is the Lord your God Who gives you the power to get wealth. If you do forget the Lord your God, I warn you this day that you shall certainly perish.* —The Torah
> (Deuteronomy 8:11-20)

Easter Week, Monday

It is always too soon to quit! A man may quit because he feels the thing he's doing is not worth finishing. What he's doing may not be important, but he is. It's what quitting will do to him that matters. Inspiration gone? The excitement and idealism with which the project began has faded? Finishing doesn't seem worth the effort? Who cares? Maybe it doesn't make any difference to others if he quits, but it will make a great difference to himself; he's learning to be a quitter. It will be easier to quit next time. When things go stale, after the inspiration is gone, that is the time to dig in and finish the job simply for the sake of finishing.

Progress is made by the men who see a thing through after the quitters have dropped out. Jesus Christ is the supreme example. He went all the way to the cross, "set His face like a flint" to suffer crucifixion. He finished the work God gave Him to do and gave the world its ultimate hope! In that finish is God's complete forgiveness— eternal life for all who will receive it. Jesus said,

> *They (men) should always pray and not*
> *give up.*   —Luke 18:1

Easter Week, Tuesday

Much social action, so far as goals are concerned, denies the very human dignity by which it professes to be motivated, for it is wholly materialistic. Its rationale is the good of man this side of the grave. And if man has no eternal value, man is not man!

If all man's hope lies this side of death, man is hopeless and "most to be pitied." If there is nothing beyond the grave, morality is an illusion. Why be good when so many evil men prosper? And so many good people suffer?

What of the millions who have perished, who knew nothing but poverty while they lived? What of the millions whom life has cheated by cruel disease, by accident, by tragedy?

If there is no life beyond the grave, the death of Jesus Christ was wasted; the Resurrection of Christ was a cruel deception. Peter and Paul and the others were liars! If the grave is the end, eat, drink, and be merry, for tomorrow we die!

> *But Christ has indeed been raised from the dead!* —1 Corinthians 15:20

Easter Week, Wednesday

God is dead? That's a contradiction in terms, like saying white is black, or love is hate, or straight is crooked, or light is darkness. That's like saying that life is dead!

The god of man's imagination is dead: the god we invent with our intellects, the god we insist on equating with our dogma, the god who is small enough for us to comprehend is dead; he's never been alive. The god we keep in a theological box is dead! But God is not dead! God is deathless! He is life itself. He is eternal. He is the great "I Am"!

He ever was and ever shall be. He is "the same yesterday, today and forever." He is the unchanging, unbegun, unending, perpetual Father of whom Jesus Christ is the only unchanging, unbegun, unending Son. He is the One who suffered profoundly, patiently when His Son hung on the cross. He was there to raise Him from the dead. The "God-is-dead" idea is a theory, a manmade theory, a human invention as irrelevant (as dead) as all the other theories about God, however sophisticated, conceived by man's intellect. We all tend to whittle God down to superman size by our dogma, but this is the absurd ultimate to which man's intellect leads in the reduction of God.

Who is this that darkens counsel by words without knowledge?   —Job 38:2

Easter Week, Thursday

Where was the body? Jesus' enemies would

have paid any price to recover it, for that would settle once for all Jesus' incredible claim that He would rise from the dead, and it would silence permanently His disciples. But their only recourse was to pay the guards to perjure themselves. And what a lie! "While they slept the disciples stole the body." If they were asleep, how did they know? (In their futile efforts to discredit the Resurrection, scholars have never fabricated a more satisfactory explanation.)

Jesus' enemies, remembering His promise to rise from the dead, took every precaution to prevent it, actual or contrived. Three days later the seal was broken, the stone rolled away, the body gone. The burial linen remained in the tomb like a cocoon.

For six weeks Jesus revealed Himself time and again in ways which left no doubt whatsoever that He was alive (see 1 Cor. 15:5-8). His disciples did not convince easily! They thought He was a ghost. He invited them to handle His body; He partook of their food. Thomas refused to believe unless He could feel the wounds of the nails and spear. Jesus submitted to Thomas's test leaving Thomas with no doubts. Jesus even prepared a breakfast and dined with His disciples (John 21:9-12).

It is inconceivable that the disciples tricked the guards, stole the body, buried it in an unknown grave, waited fifty days for a cooling-off period, and then, in spite of every kind of threat and intimidation, preached the Resurrection with conviction and power. That is more difficult to accept than the Resurrection itself! Nor is it conceivable that the church, generation by generation, for nineteen centuries, has been deluded in its testimony to the Resurrection. Easter Sunday may be perfunctory to many, but to millions it is the celebration of an historical fact which has been confirmed in personal experience.

> *After his suffering, he showed himself to these men and gave many convincing proofs that he was alive.* —Acts 1:3

Easter Week, Friday

It is certainly not missing the mark to say that Jesus was the most captivating, the most fascinating personality who ever walked the earth. The record of His life indicates that there was a magnetism about Him that drew great crowds. During His brief ministry, He was hardly ever free from the multitudes, even when He deliberately avoided them and sought isolation. His fame spread to the four corners of Palestine: "No man ever spoke like this man," they said of Him. "He speaks as one having authority. From whence has this man such learning?" they inquired.

Whence this magnetism, this irresistible attraction, this power of word? It is an open secret. He did not hesitate to share it with those who were interested. He disclosed again and again the source of His powerful ministry. He said His words were not His own, but His Father's. He insisted His works were not his own but the Father's. The Father spoke the word and did the work through Him by the agency of the indwelling Holy Spirit. Jesus Christ the man was strictly obedient to the Father's will—and filled with the Spirit of God (Luke 4:1). Before Jesus ascended following His Resurrection, He promised to His disciples the same Spirit who had filled His life and employed Him to do the will of the Father. On the basis of this promise He was able to say to His disciples, "Anyone who has faith in me will do what I have been doing. He will do even greater things than these" (John 14:12).

Fifty days after Passover came Pentecost. At Pentecost every disciple of Jesus was "filled with the Spirit of God," and that loose band of individualistic disciples was forged into an absolutely unique and unprecedented social unit—the church, the Body of Christ.

Be filled with the Spirit. —Ephesians 5:18